Darrell Bates

The Abyssinian Difficulty

THE EMPEROR THEODORUS AND THE MAGDALA CAMPAIGN 1867–68

Oxford New York Delhi Nairobi
OXFORD UNIVERSITY PRESS

1979

Oxford University Press, Walton Street, Oxford OX2 6DP
OXFORD LONDON GLASGOW
NEW YORK TORONTO MELBOURNE WELLINGTON
KUALA LUMPUR SINGAPORE JAKARTA HONG KONG TOKYO
DELHI BOMBAY CALCUTTA MADRAS KARACHI
NAIROBI DAR ES SALAAM CAPE TOWN

British Library Catalogue Data
Bates, *Sir* Darrell
The Abyssinian difficulty.
1. The Abyssinian Expedition, 1867–1868
I. Title
963.'04 DT386.3 79-40502

ISBN 0-19-211747-5

Set, printed and bound in Great Britain by
Fakenham Press Limited,
Fakenham, Norfolk

Contents

List of illustrations

Between pp. 176 and 177

Between pp. 208 and 209

List of maps

A note on origins and sources

The idea of writing a book about General Napier and his Abyssinian campaign first came to me when I was Colonial Secretary at Gibraltar some twenty years ago. Napier had been made Governor of Gibraltar in 1876 as a sort of golden handshake at the end of a distinguished military career, and while he was there he had been involved in a number of incidents which seemed to provide promising material for a book. This, added to the fact that I had been in Ethiopia during the 1939–45 war and knew much of the country in which Napier and his antagonist the emperor Theodorus had operated, led me on to think in terms of general biography. In pursuit of this idea I discovered that Napier, who was born in 1810, had at the age of 71 fathered a son while he was Governor, and that this son, the Hon. Albert Napier, was then still alive in his eighties. I went to see him in London, and he kindly encouraged my interest and gave me access to a large box of his father's papers, which we eventually traced to the National Register of Archives in Chancery Lane. These papers, together with contemporary records in the old India Office library, gave me an indication of the wealth of original and largely unused material which was available, particularly about the Abyssinian campaign and its causes. An additional attraction at this stage was a quick reading of the series of entertaining and exciting reports sent back by the special correspondent whom *The Times* had attached to the expedition.

It was some years before I was able to undertake the necessary research for such a project, and when I did so, with the help and encouragement of Richard Brain of the Oxford University Press, it was the campaign itself and its bizarre causes, and the character and history of the Abyssinian Emperor Theodorus, which seemed to provide the best subject for a book. 'The Abyssinian Difficulty' was the euphemism which Disraeli and others used at the time to describe the chain of machiavellian makeshifts and official malfeasance which occasioned the Abyssinian campaign of 1868.

I discovered the existence of other original material as I went along, and in the end the research and the writing took about two years. Other reasons why it took so long were that most of the material was in or near London while I inconveniently lived a long way away in Cornwall, and that much of it was in handwriting of varying legibility. This applied particularly to the old Foreign Office records, of which there were in all 29 volumes, all thick, heavy, dusty, and yellowed. An easier and quicker way of consulting this material is to use the few remaining copies of the Confidential Prints which were made for easy reference by the ministers and officials of the F.O. when the Abyssinian difficulty and its causes became heatedly controversial. There are two main and three supplementary volumes of these Confidential Prints in the Public Record Office, but they are a poor substitute for the originals as they are both incomplete, and lack the personal touches provided, for example, by Lord Palmerston's laconic scribbles in pencil on the back of incoming despatches, and the elegant minutes written with quill-pens by the scholarly and cynical officials of the Foreign Office. An even easier and considerably less complete version of the original files is contained in the single volume, *Papers Connected with the Abyssinian Expedition 1866–68*, which was compiled rather hurriedly for members of parliament, the Press, and the public in 1868. Sixteen other White Papers and Blue Books dealing with Abyssinia were issued between 1867 and 1870, which gives a fair idea of the importance attached to the matter at the time. The most bulky and interesting of these papers is the *Report of the Select Committee* which looked afterwards hopefully but fruitlessly into the cost and the causes of the war.

The India Office library, now housed in Blackfriars Road, has much valuable material, including the Napier papers referred to earlier, and a particularly evocative collection of letters in English, Arabic, and Amharic known as the Rassam Donation. Although the India Office seemed to have started using typewriters long before the Foreign Office, much of this material is also in manuscript, and some, like papers from the old Aden Residency, are in a delicate state and need to be handled with care. The personal letters which General Napier wrote in his own hand to the commander-in-chief of the British army during his campaign in Abyssinia are, as the Duke of Cambridge was a Royal Duke, in the Royal Archives at Windsor Castle. Also in the Royal Archives are a series of letters dealing with the sad history of the Abyssinian emperor's son Alamayu who was brought to England at the age of seven, and in whose education and welfare Queen Victoria took a close interest.

The National Army Museum in London has made a useful collection of the letters and journals of those who took part in the campaign. Some are in manuscript too, but others are copies of papers still in regimental and private hands. Other original material known as the Hertslet Papers is in the archives of the Royal Geographical Society. The Church Missionary Society has a fine collection of early letters from its overseas missions, and the records of the old London Society for Promoting Christianity among the Jews are in the Bodleian at Oxford. Humphrey Napier-Gore kindly let me browse through a boxful of family letters handed down by his mother, who was one of Lord Napier's daughters and used to recount how, when she sat on her father's knee as a child, she had to be careful to avoid the one where he had been wounded.

Contemporary printed material is also plentiful. Apart from the splendid reports which, as already mentioned, were sent back to *The Times* by its own special correspondent, there are the less accurate and generally less readable reports and accounts of other Press correspondents like the more famous H. M. Stanley and G. A. Henty. The *Illustrated London News* sent out an artist to accompany the expedition, but in the end he arrived too late to be present himself at most of the stirring events which were so graphically depicted week after week in that paper. These engravings, based on the artist's sketches and notes, were later all reproduced in a handsome volume with text by Henry Acton. A very thorough and detailed official history of the expedition written by Major Holland and Capt. Hozier was published by the War Office in 1870.

Many of the persons involved in the campaign and in its causes subsequently wrote books or issued apologies of one kind or another. As is apt to happen in such cases, some are considerably more impartial and reliable than others. Among the best are the first-hand accounts written by Dr. Henry Blanc and by Hormuzd Rassam, and a volume of memoirs written in almost biblical English by Theophilus Waldmeier, one of the German brothers sent out to Abyssinia by the Church Missionary Society, who became the emperor's special assistant and friend.

For histories and studies of the emperor Theodorus, and of the events dealt with in this book, based on Ethiopian sources or which give an Ethiopian point of view I am indebted to Professor Sven

Rubenson and a number of his colleagues at the old Haile Sellassie University in Addis Ababa. Rubenson's own book *Tewodros of Ethiopia* was published by that university in conjunction with the Oxford University Press in 1966, while the work of other Ethiopian scholars of that period like Stanisław Chojnacki, Donald Crummey, Czesław Jeśman, Margaret Morgan, and Richard and Rita Pankhurst appeared in periodicals such as the *Journal of Ethiopian Studies* and the *Ethiopian Observer*. And, like all those who write about Ethiopia, I am also greatly indebted to the massive research and scholarship of Professor Edward Ullendorff.

It was by gracious permission of Her Majesty the Queen that I was able to use the material in the Royal Archives in Windsor Castle. I should also like to record my appreciation of the kindness and help of the staff of the Royal Archives, and of the Public Record Office both in Chancery Lane and at Kew; and of the staff of the libraries of the Department of Oriental Printed Books at the British Museum, of the Foreign Office, India Office, and Ministry of Defence, of the National Army Museum and the School of Oriental and African Studies, and the staffs of the library and map room of the Royal Geographical Society. I must also thank the library staff of the Guildhall in London, and the ever obliging staffs of the Penzance public library and the Penzance subscription library near my home in Cornwall.

Through the good offices of Sir George Sinclair I was enabled to use the library of the House of Commons for Hansard and other parliamentary papers; and I am also indebted for special help to Gordon Phillips, the archivist of *The Times*, my son Nicholas Bates, Major J. M. A. Tamplin of the Ogilby Trust, and the Revd. Walter Barker of the Church's Ministry among the Jews; and on medical matters to Dr. Ronald Seaton of the Liverpool School of Tropical Medicine and Colonel A. V. Tennuci of the R.A.M.C. Historical Museum.

A list of the manuscript material, official papers and publications, articles, and printed books used is given in the Bibliography at the end.

A note on transliteration of Amharic names

The transliteration of Amharic names and words presents even more difficulty than the better-known problems associated with other Semitic languages like Arabic. As explained in Chapter I, there are 31 consonants and 7 vowels in Amharic, which allows considerable latitude when it comes to rendering them into less well-endowed languages like French and English. Rather than risk confusing the ordinary reader with phonetic and accented equivalents like Meqdela and Meqdalā, Tegrē and Tigré, I have used more commonly accepted forms like Magdala and Tigrai. Where in doubt I have generally followed the example of Professor Edward Ullendorff.

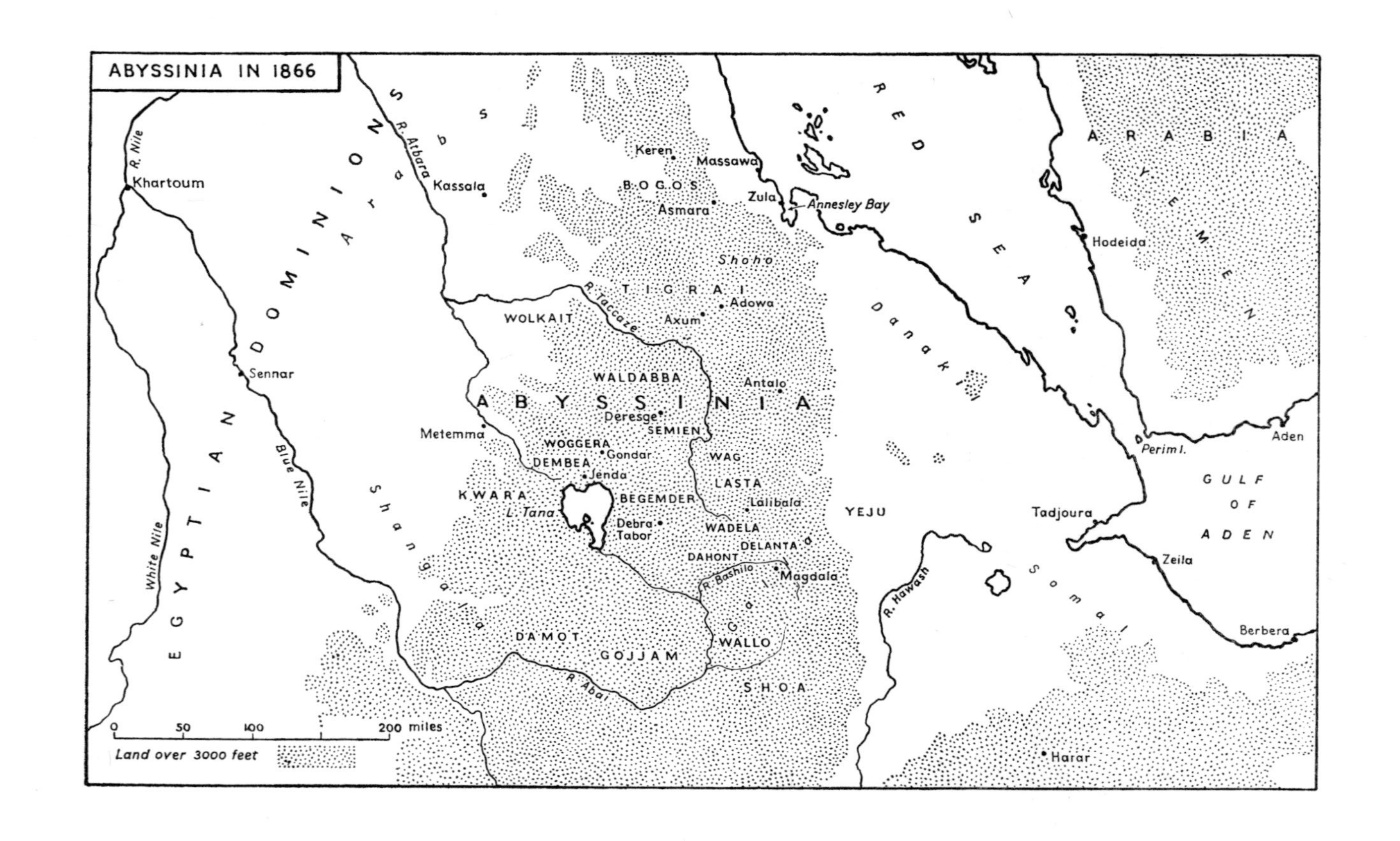
ABYSSINIA IN 1866
EGYPTIAN DOMINIONS
Arabs
R. Nile
Khartoum
White Nile
Blue Nile
Sennar
R. Atbara
Kassala
Keren
Massawa
BOGOS
Asmara
Zula
Annesley Bay
RED SEA
ARABIA
YEMEN
Hodeida
Shoho
TIGRAI
Adowa
Axum
R. Taccaze
WOLKAIT
WALDABBA
Antalo
ABYSSINIA
Deresge
SEMIEN
Metemma
WOGGERA
Gondar
DEMBEA
Jenda
WAG
LASTA
KWARA
L. Tana
BEGEMDER
Lalibala
Debra Tabor
WADELA
DELANTA
DAHONT
R. Bashilo
Magdala
Galla
WALLO
DAMOT
GOJJAM
R. Abai
SHOA
Shangalla
Danakil
YEJU
Perim I.
Aden
GULF OF ADEN
Tadjoura
Zeila
R. Hawash
Somal
Berbera
Harar
0 50 100 200 miles
Land over 3000 feet

CHAPTER I

The background

In the north-west corner of the Chapel Royal at Windsor there is a brass plaque set in the wall. The inscription reads:

Near this spot lies buried
ALAMAYU
the son of Theodore King of Abyssinia
born 23 April 1861
died 14 November 1879
This tablet is placed here to his memory by
Queen Victoria

Prince Alamayu had been in England for eleven years when he died, having arrived when he was seven. He came from Ethiopia, or Abyssinia, as it was then generally known, and it is there that one must go for his antecedents and for the events which occasioned his arrival in England, without parents or prospects, in the summer of 1868.

His father, who was known to Europeans as Theodore or Theodorus, and to his own countrymen as Tewodros, was already on the throne when Alamayu was born. Theodorus described himself in official communications as the Elect of God, the Slave of Christ, the King of Kings and Emperor of all Abyssinia, and he claimed descent from King Solomon and the Queen of Sheba. Whether or not Theodorus' claim to this ancestry was well based is open to question. What is certain is that he had to establish it in the course of his rise to power. It had for generations been a basic rule of succession to the throne of Abyssinia that descent from the Solomonic line had to be proved, and as recently as 1955 a new constitution in Ethiopia[1] reiterated that the throne must always be occupied by a descendant of Menelik I, 'the son of the Queen of Sheba and Solomon of Jerusalem'. The traditions on which this rule of succession was based may not be historically correct in all their detail, but they offer an explanation of the origins of the people who live in Ethiopia, and of the dynasty which ruled there until the deposition of the Emperor Haile Selassie I in 1975, which are as credible and as

[1] See page 4.

plausible as the traditions and myths on which many of the world's most respectable religions and political institutions are founded.

The orthodox Ethiopian version of the legend is contained in a fourteenth-century composition called *Kebra Nagast*, or 'Glory of the Kings', but the story is a very ancient one. It has taken many different forms, but the more lively and uninhibited are those which have escaped the corset of the written word, and are still handed down from generation to generation by word of mouth and popular pictorial representations.

In the beginning, the story goes, there was a serpent. The serpent tyrannized the people and demanded of them the sacrifice of a virgin every seventh day. Until the time came when the king's own daughter was the chosen victim, and a man arose, Georgis by name, and slew the serpent and saved the damsel.[1] In gratitude the king set Georgis on the throne and gave him his daughter in marriage. They founded a dynasty of kings and queens in Ethiopia which lasted seven generations; and the last of the line was Bilkis, Queen of Sheba. King Solomon was ruling in Jerusalem at the time, and in his wisdom he sent a trusted bird, a *hud* or hoopoe, to spy out distant lands, and the bird brought him news of the land of Sheba and of the beauty and wit of its queen. So he sent word and invited her to visit him.

King Solomon had heard that the queen had one foot deformed, and always kept it covered for this reason. So Solomon had a floor made of glass so that the queen would think it was water and lift her robe. And she did so, and revealed her deformity, and Solomon set his wise men to cure it. There is a window in King's College Chapel at Cambridge which shows the Queen of Sheba standing in pale blue glass marked with wavy lines like water, while in the Cathedral glass at Chartres her deformity is revealed as a webbed foot. There are still restaurants in France called *La Reine pédauque* (or 'goosefoot').

At the end of her visit King Solomon gave a banquet in her honour, and invited the Queen of Sheba and her dark-skinned maid to spend the night as his guests in his palace. She said she would provided he gave his word that he would not molest them. He gave his word but insisted in return that she gave hers that neither she nor her maid would steal any of his possessions. Solomon then had a banquet prepared with food that was heavily spiced. Afterwards the queen woke up in the night

[1] The same tradition, of course, emanating from the Middle East during the Crusades, gave birth to the legend of St. George and the Dragon.

with a terrible thirst, and she sent her maid to get some water. But Solomon had arranged that the only water in the palace was in a jar by his bed. When the maid started to draw water from the jar Solomon reached out and caught her hand, and drew her into his bed and lay with her. He then told her to lie under the bed and be silent. And Bilkis, being thirsty beyond endurance, came herself in search of water. And thinking Solomon was asleep she began to draw it from the jar. And Solomon caught her hand and said, 'You have broken your promise.' And the Queen of Sheba said, 'Water is not a possession: it belongs to everyone.' 'In your country perhaps,' King Solomon replied, 'where water is plentiful, but here it is scarce; it is man's most precious possession. But drink first, take your fill. Then, as you have broken your promise, so shall I break mine.' And when she had drunk he took her into his bed and lay with her.

In the morning the Queen of Sheba departed from Jerusalem and in due course, being returned to her own country, she gave birth to a son and called him Menelik. When he was grown up she sent him to Solomon's court in Jerusalem to learn his wisdom, and when he came back he brought with him the eldest sons of a hundred of Solomon's elders to help him govern his kingdom wisely. And just as the emperors of Ethiopia are the descendants of King Solomon and the Queen of Sheba through their son Menelik, so all the tribes of the light-skinned Amhara are the descendants of the hundred sons of Israel sent to Sheba by Solomon. At the same time as the Queen of Sheba bore a son, so too did her dark-skinned maidservant; and the Galla peoples[1] of Ethiopia, being less fair than the Amhara and less dark than the Shangala and the people of the Nile, are the descendants of the son she bore to King Solomon of Jerusalem.

The importance of this legend lies of course not in its truth but in the fact that at that time it was widely believed. Scholarly theories about the origins of the peoples and dynasties of Ethiopia are just as prone to uncertainty as the legends. While there may well have been some kind of contact between King Solomon's Israel and the people of Sheba in the tenth century B.C., it is improbable that the land of Sheba was in Ethiopia or indeed anywhere in Africa. It was more likely to have been the area known to the Arabs as Saba in the highlands of the Yemen in southern Arabia. What is established fact is that over a period of about

[1] Although Galla is the name by which they are commonly known, the Galla themselves prefer to be called Oromo.

a thousand years from about 500 B.C. to 500 A.D. some of the inhabitants of Saba left their cool and fertile highlands in Arabia and settled in the equally cool and fertile highlands of Ethiopia.

The people of Saba, known to archaeologists as Sabaeans, were sophisticated people who spoke a Semitic language similar to Arabic and Hebrew but with its own distinctive script. Their culture, and especially their religious beliefs and practices, showed marked Jewish influence, the result no doubt of trading contacts with Israel dating back to Solomon's time and to the existence of ancient Jewish settlements in the Yemen. When the Sabaeans crossed the Red Sea they found both the African coast and the hinterland already populated by Hamitic peoples of mixed blood who were themselves the descendants of earlier invaders from southern Arabia, copper-skinned people similar in language, looks, and nomadic habits to the present-day Somali and the Masai. The pale-skinned Sabaeans may never have been very numerous but they soon dominated the highland areas with their superior culture and military strength, and they laid the foundations of a kingdom based on the town of Axum which by 300 A.D. not only controlled the highlands of northern Ethiopia and the lowland areas as far west as the Nile, but by reconquest the highlands in southern Arabia from which they had come as well. In the fourth century A.D. one of their rulers named Ezana described himself on a carved obelisk at Axum as 'King of Axum and of Himyar and of Raydan and of Ethiopia and of Saba and of Salhen and of Tseyamo and of Bega and Kasu, the King of Kings, the son of the invincible god, Ares'. Not all these places can be identified now but Himyar and Raydan were in the Yemen while Bega and Kasu were probably lowland areas north and west of the Abyssinian highlands in what is now the Sudan.

The invaders from Saba who founded the Axumite kingdom and spread all over the highlands became known as the *Habash*, an Arabic word said to be derived from *Habashat*, the name of the Sabaean tribe to which they had mostly belonged.[1] Whatever its origin, Abyssinia was the name by which the country soon became known throughout the Middle East. The Greeks, however, called all the people who lived south of Egypt 'Ethiopians', or people with burnt faces, in the same arrogant way in which they called all those who lived north of Greece 'Celts', or barbarians. It seems likely therefore that when the kings of

[1] Another theory is that it comes from the Arabic *habsh*, meaning a mixture or confusion of races.

Axum, who prided themselves on their pale Arabian skins, styled themselves 'Kings of Ethiopia', they did so because they had extended their rule by conquest over the neighbouring lowland areas inhabited by dark-skinned peoples. Although 'Ethiopia' continued to be used both inside the country and in Europe, 'Abyssinia' became the name most commonly used, and was certainly the one by which the country was generally known in the nineteenth century. 'Ethiopia' is now back in fashion, and, despite its racial origins, is the name by which the proud people of the country like it to be called.

When the Sabaean people settled in the highlands on the African side of the Red Sea they took with them not only their physical characteristics but their legends, their language, and their religion. Over the years there was considerable intermingling both of blood and of culture between the Semitic newcomers and the existing inhabitants, and by the fourth century A.D. the kingdom of Axum had developed its own hybrid language and script called Ge'ez. It differed from Sabaean and other Semitic languages like Arabic and Hebrew in being written from left to right, and in having the vowel signs incorporated in the consonants. With 31 consonants and 7 vowels, that made a total of 217 characters in the alphabet. This was still the religious and literary language of Abyssinia in the nineteenth century, although Amharic had long since become the tongue in most common use.

In the same way, the religion that the invading Sabaeans brought with them, which was a strange mixture of pagan practices and Jewish rituals, became influenced by the pagan beliefs of the indigenous Hamites. But a new element was introduced in the fourth century A.D. when two Syrian missionaries named Frumentius and Edesius persuaded the king of Axum of the superior merits of the Christian faith; the practical advantages of a spiritual affinity with the powerful Christian emperor of Constantinople may have appealed to him too, at a time when a Persian threat to his remaining Arabian dominions was emerging. The conversion of the king's often inaccessible subjects to Christianity was a slow and difficult process, and this may account for the persistence both of pagan and of Jewish beliefs and practices in some parts of Christian Ethiopia for hundreds of years.

The emergence of Islam in the seventh century as a religious and political force in the Middle East coincided with a decline in the vitality of the Axumite kingdom, and for a time cut off Christian Abyssinia from the outside world. 'Encompassed on all sides by the enemies of their religion the Aethiopians slept near a thousand years, forgetful of the world by whom they were forgotten.' The isolation was not as complete as suggested by Gibbon's rounded prose but it did have the effect off preserving the nation's institutions, like cultural fossils, from the changes wrought by Renaissance and Reformation elsewhere. During the period, Abyssinia was messily occupied with baronial feuds, like western Europe, and with imperialistic excursions blessed by the Church, not unlike the Crusades. Having lost its dominions in Arabia and in the lowland plains to the forces of Islam, the Abyssinians started to compensate by pushing south, and compelling the less sophisticated peoples whom they encountered to adopt their culture and their religion.

It was during the sixteenth century, however, that events took place which etched themselves more firmly on the eager and receptive mind of the youth who was to become the Emperor Theodorus. Between 1527 and 1541 the dominions of the Ethiopian empire were overrun by Muslim forces under the leadership of Ahmed bin Ibrahim el Ghazi, better known by his Amharic nickname of 'Granye', the left-handed. This remarkable young man, whose major victories were achieved when he was still in his twenties, came from the Horn of Africa, and drew his support from the Danakil, or Afar, and the Somali. When the Muslim forces, with the help of Turkish cannon and Arab muskets, had occupied most of the Abyssinian highlands, the Abyssinian emperor, Lebna Dengal, decided that he needed outside help. The emperor, whose name meant 'Incense of the Virgin' and who customarily received foreign visitors half-hidden behind a curtain of green taffeta like a deity, sent an envoy to the Portuguese, who had shown an earlier interest in Abyssinia, with an offer to submit the Ethiopian Church to Rome in exchange for what we would now call technical aid and military help against his Muslim invaders.

The help did not arrive until after his death, but when it did come, in the shape of 400 Portuguese soldiers under Vasco da Gama's youthful kinsman Cristovão da Gama, it was most effective. Within two years Granye and his main force had been destroyed. Although the Portuguese fulfilled their side of the bargain, the Abyssinian emperor and his successors were reluctant, when it came to the point, to sever their ancient ties with the See of Alexandria or to abandon the many distinctive features of the Ethiopian Church of which Rome disapproved. It took nearly a hundred years of persuasion and pressure by Portuguese missionaries, and a withholding of military supplies, before a formal submission was made. But the methods which the Jesuits' missionaries employed in this period were to sow the seeds of their own destruction. They attacked as heresies many of the Old Testament practices and beliefs to which the Abyssinian Church was particularly attached, like observance of Saturday as the Sabbath, ritual circumcision, and many detailed prohibitions in matters of food and sex. Within a few years of the emperor Susenyos' formal submission to Rome in 1626, he was forced to repudiate it and abdicate, in such a violent upsurge of local religious fervour and xenophobia that all the Jesuit missionaries were expelled and other traces of Portuguese influence removed. It was largely because of these events that suspicion of Europeans, especially those seeking favours for the missionaries of their choice, became so deep-rooted that it was nearly two hundred years before Abyssinia was to emerge from that period of isolation.

The fighting between the Abyssinian Christians and the Muslims did not end with Granye's defeat by the Portuguese, and it was for many years a recurring feature of the Abyssinian scene. The Galla peoples of the southern and western highlands watched this struggle with interest. They had suffered in their time from both parties, and were waiting in the wings for opportunities to exact revenge and to recover lands which had been taken from them. The Galla were a very ancient race, the indigenous stock, perhaps, on which most other peoples in this part of eastern Africa had been grafted. Darker in skin than the Amhara, less negroid in features and colour than the Nilotic races of the Sudan, the Galla were tall and handsome and strongly built, and excellent fighters. They were originally stock-owning nomads, used to protecting their cattle from lion and rival clans with knives and spears, and they were brought up from boyhood to the notion that the respect of their elders and the favours of their womenfolk only went to those who had tangible proof that they had killed a lion, an elephant, a buffalo, or a man.

As the Christians and Muslims dissipated their energies and resources in internecine warfare, the Galla advanced and often settled as farmers on the land they took until, by the middle of the nineteenth century, they had occupied most of the sultanate of Harar in the south-east, and large parts of the southern and central Abyssinian highlands. Their advance was initially the cause, and finally the result, of the decline of the Abyssinian monarchy. After the defeat of Granye and the subsequent expulsion of the Portuguese, the emperors moved their headquarters to Gondar, a few miles north of Lake Tana, the reservoir of the Blue Nile. It was an agreeable place, with a happy climate of warm days and cool nights, and safely tucked away, it seemed, from the menace of the Galla and their cruel knives. It was also, however, a long way from some of the imperial dominions like Tigrai and Shoa, and from the encampments of the powerful barons, the *rases*, who ruled their provinces with the pomp and style of princes, and increasing independence of the emperors.

While the *rases* built up their forces and lessened their ties with the central government, the emperors concentrated for the most part on building and gilding an imperial city and castle at Gondar. In its prime the city had twelve gateways, and walls thirty feet high, a mile in circumference. Although both city and castle owed a debt in style and construction to the Portuguese, they became increasingly subject to Byzantine and Moorish influence. The great mosques of Constantinople and Cordoba, and the palaces and harems of Cairo and Damascus, gradually became the model for the churches and courts of the Abyssinian emperors. Even the names of the city gates seem to have been taken from *The Thousand and One Nights*—the Gate of the Musicians, the Gate of the Spinners, and the Gate of the Pigeons; near the delicately tiled Turkish baths there were the Brocade House and the House of the Hens. This was the setting for the elegant indolence, the corrupt decadence, and the resigned impotence of the emperors during the period of anarchy between the middle of the eighteenth century and 1855 known in Ethiopian history as the *zemene mesafint*, the period which was likened to the era in the *Book of Judges* when 'there was no king in Israel; every man did that which was right in his own eyes'.

When Bruce[1] went to Abyssinia in 1769 he found Gondar already in decline and falling into ruin. The stone and brick buildings had become barely habitable from neglect; the carpets and silk hangings, the chipped Venetian mirrors, and the once fashionable furniture of cane and ivory

[1] James Bruce of Kinnaird, who travelled to Gondar in 1769, and whose *Travels*, written many years later, are best known for their accounts of Abyssinian feasts at which the guests were said to cut pieces of meat from living beasts, and to pleasure themselves at table with the ladies, screened only by shawls held up by obliging neighbours. Many later travellers and missionaries tried hard to witness such goings-on but never with success. The reason may well have been that Bruce was, as Samuel Johnson put it, 'not a distinct relater'.

had been moved into huts made of sticks and clay and thatched with reed. For occasions of state the emperors used tents and pavilions of red silk. The imperial throne changed hands twenty-seven times during this period of 105 years. The incumbents were often very old men or short-lived boys chosen for their incapacity from the assortment of legitimate and illegitimate males who were kept, as Samuel Johnson depicted in *Rasselas*, in polite and poverty-stricken confinement in a mountain stronghold. One was reputed to be 96; another, who was not allowed to ascend the throne until he reached his seventies, had a hand cut off by his brother to reduce his activity. Another was a young boy, small, slender, and effeminate, who cultivated apricots and pomegranates in the gardens of Gondar. Bruce described one who had managed to preserve some of the dignified, almost mystical presence of his forbears. 'The king,' he wrote, 'was seated upon the throne, very richly dressed in brocade, a very fine muslin web wrapped loosely round him so as to hang in plaits, and in some parts to show and in others to conceal the flowers of the cloth of gold of which his waistcoat was composed. His hair was loose, combed out to full length, and a fork made of rhinoceros horn, with a gold head on it, stuck through his hair; he was perfumed with rose water, and two people stood on opposite sides of the tent each of them with a silver bottle. . . .'

In this era of imperial decline and anarchy, two of the most vivid and commanding figures in the palace of Gondar were women. Perhaps it was more than coincidence that they both had Galla blood. One, who also claimed a residue of Portuguese blood, was nicknamed Mentewab, which meant 'How beautiful she is!' She lived to a great age, and as a dowager empress made a great impression on James Bruce, and he, it was said, on her. The other woman was Itege Menen, the mother of Ras Ali, who married two emperors and outlived them both, and led her own troops into battle.

As the power of the emperors faded, the strength of the *rases* grew. It suited them to preserve the imperial throne while keeping its incumbents weak and dependent on their goodwill for sustenance and the appurtenances of pomp. Apart from the importance still attached by the Church and public opinion to the continuity of the Solomonic line, any attempt by one *ras* to usurp the throne himself would have aroused the jealousy of other *rases* and led to civil war. They were satisfied therefore, for the most part, to pay nominal homage to a powerless emperor, although they did not always agree on who should wear the emperor's clothes. At one time there were said to be as many as six emperors or ex-emperors living simultaneously. The *rases* used them sometimes for show on ceremonial occasions, like a regimental goat, or took them into battle as mascots to bring them luck. No one took them very seriously. The traveller Nathaniel Pearce, who was schooled in Yorkshire, noted of one emperor that when he died 'the *ras* only kept one day's cry for him'. In this period of national decline and shame the scribes of the Royal Chronicles addressed themselves to the causes. 'How is it that the kingdom has become contemptible to children and to slaves? How is it that the kingdom is a laughing-stock to the uncircumcised? How is it that the kingdom is the image of a worthless flower that children pluck in the autumn rains . . .?'

It was in this situation that Prince Alamayu's father was born in the early part of the nineteenth century.

CHAPTER II

The rise to power

Alamayu's father was not born with any silver spoon in his mouth. All he would have had, like any other Abyssinian boy, was the tip of a lance thrust between his lips to ensure that he had courage, together with his proper ration of joyful cries from the womenfolk—twelve for a boy and three for a girl. His circumstances did not warrant any record being made of the date or the place of his birth, and Ethiopian and European scholars differ on both these points. The most that can be said is that he was born sometime between 1818 and 1820 somewhere in north-west Ethiopia. There are similar doubts about the circumstances and even the names of his parents. It would probably not have seemed to matter much at the time but the details of his parentage became a question of considerable importance later on. His father is known to have been a man of authority in the district of Kwara, west of Lake Tana, whereas some authorities merely refer to his mother as 'a lady of Attitegeb', and others as a woman of humble birth. When he became emperor claims were made that one or even both his parents were of royal descent, but a sympathetic study published in Addis Ababa in 1966[1] reached the conclusion, after careful research based on land records and family trees, that none of the known genealogies brought Theodorus 'within range of a ruling monarch for seven generations'.

Kasa, to give him the name his parents gave him,[2] grew up without expectations. His father died when Kasa was a child, and it was to the well-established family of his father's first consort, Welette Tekle, rather than to his own mother, that he turned. Under the powerful

[1] Sven Rubenson, *King of Kings, Tewodros of Ethiopia*, published by Haile Sellassie I University in association with the Oxford University Press.

[2] Clement Markham wrote in 1869 that in Abyssinia 'a child generally receives a name of endearment from its mother, such as Warkye (My Gold), Negusye (My King), Alamye (My World), Oobye (My Beauty), or Kasai (My Substitute, given to the second child when the first-born has died). At its baptism a child receives a Christian name, as Walda Yasus (Son of Jesus), Gabra Mikhael (Slave of St. Michael), Tekla Georgis (the Plant of St. George), or Tesfa Tsion (the Hope of Zion). . . . In addition to these the Abyssinians are often called by the name of their favourite horse with the prefix Abba (Father). Kasa, present ruler of Tigre, is Abba Buzbuz.'

protection of his half-brother Kinfu he received a good education in the local church schools. At this and another school, where he remained until he was sixteen, he seems to have absorbed as much knowledge of the history, law, literature, and legends of his own country as most of the foreigners he was to meet afterwards knew of theirs. He certainly learnt more than they did about the biblical and dialectical foundations of the beliefs and practices of his own religion: even among the Catholic and Protestant missionaries he encountered later there were few who could hold their own when it came to discussion of esoteric matters like the true nature of Christ or the substance of the Trinity. At the same time he got a good grounding in the skills and strengths of manhood. He was a first-rate horseman, a marksman with firearms, and so skilled with a sword or a spear that it was said that in his youth he would charge elephants on horseback armed with no more than a lance. His education was widened by active participation in the sporadic campaigns which Kinfu conducted during the conventional fighting season between the rains, when the ground was dry and the rivers were fordable. This all-round education, coupled with his legendary courage and powers of endurance, and his great physical strength, made him a formidable young man by the time his half-brother Kinfu died in 1839.

It was at this time, according to Zeneb, who was Kasa's companion and scribe during this period, that Kasa took to the hills and became a *shifta*, an Amharic word which, like our *guerrilla*, means patriot to some and brigand to others. He already had the habit of command, and soon gathered round him a band of men from both the highland and the lowland areas whose knowledge of the terrain helped him to become a rich, powerful, and much feared figure in the Abyssinian borderlands between Lake Tana and the Nile. It was an uncertain and itinerant existence, living in tents with his followers and being hunted from time to time by the forces of law and order; there were occasions, Zeneb reported, when they lived in the wilderness on the margins of starvation and 'ate the fruit and wild honey of the trees'. There were also moments of power and plenty when Kasa stood outside his tent and surveyed the booty of his brigandage—horses and mules, carpets and cooking-pots, elephant tusks and rhinoceros horn, hoards of heavy Maria Theresa dollars,[1] stocks of grain, cattle, sheep, and goats, war drums, matchlock muskets, butter, honey, and huge jars of beer and

[1] See page 106.

mead. Divided among his followers, they helped to cement their loyalty, and Kasa was wise enough to share his booty too with the villagers and peasants of the places where he drew his supplies. He even gave them seed so that there would be crops for him to share, if need be, the following year.

By 1845 Kasa was too successful to be ignored and too strong to be subdued. The governor of the area in which he was operating decided that it was time to come to terms with him. The area was known as '*Ye Maru Quimis*', 'the land that Maru tasted', that is to say the province in which Dejazmatch Maru had taken his dues in tithes and taxes. The governor at that time was Itege Menen, the second of the two formidable women mentioned on page 9. She had acquired the governorship from her own son Ras Ali, who had grown up to become one of the most powerful rulers in northern Abyssinia. Menen derived her title of Itege, or empress, from marrying one of the many weak figureheads who occupied the imperial throne at Gondar for a brief period, but her standing and her power stemmed from her own indomitable and devious character. Her offer to Kasa was to allow him 'to come in', as the Amharic saying went, in exchange for an amnesty for himself and his followers. Kasa, who knew what such promises might mean in practice, declined the bait until it was replaced by something more tangible. When it came, it was itself a measure of Kasa's success. He was offered Ras Ali's daughter as a wife, and the district of Kwara as his fief. Whether she was Ras Ali's daughter or his half-sister, as some assert, the lovely Tewabach became a most devoted and much cherished wife. But neither this close relationship nor the governorship of the rich province of Kwara was enough to deter Kasa from taking up arms in the end, first against Itege Menen, and then against Ras Ali himself.

Nor did he wait long. Early in 1847, taking advantage of Menen's absence on a raid, he appeared with a show of force at Gondar, and demanded the dues and the deference formerly paid to the empress. When Menen returned and tried to restore her authority by force she was defeated and taken prisoner. With Itege Menen as his prisoner, Kasa learnt, though not perhaps for the first time, the value of having in one's hand persons of sufficient worth for a price to be asked for their release. It did not matter to the pragmatic Kasa whether it was filial affection, pride, or purely practical considerations that moved Ras Ali to pay a ransom for his mother. What mattered was that Kasa was able to demand and to get the whole of the land that Maru tasted, a huge and fertile province which embraced all the highlands and borderlands from the Taccaze river in the north to the Abai, or Blue Nile, to the south, and which had as its centre the imperial city of Gondar.

For five years after his defeat of Itege Menen in 1847 Kasa concentrated on consolidating his position. He made his peace with Ras Ali for their mutual benefit. Ras Ali was busily and bloodily engaged at that time in trying to assert himself as the dominant ruler in the Abyssinian highlands from Gojjam to Tigrai. Tigrai was particularly important as it controlled his only route to the sea and his contact with the outside world through the port of Massawa. Apart from his need of firearms from the Turks and the Arabs, Ras Ali was at that time trying to get some political and material support from Britain through the medium of Walter Plowden, the British Consul at Massawa.

In 1852 relations between Ras Ali and Kasa deteriorated, and fighting began. It was Kasa who provoked the confrontation, partly because he now felt strong enough to win, and partly because Ras Ali, encouraged by the recognition and arms he was getting from Britain, was becoming increasingly ambitious and was setting his sights on the imperial crown. Although Kasa still had only a few hundred firearms, he had become a good tactician, and now, in eighteen months of skilful campaigning, he defeated all the forces which Ali sent against him, and finally routed Ras Ali's own army in a decisive battle in Gojjam.

The elimination of Ras Ali left Kasa with two main rivals in central Abyssinia—Ras Biru in Gojjam and Ras Ubye in Semien and Tigrai. He decided that the time had come for him to seek the blessing and co-operation of the established Ethiopian Church. The chief dignitaries of the Church, having been expelled from their customary place close to the court of the nominal emperors at Gondar by the Muslim Ras Ali, had for some time been living under the wing of Ras Ubye in Tigrai. Kasa now successfully used all his powers of persuasion and pressure to induce them to return to Gondar, and to abandon any idea they had of consecrating the ambitious Ubye as emperor. One of the inducements he offered them, in addition to the usual material rewards, was a promise to expel their spiritual rivals, the Catholic missionaries who were established in Gondar. It was a promise which Kasa was quick to honour; and in September 1854, after defeating Biru, he had little difficulty in getting the blessing of the Church for a significant change in his own status. He exchanged the subordinate title of *dejazmatch*, which had been appropriate to his command of a province, for that of *negus*, or king. At the same time he took another step which established himself even more firmly in the favour of the Church. He took Holy Communion in public with his wife. This not only confirmed his marriage in the most formal way, but it was also, in the eyes of the Church, a public affirmation of Kasa's regard for the Christian principle of monogamy, a principle which, while accepted in theory by both princes and priests in Ethiopia, was not always followed in practice by either.

Less than six months later, in February 1855, Kasa defeated Ubye in another decisive battle at Deresge, in Ubye's ancestral province of Semien. Two days after the battle Kasa was anointed and crowned *negusa negast*, 'king of kings', by Abuna Salama, the Coptic metropolitan of the Ethiopian Church. The ceremony took place in the local village church. Most village churches in Abyssinia were too small and too flimsy to allow for any degree of pomp and dignity but, by a happy coincidence, this church was a substantial building which had been erected for Ras Ubye by a versatile German botanist named Schimper, who had spent many years collecting plants in the highlands of Abyssinia and had made his home in the country.

Although it was not until some years later that the new emperor felt it necessary to assert his royal descent from Solomon and Sheba in public, he lost no time in presenting his other credentials. He did it in a way which he knew everyone in Abyssinia would understand. He had himself crowned as Tewodros, transcribed into English as Theodorus when it was officially reported to the Foreign Office by the British Consul. He chose this name because of a well-known legend. The legend took several forms, but its essence was that a Messiah-like king with the name of Tewodros would be raised up by God to free the country from oppression and tribulation, and to lead it into an era of peace and plenty. This was projected by the new emperor and his supporters to mean that it would end the long period of *mesafint*, during which Abyssinia had been ruled by impostors, idiots, and women, and in which corruption, injustice, and moral perversity had flourished; and that, having first destroyed all those who had encircled or encroached on the ancient dominions of Ethiopia, he would restore the country to its old greatness. Kasa was wise enough not to confine himself to the promises of liberty, equality, and prosperity usually made on such occasions, but to undertake to right specific wrongs, such as soldiers' taking grain from villagers without payment, and offenders' being handed over for punishment to the family of the victim, both of which he knew were great public grievances. He had to be called Tewodros the Second because of another Tewodros who reigned very briefly in the fifteenth century.

The gradual encroachments of the Galla had profoundly disturbed and offended the Christian people of Abyssinia, and the position of power which had been achieved by the Galla and Muslim Ras Ali in the very heartlands of the Amhara had a similar effect. The emergence of Mohamed Ali as a strong man in Egypt in the first half of the nineteenth century presented a threat to Christian Abyssinia from another quarter, and the Abyssinians watched with growing apprehension as his well-drilled and well-armed troops pushed southwards up the Nile and its Abyssinian tributaries in search of slaves, ivory, and gold. It was not only to these northern and western borderlands that the Egyptians posed a threat: Mohamed Ali had, for a consideration, been appointed *wali*, or governor of Abyssinia, by the Sultan at Constantinople, and this gave him the control of the Red Sea port of Massawa and a virtual stranglehold on Abyssinian trade and communications with the outside world.

The political and the religious future of Abyssinia was thus in danger. Another reason why a strong central government was needed was the increasing interest being taken in Abyssinia by a number of European powers. Ras Ali and others had indeed encouraged such an interest, particularly by Britain and France, in the hope that, as Christian nations, they might afford some protection against the infidel Turks and Egyptians. There were, however, dangers as well as advantages in such approaches. The rulers of Abyssinia had had little experience of European intervention in the past but they were cynical enough to assume that it would be designed to serve European rather than Abyssinian interests, and that calling in European doctors, so to speak, might be more of a danger to the Abyssinian patient than to the ills they were meant to cure. The danger would clearly be increased by any disunity inside Abyssinia which the Europeans could use to play one ruler off against another. If there was only one strong ruler in Abyssinia, not only would this danger be diminished but a clever man could turn the tables and take advantage of the rivalries and jealousies which existed between the British and the French not only in matters of political influence and commercial advantage but in questions of religion as well.

It was not only these external dangers which made the time ripe for a

The Emperor Theodorus, by Baudran

European hostages after their release from Magdala

Gondar

Messiah. The absence of a strong central government, and the constant warring of the barons had their inevitable consequences in terms of misery, starvation, insecurity, and injustice. The internal situation in Ethiopia in the middle of the nineteenth century was thus more than ready for an upheaval. Kasa may have been a man of such quality and driving force that he would have risen to the top in any circumstances; but the combination of grievances and unrest inside the country, and of pressures and dangers from outside, were such that, if Kasa had not been on hand, then someone else would probably have appeared to take his place and play a similar role.

It is doubtful, however, if the forces of history could have been relied upon to produce a man quite as extraordinary as the new emperor. Walter Plowden, the British Consul at Massawa, who knew him well, sent this report to the Foreign Office soon after his coronation:

> The King Theodorus is young in years, vigorous in all manly exercises, of a striking countenance, peculiarly polite and engaging when pleased, and mostly displaying great tact and delicacy. He is persuaded that he is destined to restore the glories of the Ethiopian Empire, and to achieve great conquests; of untiring energy, both mental and bodily, his personal and moral daring are boundless. . . . When aroused his wrath is terrible, and all tremble; but at all moments he possesses a perfect self-command. Indefatigable in business, he takes little repose night or day; his ideas and language are clear and precise; hesitation is not known to him; and he has neither councillors nor go-betweens. He is fond of splendour, and receives in state even on a campaign. He is unsparing in punishment—very necessary to restrain disorder, and to restore order in such a wilderness as Abyssinia. He salutes his meanest subject with courtesy; is sincerely though often mistakenly religious, and will acknowledge a fault committed towards his poorest follower in a moment of passion with sincerity and grace.
>
> He is generous to excess, and free from all cupidity, regarding nothing with pleasure or desire but munitions of war for his soldiers. He has hitherto exercised the utmost clemency towards the vanquished, treating them rather as his friends than his enemies. His faith is signal; 'Without Christ,' he says, 'I am nothing; if He has destined me to purify and reform this distracted kingdom, with His aid who shall stay me?'

CHAPTER III

The protagonists: the barons and the priests

The first objective which the new emperor set himself was proclaimed at his coronation: 'I swear by this crown of my ancestors that I shall gather under my authority all the provinces which in the past belonged to this Empire.'

He was as good as his word. Within a week of his coronation Theodorus was on the move with an army of between fifty and sixty thousand men, their arms considerably increased by 7000 rifles taken from his opponents at the battle of Deresge. He made a departure from tradition by campaigning in the rainy season, and to this startling military innovation he added another by keeping his troops on the move both in Lent and at Easter. By the end of that year (1855) he had broken the power of the Galla chiefs who for generations had cut off the province of Shoa from the rest of Christian Abyssinia, and had taken from them the superb natural and man-made fortress of Magdala, which he was later to make into his own private stronghold. From there he moved south to Shoa itself. When eventually he returned to Gondar in July 1856 he had gone a long way in his first year towards fulfilling the promise made at his coronation; but as security for Shoa's good behaviour in the future he had taken the precautions of abducting the king of Shoa's eldest son, Menelik, and keeping him as a hostage.

The following year he planned to complete the subjugation of Tigrai, and to recover possession of the coastal areas and the port of Massawa which had for many years been in the hands of the Turks. 'After that,' Plowden blandly told the Foreign Office, 'he wishes to reclaim all the provinces lately conquered by Egypt along his northern frontier; even to Khartoum, as his by right: nor does his military ardour hesitate to dream of the conquest of Egypt and a triumphant march to the Holy Sepulchre.'

During the long period of anarchy the hereditary rulers of the provinces had grown to enjoy their independence and their freedom from obligations to a central government. As soon as Theodorus had gone south to attack the Galla, two brothers named Negusye and Tesemma, who were closely related to the defeated Ras Ubye of Tigrai, had taken advantage of the emperor's absence to try and assert their independence by raising the standard of revolt in Tigrai and Semien. For the next five or six years Theodorus had this problem intermittently on his hands. It was one that became increasingly important when the French, for good reasons of their own, recognized Negusye as king of Abyssinia and encouraged him to persist in his revolt. In the end it took Theodorus six years to complete the subjugation of Tigrai;[1] in anger and exasperation at this frustration of his dreams, he finally left Negusye to die a slow and horrible death on the battlefield.

When Theodorus was in the south, there was also a rising against his authority in the province of Gojjam. He returned to deal with this rebellion, and the Galla chiefs took up arms again, led by the very man that the emperor had appointed to keep them in check. Theodorus returned in all seven times to the Galla lands, declaring amnesties and pleading with the people to lay down their arms in the interests of national unity. In the end he reverted in desperation to the traditional and better understood formula of massive retribution; in this case it was more than an eye for an eye. After one battle, his Abyssinian biographer Zeneb recorded with admiration that the Emperor Theodorus cut off the hands of 787 prisoners.

For three years the governor he had left behind in Shoa to keep the peace had remained loyal, but in 1859 the emperor had to go south again to quell a revolt there too. He did not lose control of his dominions in those early years but he became saddened and disillusioned, and finally exasperated and angered by the constant rebellions and disloyalties of those he was trying to unite or those he believed he could trust, by the waste of having to contain his Christian compatriots at home when he should have been fighting infidels abroad, and by the years of precious time and youthful energy spent on campaigning instead of on the much needed work of reform.

Theodorus knew that he had to destroy the power of the barons before he could carry through the domestic reforms he had in mind. Plowden reported that

> the arduous task of breaking the power of the great feudal Chiefs, a task only achieved in Europe during the reigns of many consecutive kings, he has commenced by chaining almost all those who were dangerous, avowing his intention of liberating them when his power shall be consolidated. He has

[1] Transcribed by the French as Tigré, a spelling now commonly and misleadingly used without the accent. See note on p. 134.

placed the soldiers of the different provinces under the command of his own trusty followers to whom he has given high titles . . ; thus in fact creating generals in place of feudal chieftains more proud of their birth than of their monarch, and organizing a new nobility, a legion of honour dependent on himself and chosen especially for their daring and fidelity.

To those he gives sums of money from time to time, accustoming them to this intention of establishing a regular pay; his matchlock-men are numbered under officers commanding 100 to 1000, and the King drills them in person. In the common soldiers he has effected a great reform, by paying them, and ordering them to purchase their food but in no way to harass and plunder the peasants as before: the peasantry he is gradually accustoming to live quiet under the village judge, and to look no more to military rule. As regards commerce, he has put an end to a number of vexatious exactions, and has ordered that duties shall be levied at only three places in his dominions. All these matters cannot yet be perfected, but he intends also to disarm the people, and to establish a regular standing army, armed with muskets only, having declared that he will convert swords and lances into ploughshares and reaping-hooks, and cause a plough-ox to be sold dearer than the noblest war horse.

The feudal system in nineteenth-century Abyssinia was much like its counterparts in medieval Europe. It was built on a complex set of obligations and rights in which, in theory, everyone from king to peasant had a share of both. It was a system which at its best gave rise to the concept of *noblesse oblige*, and at its more common worst to a concentration of rights at the top and obligations at the bottom. We are indebted to Plowden again for a vivid picture of what the system involved for the peasants in practice:

They pay a certain portion in kind to the *ras* or other great chief and sometimes a regular tax in money; besides this, they must furnish oxen to plough the king's land. Their immediate governor then takes his share in kind of every grain, say a fifth, and feeds besides a certain number of soldiers at the expense of each household; he has rights to oxen, sheep, goats, butter, honey and other requisites for subsistence; he must be received with joy and feasting by his subjects whenever he visits them and can demand from them contributions on fifty pretexts—he is going on a campaign, or has just returned from one; he has lost a horse or married a wife, his property has been consumed by fire, or he has lost all in battle, or the sacred duty of a funeral banquet cannot be fulfilled without their aid. . . .

Theodorus also sought to deal with these abuses by dividing each of the provinces in his dominions into small administrative units, and putting his own representatives in charge. They replaced the hereditary headmen, called *chikka shum*, whose office was generally derived from ownership of land. While they had in many ways been the backbone of the country's administration, maintaining law and order, and providing a rough-and-ready system of justice, increasing demands from above for taxes and conscripts and supplies meant too often that the obligations imposed on them were used as opportunities for their own private gain.

For these reasons the new emperor went out of his way to identify himself with the peasants rather than the barons. In a court of rich robes and dandified fashions he went ostentatiously barefoot and hatless, and revelled in wearing soldier's clothing. He turned his back in other ways too on the meaningless fripperies and ritual postures of the old court in the insanitary ruins of the palaces and castles at Gondar; when he had to be there he lived in a tent in the palace gardens. Mostly he avoided it, and lived in the field with his troops, forty or fifty thousand of them together with something like ten thousand official attendants and a host of menial camp followers—porters, men to cut grass for the horses and mules, women to grind corn and brew beer, and many others down to the small boys, the *wisht ashkeriotch* described by the English traveller Parkyns, whose duties ranged from brushing away the flies to acting as cushions for the feet. They made up a huge concourse which, when it was on the move, looked like some chaotic tribal migration.

It was in fact more orderly than it looked. Everything down to the smallest detail was regulated by traditions and customs which had their roots in ancient Sabaean and Judaic cultures. The concourse was continually on the move, enabling the emperor both to see things for himself and to be seen, to hear complaints, and to dispense justice in public as a final court of appeal. Punishments were administered on the spot and in public, *pour encourager les autres*, just as in London convicts were still being hanged in public at Newgate.[1] In his own fashion Theodorus simplified and humanized the old penal codes: the only punishments he permitted were, according to Plowden, chaining, flogging, mutilation, and death; this, Plowden explained, anxious as always to impress the emperor's virtues on a startled Foreign Office, excluded such refinements as 'flaying alive, splitting down with an axe, cutting up by bits (as a finger or toe each day), burying to the neck alive in the earth, binding the victim naked on a black anthill anointed with honey or butter. . . .'

Theodorus took his judicial functions very seriously. He often began

[1] The last public hanging at Newgate was in 1866.

his hearings at four in the morning, and interspersed the harshness of some of his sentences with acts of quixotic generosity and kindness. Nor was it only criminals who had cause to fear his judgments. He treated thieves and highway robbers with great severity, but he was even more severe when he found the ruling of a judge to be wrong or to have the taste of corruption. An appeal court moving about the country made justice easier and quicker and cheaper, but its advantages were probably more apparent to those with claims and grievances than to those who administered the law. It certainly added to the new emperor's growing unpopularity with the political and judicial establishment. There were seventeen attempts on Theodorus' life in the first two years of his reign, and he was wounded on six occasions. It was no wonder that he always wore a sword and a revolver, and carried a lance in his hand; for the same reason, perhaps, he decreed that the emperor was the only person allowed to keep a lion, an imperial practice which Haile Selassie was to follow up to the end of his rule.

When Theodorus decided to take the title and responsibilities of emperor he needed the support of the Church. He needed it not only because he knew that no one inside or outside Ethiopia would accept him as *negusa negast* unless he had been anointed and crowned by the head of the Ethiopian Church, but also because the Church had both influence and wealth. For centuries Church and State had worked closely together in Abyssinia and had served one another's interests. As the Catholic archbishop David Mathew put it,

> the nobility supported the clergy by giving endowments to churches and monasteries, setting up churches in newly conquered lands, and observing religious ceremonies as state functions. The clergy in turn served secular authority by providing a communications network for relaying and supporting official policies, excommunicating enemies, and providing counsel and morale in connection with military expeditions.

The alliance had worked well in the past, and the new emperor naturally hoped that it would continue to do so in the future.

The two key figures at the head of the Ethiopian Church were the *abuna*, or bishop, who was appointed by the Coptic Patriarch of Alexandria, and the *etchege*, or premier monk, who was appointed by the emperor. The latter was always an Abyssinian, and in practice often exercised greater power and influence than the bishop, who, by a custom going back to the beginnings of Christianity in Ethiopia, was always an Egyptian Copt and a stranger therefore to the language and customs of the country in his charge. The Ethiopian Church needed a bishop with apostolic succession. This called for consecration by the hands of a patriarch of the Orthodox Church, and the nearest one had his seat at Alexandria. An additional reason, from an Abyssinian standpoint, for bringing in a bishop from outside was that he alone had the power to anoint and crown the emperor, and there were obvious advantages in not allowing so great a power to lie in the palm of a native Abyssinian with family and other local connections. Taken together, these advantages were such that the patriarchs at Alexandria saw in them an opportunity to exact payment from Abyssinia for their services. As these payments soon became their largest single source of income, the patriarchs had a strong vested interest in continuing the arrangement. Since the seventh century, however, Egypt had been under Muslim control, and the Islamic rulers in Cairo saw no reason why they too should not receive some benefit from an arrangement which was of such clear advantage both to the Christian Patriarch of Alexandria and the Christian rulers of Ethiopia. Egypt had lived since time immemorial under the fear that Abyssinia could impede the flow of the Nile; on this basis therefore a tacit understanding was reached whereby neither the flow of the Nile nor the supply of bishops from the see of Alexandria was impeded. The mutual advantages of this arrangement were so exactly and delicately balanced that it lasted for over 1500 years, and it was not until 1950 that for the first time a native of Ethiopia was made head of the Ethiopian Church.

The bishop who crowned Kasa as Emperor Theodorus II had been educated at a Church Missionary Society school in Cairo before he enrolled as a monk in the Coptic monastery in Egypt from which the bishops of the Ethiopian Church were traditionaly chosen. He was selected for this difficult and far from popular post when he was 21 years old. He took the title of Abuna Salama III, and when he learnt of the sum which the Patriarch of Alexandria had received from Abyssinia for his consecration and despatch to a life of permanent exile in a strange and seemingly barbarous country, the new bishop, who was not without a sense of humour, observed that at seven thousand silver dollars he was probably the highest priced slave in the world.

Abuna Salama arrived in Abyssinia in 1841. Finding the emperors to whom he was accredited living in impotent decadence and poverty at

Gondar, this quick-witted and ambitious prelate soon allowed himself to be caught up in the web of intrigue and tussle between the rival barons, Ras Ali, Ras Ubye, and Ras Kasa. It was a tangled web still further tangled by the rivalries and jealousies of Catholic and Protestant missions which had managed to secure precarious toe-holds in various parts of Abyssinia. Although the bishop held a spiritual position of almost mystical proportions it was not without its material opportunities. As Plowden put it,

his person is sacred to the highest degree, and wisely much hidden from the vulgar gaze. . . . He is also supposed to be pure from all defilement from his youth up, and is always veiled even on reception days when he blesses the prostrate multitude. . . . He obtains money from the people who sometimes come from the most distant parts of Ethiopia for remission of sins and absolution or to be made deacons, for which they pay a small sum.

The rivalries of the barons and the foreign missions provided other opportunities, and by the time he had been induced to abandon Ras Ubye, and crown Kasa as emperor in 1855, Abuna Salama was a rich man and a large landowner. The alliance he formed with the new emperor was of benefit to them both. Like Theodorus, however, Salama was a man of strong and independent character, and clashes of personality and interests began to occur. These clashes were brought to a head in a dramatic way by a visit from the Patriarch of Alexandria at the end of 1856.

Plowden reported to the Foreign Office that the emperor who was 'a man of fervent, even fanatic religious temperament', had expected to see in a patriarch 'the representative of Christ upon earth, one with his ideas wholly bent on religious matters, who would bless his efforts to extirpate Paganism and Islamism, and give spiritual counsels to himself and his subjects . . . '. In the flesh the patriarch was a disappointment.

Instead of in some measure accommodating himself to the material forms of Abyssinian worship, he spoke slightingly of their reverence for the Cross, of their prostrations to the Church, and of their saints and holidays; he pressed the King constantly to review his troops, and after a stay of a week he began to insist on returning to Cairo.

As a result, even the rich presents which the patriarch had brought with him were regarded with suspicion. Theodorus feared that 'the crown of a thousand sequins' was meant as a sign of fealty to Said Pasha, the Turkish viceroy in Egypt. He began to suspect that the reason for the patriarch's repeated requests to review the emperor's troops was that he wanted to look for points of weakness, and he even started to wonder if the patriarch was not acting as a spy for the Egyptians. His fears seemed to be confirmed when he discovered that the patriarch and Salama had together concocted a letter for him to send to the viceroy. The letter proposed an exchange of forty Abyssinian mules for 'three Turkish officers to discipline the Abyssinian troops, regimental bands, pioneers, sappers, engineers, bakers, doctors and medicines, cannons and muskets'. Much as Theodorus wanted these things, he had no wish to become dependent on his Egyptian neighbours or to allow them to infiltrate his country in any way. The seal seemed to be set on the emperor's suspicions when news reached him that Egyptian troops were massing near the frontier. The news was false but it was not the first, nor the last, time that Theodorus reacted to reports of this nature. He publicly accused the patriarch of being a crypto-Muslim and an agent of the viceroy, and confined him to his quarters. The patriarch countered by excommunicating the emperor. Theodorus then riposted by accusing the prelate, apparently with good reason, of engaging in the slave trade on the side. Caught between his obligations to the patriarch who had appointed him and the emperor under whose regime he had to live, Abuna Salama found himself in an awkward position. His efforts to please each in turn by excommunicating the other had the effect in the end of antagonizing both. Theodorus, who had a low opinion of high ecclesiastics in general, had the ultimate satisfaction of confining both prelates to their quarters in separate compounds within earshot of one another; he then lay concealed, and listened to their mutual abuse. It was not long, however, before Plowden reported that the emperor and the patriarch had been reconciled with ceremony, and sworn to peace and friendship. In the end the patriarch stayed for nearly a year in Abyssinia, and when he left, with a handsome present of ivory for himself, he carried a friendly letter for the viceroy proposing an exchange of Abyssinian mules and horses for Turkish arms and cannon.

One of the reasons why relations between Theodorus and the ecclesiastical authorities were strained during the patriarch's visit was that the emperor was trying to persuade them to make a contribution to his revenues. The Ethiopian Church had over the years acquired immense holdings of land which were free of tax, and used to provide a living for large numbers of priests, monks, and deacons. By an ecclesiastical equivalent of Parkinson's Law their numbers had grown as the Church's lands increased until it was said that they comprised as much as one in four of the Christian population. Theodorus' plan was to limit each individual church's holding of land to what was necessary to support the two priests and three deacons, this being the minimum required to perform the elaborate rituals of the Ethiopian eucharist. As some churches were supporting more than a hundred ecclesiastics of one kind or another, this would have meant a considerable reduction in numbers, and the return to taxable civil use of large amounts of tax-free Church land. This step would have obliged large numbers of clergy to follow other occupations in which they could also be taxed. Theodorus was interested in revenue as well as reformation.

Another complaint which he had against the Church was that traditionally some of its lands and buildings temporarily provided sanctuary for fugitives and rebels. As a bandit he had had occasion to appreciate their worth in the past, but as an emperor he naturally saw an arrangement which allowed criminals and political offenders to lick their wounds and regain their strength in a different light. To avoid a rupture with the Church while he was establishing his position Theodorus did not press his claims too far during the patriarch's visit, but four years later, in 1860, when he felt more secure, he was to start putting his proposals into effect, and to risk incurring the enmity of Abuna Salama and the whole Ethiopian Church.

CHAPTER IV

The protagonists: the missionaries and the consuls

Abyssinia presented a problem to missionaries which was almost unique. Had it been an infidel country the challenge would have been clear, and if it had been clearly and universally Christian it could have been left to its own devices. The trouble was that it seemed to be neither the one nor the other. Apart from its non-Christian peoples—the Muslims, the so-called Black Jews,[1] and the pagan tribes—the Coptic Church of Ethiopia itself seemed, to European eyes, to constitute a strange mixture of animistic, Judaic, and Byzantine elements. Persistent belief in old gods and ancient spirits was reflected in the existence of 192 feast-days in the calendar of the Ethiopian Church; Judaic practices included the observance of the Saturday Sabbath, ritual circumcision, and a number of Old Testament distinctions between clean and unclean foods; while the debt to the eastern Orthodox Church was evidenced not only in such matters as the elaborate liturgy of the eucharist, and veneration of the Virgin and of innumerable saints, but also in its central monophysite belief in the single divine nature of Christ as opposed to the dual human and divine natures recognized by Catholics and Protestants. This confusing mixture was epitomized both for missionaries and for ordinary travellers by the observance in Abyssinia of both the Christian Sunday and the Jewish Saturday as days of rest, with the result that, as Plowden discovered to his annoyance, 'water cannot be drawn, nor wood hewn from Friday evening to Monday morning'. There were times indeed when those brought up in the domesticated usages of the Church of England found it difficult, and even distasteful, to believe that they and the Abyssinians shared a common faith. Similar reservations were felt, though not always for the same reasons, by Catholics and Evangelicals.

Although it was not undeserved, the expulsion of the Portuguese Jesuits from Gondar in 1653 discouraged missionary enterprise for two hundred years, and it was not until the 1830s that foreign missions sought to establish themselves again. This time Protestants as well as

[1] See p. 32.

Catholics were involved. In an attempt to avoid the mistakes of the Jesuits, who had been intolerant of local usages, the new Catholic effort was directed into two separate channels. The Capuchins were charged in the usual way with converting pagans and using Latin, while the Lazarists were to work more subtly within the framework of the indigenous Ge'ez rites in an attempt to amend the heresies of the Ethiopian Church. The distinction stood them in good stead when the Emperor Theodorus expelled the Lazarists from Gondar in 1855. The Capuchins were left free to continue their activities, particularly in the area of Bogos and Keren in the north where Father Giovanni Stella was constantly using his compelling personality to get help in warding off unwelcome interference, whether it came from his Egyptian neighbours or from ambitious Abyssinian rulers. He in turn was helped by the pleasant climate of upland Bogos, and the beauties and generally harmless charms of its girls; together they served to attract considerable attention and sympathy from foreign consular officials at Massawa, where both the climate and the women tended to be unhealthy.

Although he also objected to the alliance which existed between the Catholics and his rival, Negusye of Tigrai, the main reason why Theodorus had expelled the Lazarists from Gondar was that Abuna Salama had insisted on it before he would agree to anoint and crown him as emperor. The Catholic bishops and the French consul in Abyssinia at the time thought that Salama, whose original selection in Egypt they had strongly opposed, was prejudiced against Catholics because of his Protestant background and his close friendship in Abyssinia with Plowden. But when asked why he objected to the Catholic missions Salama's answer was that the Pope of Rome would never have allowed others to propagate their doctrines in his dominions as the Catholics had done in his. He argued that the same objection did not apply to the Protestant missionaries, who were content to work with their hands, to circulate their Bibles, and only to preach to the heathen.

It had not always been so. When the Church Missionary Society first went to Abyssinia in 1830 they were less sensitive and more ambitious. The first missionaries had tried to convert not only the pagan tribes but the Christians of the Ethiopian Church, and they had felt it was their duty to deride and uproot unprotestant things like fasting, and veneration of the Virgin and the saints. They believed, as they put it, that they had to destroy before they could build. Their attitude was typified by

Samuel Gobat, later Anglican Bishop of Jerusalem, who, after speaking to the head of the Ethiopian Church about excessive veneration of the Virgin, wrote that 'when I began to prove that she was a sinner he kindled with an indignation which he wished to hide . . .'. It was not surprising that the first Protestant missionaries to Ethiopia were quickly expelled.

Encouraged by the friendly attitude of Abuna Salama and reports of more favourable political developments in Ethiopia in the 1850s, the Church Missionary Society decided to try again. Although it was a London-based, Anglican organization, it had habitually used for its work in Abyssinia what were described as simple Swiss and German pietists. They were trained at evangelical colleges in Switzerland, and were thought to be better equipped than the English to learn difficult languages like Amharic, and to be more suited to local conditions; as one of them explained, 'Living in Abyssinia is simple, with no plate, spoon, fork or table.' The first missionaries had been ordained priests, but the C.M.S. had learnt by its earlier mistakes. It decided that this time it would send no ordained missionaries and attempt no conversions. Instead it would send a small group of pilgrim missionaries, trained artisans of exemplary character and piety who would try and establish a settlement near Gondar where, as their mentor Dr. Krapf put it in a letter,

> they should pursue their accustomed trades and endeavour to engage some young men whom they could instruct in their trades as well as in spiritual matters. As the establishment would require many servants, the Bishop thinks that there would be at once a little congregation of Abessinians, in which the Word of God could be preached, and the light and example of true christianity be exhibited before the Abessinians without attacking the Abessinian Church in a direct way, as the Missionaries ex officio and professo would do. He thinks that the Abessinians, especially the chiefs, would receive and value christian mechanics, whilst they would on the outset refuse official Missionaries or priests.

An advance party led by Dr. Krapf arrived early in 1855. It was encouraged by a chance meeting on the way with the Lazarist Bishop de Jacobis, who was sadly making for the coast after his expulsion from Gondar while the Protestants were hopefully going in the other direction, with nineteen camel-loads of Amharic Bibles. Seventeen years earlier the positions had been reversed, with Krapf and his fellow missionaries being expelled from Tigrai and the Catholics being welcomed. This change of fortune caused Krapf to write home, with unecumenical satisfaction, that 'the contemplation of these remarkable changes strengthened our confidence in Him who will finally overthrow the schemes of all the enemies of the gospel'. It soon became clear, however, that Theodorus was much more interested in the newcomers' technical skills than in their piety or their zeal. He set the stage for the parts they were to play from the start. He received the missionaries reclining on a cushioned couch with the Coptic bishop by his side, while they were politely but firmly seated on the ground and informed that, instead of the improving handicrafts of weaving, joinery, and masonry which they had in mind, he wanted a gun-maker, a printer, and an architect. After hearing stories of a steam plough he later added that 'one of the labourers shall bring the thing that ploughs with a fire-screw'. The missionaries had been advised to say nothing at that stage about religious matters, and in the end Krapf had to report to the Anglican Bishop of Jerusalem, who was superintending the operation, that instead of getting permission to establish a small settlement where they could propagate their faith by example and teaching, they had somehow found they had agreed to provide a specific number of specified artisans to work for the emperor. It was not surprising that when they heard about this arrangement, three of the seven men who had been trained for work in Abyssinia withdrew. Two others, named Flad and Bender, decided to continue in the hope that the venture might prepare the way for a proper mission later to convert the heathen or the Black Jews. The other two trainees, Mayer and Kienzlen, who were more adventurous, had no such reservations, and they were joined in 1858 by Waldmeier and Saalmüller, and a gunsmith called Schrol.

Having made his position clear, Theodorus began to use his considerable charm, and a persuasive mixture of rewards and threats, to get the missionary artisans to concentrate their efforts on important matters like mending muskets, making roads, blasting rocks, and constructing a machine for the manufacture of gunpowder. The threats he made were disturbing enough in themselves to get results, but compliance and success were rewarded with a dazzling amiability, and with kindnesses and acts of generosity which took a variety of forms from encouraging invitations 'to partake of the Lord's supper together' to offers of local ladies on a temporary or permanent basis. The emperor was especially touched by the care and trouble which the missionaries took to try and save the life of his beloved wife Tewabach in 1858. Their efforts and their compliance with his wishes were finally rewarded two years later when the emperor gave them a place of their own at Gaffat, near his own new headquarters at Debra Tabor, where they could at last build themselves proper houses, a workshop, and a school. He often came there to share their simple meals, and spent long hours talking to them both about practical matters and about questions of religious belief. Although Theodorus tended to regard Europeans generally as barbarians who, by some inexplicable dispensation of providence, possessed technical skills and equipment, he came to rely more and more on the company and even the advice of these down-to-earth Swiss and German workmen. They for the most part developed feelings of admiration and respect for the emperor, feelings tinged occasionally with affection and always with awe. Kienzlen said of him that 'he was the only man in Abyssinia who possesses the fear of God'. There were even times, as Theodorus bemoaned the archaic obstinacies and the moral weaknesses of many of his own priests, when these hopeful missionary artisans began to think that the emperor was attracted by their own pietist beliefs.

The emperor's attitude to European missionaries was usually more detached. It was summed up in the reply he gave to Gilbert, the French consul, when he was asked to reconsider his expulsion of the Lazarists: 'It is truly scandalous,' he said, 'that Christendom should be divided into five or six mutually hostile denominations while Islam remains a compact body. Why should not an ecumenical council be convened in order to agree on a doctrinal formula which the whole of Christendom should then be bidden to adopt? . . . I am ready to submit myself to the decree of such a council; but until it is convened I shall remain in my old faith, and I will not allow that another one be preached since there should not be two religions in a well-ordered State.' This did not mean that he refused to tolerate other beliefs. But freedom of worship was one thing, and the right to proselytize was another. As he later explained in a letter to Gilbert:

I can give you an assurance then that neither your people nor those of our people who profess your faith will ever be molested or tormented in the countries of which Divine Providence has made me master; for not only Christians, our brothers, but also Muslims and Jews can live in our countries on condition that they behave in conformity with the laws of the country and obey the wishes of the sovereign. But if there are people who want to teach another faith, I will inform you that we have a bishop and a clergy, and that we cannot renounce the beliefs of our fathers.

His attitude to missionaries was again put to the test when he was approached early in 1860 by a representative of the London Society for Promoting Christianity among the Jews. Its purpose was to convert Jews to the beliefs and practices of the Church of England. It started work in the East End of London but eventually extended its operations to Jewish communities in India and the Middle East. It was a well-organized and well-supported mission, and it was fashionable in the middle of the nineteenth century for daughters and aunts to do crochet-work and flower paintings for what was known as 'the Jews' basket' at church fêtes and charity bazaars. The object of the Society's interest in Abyssinia were the Falasha, or Black Jews, a distinctive community which then numbered about 250,000 people who lived in settlements in and around Gondar and in remote mountain valleys in the province of Semien. They regarded themselves, and were accepted by others, as Jewish by race and religion; some of them indeed claimed that they were one of the lost tribes of Israel. Recent research[1] has thrown doubt on such claims, and it seems more likely that the Falasha are the descendants of indigenous pagans who had absorbed a number of early Judaic beliefs and usages from the Sabaean ancestors of the Abyssinian people, and later resisted the general conversion to Christianity. They thus acquired the Jewish elements of their religion some two thousand years ago. As they were subsequently virtually cut off from contact with the outside, this meant that they were untouched by the important body of later Jewish writings known as the Talmud. The result was that the Falasha were still practising in Abyssinia in the nineteenth century a religion mainly derived from the Old Testament, and were observing rituals and prohibitions which had remained unaltered since the time of Abraham and Moses.

The fact remains that in 1860 the Falasha were regarded as Jews both in missionary circles in Europe, and inside Ethiopia itself where the word *falasha*, meaning exile, reflected their outcast status as unbelievers living in a Christian world, relegated to the practice of useful but menial tasks like masonry and ironwork. It was largely due to the pietist Flad, who saw in the Falasha an opportunity for preaching the gospel which was denied to him at Gaffat, that interest in the Black Jews of Abyssinia was aroused in Britain. The first body to respond was the Jewish Mission Committee of the Church of Scotland, but for various reasons

[1] See W. Leslau, *Falasha Anthology*, New Haven, 1951, and *Coutumes et croyances des Falachas*, Paris, 1957.

their chosen German representatives, Staiger and Brandeis, did not reach Abyssinia until 1862, two years after they had set out from Europe. In the end the first to arrive and present himself to the Emperor Theodorus and Abuna Salama was the representative of the London Society. His name was the Revd. Henry Stern.

Henry Aaron Stern was by birth a German Jew. He came to England when he was 19 to improve his lot, but finding himself destitute and unemployed in the East End of London in 1839 he sought admission to the Operative Jewish Converts' Institution, which had been established in Bethnal Green by the London Society for Promoting Christianity among the Jews. There he learnt the trade of a printer, and was eventually baptized as a member of the Church of England. He trained as a missionary and served the Society in various parts of the Middle East, where his zeal and his pushful manner earned him several converts but few friends. His efforts in foreign parts led the London Jews' Society, as it was known for short, to select him as their emissary to Abyssinia.

When Stern explained that his object was to start schools, circulate Bibles, and convert the Falasha, the emperor and the bishop were pleased. To bring the stubborn Falasha into line in religious belief and political conformity had long been the ambition of successive Abyssinian rulers. When, however, Stern went on to say that by Christianity he meant the usages of the Church of England, both the emperor and the bishop objected. As Salama put it, 'I do not like to have two creeds and two Churches in Abyssinia but if you . . . let the Abyssinian priests baptize your proselytes, you may teach whatever you like.' In other words, the missionaries could use what means they wished to convert the Falasha to Christianity so long as it was to the Ethiopian Church that they eventually adhered. This was not at all what the London Society had in mind nor was it the purpose for which well-meaning people in England had contributed their pennies to church collections and mission-boxes. Stern felt, however, that it would be better than nothing, and that it might one day lead to better things. So, in September 1860, he established a mission station at Jenda near Gondar. He put it in the charge of Flad and his German wife, who were happy to exchange a new mission station with a high moral tone for what they both feared was the decreasingly conventional atmosphere at Gaffat, where the artisans were not only busy mending the emperor's muskets but were living with local wives. This change of allegiance by Flad and his wife meant, however, that relations between the two Protestant bodies got off to a bad start, and provided both the emperor and Abuna Salama with opportunities to play one off against the other.

Having established his mission station, Stern returned to England to explain the position as best he could to his headquarters, and to represent matters to the general public in lectures and sermons in such a way that contributions to the venture would continue. To help achieve this objective he wrote a book which he called, after the fashion of the time, *Wanderings among the Falashas in Abyssinia with a description of the country and its Various Inhabitants*. It was published in 1862. It succeeded in its purpose, but the Revd. Henry Stern was to pay heavily, and almost with his life, for some of its contents.

One of the difficulties of being a consul in Abyssinia during this period was to know to which of the aspiring rulers one should pay one's respects. A consul could take formal note of the emperors at Gondar, but it was unsatisfactory to do business with those who had neither power nor resources. There came a time when one had to decide which of the contending barons was likely to achieve the greatest and most lasting success. Another difficulty was where to live in a country where even the most stable rulers not only changed their capitals frequently but sometimes burnt the previous ones to the ground when they moved. A third problem was what to do. Was it a consul's duty to promote trade; to protect missionaries of one's own kind; or was it, as often seemed to be the main concern of their superiors at home, simply to frustrate the ambitions of other European powers?

All these difficulties were present when Walter Plowden was appointed as Her Majesty's first consul in Abyssinia by Lord Palmerston[1] in 1848. He was directed to Ras Ali, as the *de facto* ruler, but he was instructed to try and get the signature of the nominal emperor as well to a treaty of friendship and trade. Owing to a mistake in the Foreign Office, Plowden's letter of introduction was actually addressed to 'His Highness the Ras of Tigré, Abyssinia', who was Ras Ali's bitterest rival. It was a careless and unfortunate mistake, but the staff of the Consular Department of the Foreign Office had for some time been bemused by having to deal with a variety of letters from Abyssinia, not only from

[1] Viscount Palmerston (1784–1865) was Foreign Secretary in a variety of Whig and Liberal governments between 1830 and 1855, and intermittently Prime Minister from then until his death.

Ras Ali but from 'Dejaj Oobeay of Tigré'[1] and the 'king of Shoa', all of whom addressed their missives to Queen Victoria personally in the style and self-assurance of independent sovereigns. Nor was it easy to advise how these letters should be answered. The king of Shoa, for example, wrote: 'I am about to reproach you because you did not write to me or send anyone to me at the death of my father, but now I beg of you to send me 1500 dollars.' In a postscript, after saying that he was sending the Queen 26 elephant tusks and 31 rhinoceros horns (a well-known aphrodisiac), he added, 'I also beg that you will send me persons who can make a crown, and make cannons and paint pictures, and build palaces.' Ras Ubye tried a different approach: 'You are a Christian Queen; you are powerful, and I now request your assistance and friendship, that you will not permit the Mohammedan forces to ravage and occupy my territories but will insist on their remaining content with the island of Massowah[2] (though that even they have no right to) without setting foot on the mainland . . .'. He ended with the blandest of apologies: 'My soldiers, by mistake and in ignorance, burnt the house of your Consul at Moncooloo[3] for which I was sorry.'

The question of where to live was complicated by the fact that the status of Massawa, which seemed to be the best place from the point of view of trade, was in dispute: it was claimed as of right or by conquest not only by Ras Ubye and the emperors of Abyssinia but by the Turks, the Egyptians, and a local chieftain called 'the Naib of Arkeeko'. While this question was being resolved by the legal experts in the Foreign Office, Plowden was told to keep in touch with the itinerant camps of the rival barons in the interior. It was an instruction whose issue the Foreign Office was soon to regret.

He was also to protect British trade, conclude a treaty, and 'establish friendly relations with influential Chiefs of families'. His instructions were based on a minute in Palmerston's own handwriting, dated 22 August 1847. 'I do not,' he wrote, 'think it expedient to endeavour to obtain possession of any territory in that quarter, our object ought rather to be to encourage and secure the independence of the native Rulers.'

[1] So styled in the F. O. files. He is referred to in this book as 'Ras Ubye of Tigrai'.

[2] Now generally spelt Massawa, but it appears in contemporary reports and letters in other forms such as Masua and Massowa.

[3] A village on the mainland near Massawa, generally spelt Monkullo, where the consul once had his house.

Walter Plowden was no stranger to Abyssinia. He was an adventurous young man who had started his career with the firm of Carr, Tagore and Company in Calcutta when he was 19. In the preface to an edited version of his private journal, which was published after his death, Plowden's brother wrote that 'the sedentary duties of a mercantile life being unsuited to his genius, he threw up the advantages of such a career and in 1843 embarked for England'. A confidential note in the Foreign Office files put it in a different way: 'sent out to India in a mercantile house but his habits were not steady enough and he was re-consigned to his friends.' He had spent four years in India and he was still only 23 when on his way home he met another adventurous young man in Egypt named John Bell, and joined him on the spur of the moment to look, as they said, for the source of the Nile. Their travels took them to Abyssinia and they both liked it so much that they stayed. They attached themselves to the retinue of Ras Ali, and established such cordial relations with him that in 1847 Plowden was asked by Ras Ali to accompany some envoys he was sending to England with presents and a letter for Queen Victoria. Ras Ali needed Plowden's help because, whatever route his envoys used, they had to traverse Turkish-held territory, which would have put their presents and even their lives in jeopardy. As it turned out, the journey, the whole cost of which was met by the British tax-payer, was disastrous: their Arab dhow was wrecked in the Red Sea, most of the presents were lost, and the Abyssinian envoys were so unnerved by their first experience of the sea that they left Plowden to go on to England alone, and returned to Abyssinia by an overland route. In England Plowden impressed Lord Palmerston and the officials at the Foreign Office both with the possibilities of trade with Abyssinia and with the need to counter French attempts to curry favour with Ras Ubye. When the question of appointing a consul was proposed, it was in the end Plowden himself who got the job. He had been recommended to Palmerston by a cynical Foreign Office official in the following terms: 'high spirited and full of enterprise but without the steadiness for a mercantile life. I think he might well be employed in Abyssinia.'

It was frequently impressed on Plowden in London, and in subsequent correspondence when he returned to Abyssinia, that his chief concern should be to conclude a treaty. Her Majesty's Government's enthusiasm for a treaty is difficult to understand. Plowden had made it clear that his experience of Ras Ali and his entourage indicated that, whatever provisions were included in a treaty, 'it would be difficult to induce them to see the necessity of adhering to them when they should appear to militate against their interests to the slightest degree'. Nevertheless great trouble was taken in the cold attics and dingy basements of power in Whitehall over the exact wording of this 'Treaty of Perpetual Amity and Commerce', as it was styled. In the end it was drafted in what was known in the Foreign Office as 'the simple form deemed appropriate for unsophisticated States like Spain and Greece'. With a touch of diplomatic genius it referred to the other party to the agreement as 'His Majesty of Abyssinia', thereby avoiding delicate questions such as the relative standing of the emperor, Ras Ali, and Ras Ubye, and any similar problems which might arise in the future.

It took Plowden some time to persuade Ras Ali to sign the Treaty. It was finally signed and sealed in November of 1849, something over two years after the idea was first mooted in London. Plowden reported the occasion somewhat briefly in his official despatch, but his private journal was more explicit:

Accordingly one morning I went into his inner tent, and had the Treaty read to him by my scribe. After the Abyssinian manner, he kept talking to his favourite *shoomeree*[1] about a horse that was tied in the tent and that was nearly treading me under foot half a dozen times—we all sat on the ground, the Ras inclusive. On his asking me some trifling question, in answer, I begged his attention to what was being read, to which he assented, and yawned exceedingly; however, it was got through, some points having been explained and dwelt upon by me. Whereupon the Ras said that he saw no harm whatever in the document, that it was excellent but appeared to him exceedingly useless inasmuch as he did not suppose, as Abyssinia was then constituted, that one English merchant would or could enter it in ten years.

It said much for Plowden's sources of information, and his own adaptability, that he not only managed to anticipate Kasa's rise to power, but also to establish good relations with the new emperor. Yet whereas in Ras Ali's time it was Plowden who was the ruler's closest friend and adviser, with John Bell playing a subordinate part, now Bell became the right-hand man, with Plowden playing a role of gradually decreasing importance. Theodorus was a man who demanded complete allegiance, and he could not forget that Plowden had once been his defeated enemy's closest friend. Although he knew that Plowden had responsibilities to the British Government, there were times when he

[1] An elder.

seemed to see them as implying divided loyalties. With John Bell, who had no official position, there were no such reservations. Johannes Bell, as he was known, had virtually become an Abyssinian, and was committed to the country both by affection and by interest. He had married the daughter of a noble family in Begemder and fathered several enchanting children. He owned a great deal of land, and held a number of honorific and profitable posts. He was skilled and brave in the manly activities, riding and shooting and fighting with spear and sword, which were admired and at which the emperor himself excelled; and having served in the navy, he was in demand too for training and drilling the emperor's musketeers. But John Bell was more than an ally. He was the emperor's familiar, his *likamanquas*. He slept in the emperor's tent, shared his meals, and was his confidant in private and public affairs; it was also his duty to mislead the enemy in battle by wearing the emperor's clothes. It was Bell, more than anyone else, who opened Theodorus' eyes to the technical achievements of the Western world, and who also perhaps gave him more expectations in the way of material and moral support from Britain than was wise. He introduced the emperor to Shakespeare—'Bell's Bible', as Theodorus teasingly called the book which John Bell used for his extempore translations, while Theodorus listened entranced as the plots of the great tragedies were unfolded to him scene by scene. Although he was the emperor's familiar, John Bell was also, for the other Europeans in Abyssinia, their most helpful and influential friend at court. As the Revd. Henry Stern put it, in his usual gauche way, he was 'a perfect Abyssinian in appearance and dress but a gentleman in thought and heart'.

For Consul Plowden the first years of the new emperor's reign were far from comfortable or easy. There were several things he had been told to try and settle: apart from the delicate business of trying to persuade Theodorus to ratify the Treaty concluded with Ras Ali, there were three matters to which H. M. G. attached particular importance—the suppression of the slave trade, dissuading the new emperor from attacking the Turks and the Egyptians, and persuading him to let missionaries of every kind work freely in Ethiopia. Balanced against these was Theodorus' desire to send an envoy to England, and his need of arms and technicians.

This game of diplomatic tit-for-tat was one at which Theodorus was very skilled. He realized, however, that his bargaining position would be stronger once he had completed the pacification and unification of his country. So he temporized on every issue. He did so with such bewildering switches from sweetness to anger, and from humility to arrogance, and with alternating moods of infectious hope and demoralizing despair, that it was some time before Plowden realized that he was wasting his time, and that he was unlikely to bring matters to a head either by accompanying the emperor on his travels or by waiting at Gondar for him to return from his campaigns. He was reinforced in this conclusion by a deterioration in both his health and his enthusiasm. He was no longer the youthful adventurer he had been. He was nearly 40, and he had been suffering for some years from a disease which he left unspecified in his official reports. Latterly he had said that he had been 'attacked by a pestilence of a peculiar and formidable nature'. In November 1859 he also had the misfortune to break his leg.

The Foreign Office had already noticed a diminution of the usefulness and objectivity of Plowden's reports. They had also observed that, although Massawa had now been designated as his station, he spent little time there and rarely referred to matters of trade. When Plowden told them that he was wasting his time trying to keep in touch with the emperor in present circumstances, his real object was to get permission to return to England for medical treatment and leave. But while the Foreign Office readily agreed that 'no special advantage was derived from his frequent visits to the interior', the rest of their reply to his letter was not what he had hoped for.

> You will therefore return to Massowah, which is your proper residence, and you will not leave it, unless under very exceptional circumstances, without prior orders or permission from the Secretary of State. . . . The interests of that port are intimately connected with British interests in India, and, with judicious care and encouragement, it may become the outlet of a large trade between Abyssinia and Her Majesty's dominions.

Plowden never received this letter. It took two, three, or even four months for letters to travel from Whitehall to the interior of Abyssinia, and before it could have reached him he had met his death. He died from a spear-wound, but the circumstances of his death were controversial. One theory was that a nephew of the emperor's called Garrad, having defected to Ras Negusye of Tigrai, set out in force to waylay Plowden on instructions from Negusye, or even, it was alleged, from his French allies. The French version was that Plowden and Garrad were old enemies, and that the spear-wound was inflicted by Garrad in self-defence. Whatever the cause, Plowden was wounded and captured but not killed by the spear, and Garrad took the opportunity to demand a ransom of a thousand dollars for his release. According to a report which reached Massawa on 24 March the ransom was paid 'by his friends', but Plowden died nine days later in Gondar, and was given 'a great burial after the Abyssinian manner', with thirty priests performing the rituals.

A later report said that 'the emperor is much affected, and has announced his intention to exact signal vengeance for his friend's death'. Again Theodorus was as good as his word. He pursued his nephew Garrad and his party, and as he proudly explained in a long personal letter to Queen Victoria afterwards, he exterminated them all 'not leaving one alive though they were of my own family, so that, by the power of God, I may get your friendship'. He also mentioned modestly that he had paid the ransom for Plowden out of his own pocket. In the course of this punitive operation, John Bell was also killed, while dressed, in his usual hazardous line of duty, in the emperor's attire. Plowden's death was a milestone in the progress of relations between Britain and Abyssinia; but Bell's death and the removal of his influence on Theodorus was probably even more important. There was one observer at least, the perceptive missionary Theophilus Waldmeier, who saw it as the beginning of the end.

CHAPTER V

The first captives

News of Plowden's death reached the Foreign Office in May 1860. Although the department was immediately urged to appoint a replacement by various interested parties, including a persistently tiresome expert on everything to do with Abyssinia named Charles Beke who wanted the post himself, it was eight months before it reluctantly did so; and another year before the new consul reached Massawa. His name was Charles Duncan Cameron. He had started his career as a Lieutenant by purchase in the 45th Foot, and after service in the Zulu wars in South Africa, and then in the Crimea, he had joined the consular service and spent some years in Russia. There is nothing in the Foreign Office files to show how or why he was selected. All they tell us is that, when asked if Cameron was to be given any special instructions about British policy in Abyssinia, Lord Wodehouse, the Under Secretary of State, who knew that the French had supported Theodorus' rival Negusye, replied in a brief handwritten minute, 'We have hitherto supported the Emperor of Abyssinia, as I believe he calls himself. . . . I hardly know what instructions to give Mr Cameron. He should certainly watch the proceedings of the French.' When it came to drafting the new consul's instructions the officials at the Foreign Office sensibly ignored this ministerial imprecision and added much good sense of their own. It was a lengthy despatch in which frequent references were made to the rivalry between Theodorus and Negusye, but the nub was contained in one short paragraph:

> The principles, therefore, on which you should act are abstinence from any course of proceedings by which a preference for either party should be imputable to you; abstinence from all intrigues to set up exclusive British influence in Abyssinia; and lastly, the promotion of amicable arrangements between the rival candidates for power.

There was another equally notable paragraph setting out the policy to be followed in regard to missionaries:

Her Majesty's Government are aware that religious rivalry has contributed its share to promote dissension in Abyssinia; but such rivalry should receive no countenance from a British Agent, on the contrary, his study should be to extend as far as possible general toleration of all Christian sects, as being consistent with the doctrines of Christianity and with sound policy. The British Government claim no authority to set up or advocate in a foreign country one sect of Christianity in preference to another; all that they would urge upon the rulers of any such country is to show equal favour and toleration to the professors of all Christian sects.

The despatch was signed by Lord John Russell,[1] as Secretary of State for Foreign Affairs in Palmerston's last Liberal Government.

When Cameron eventually left London to take up his post he carried with him a letter to the emperor which was also signed by Russell, and a present supposedly from the Queen in the shape of a rifle and a matched pair of handsomely engraved revolvers. Although the letter itself was only a last-minute afterthought, it and the presents were intended as gestures of thanks to Theodorus for meeting the cost of the £200 ransom paid for the wounded Plowden, and for 'the steps which you had taken to punish the men who had murdered Mr. Plowden and Mr. Bell'. Understandably no reference was made to the nature of the steps the emperor had actually taken.

Owing to what was then a not uncommon misunderstanding, the Government of India, which also exercised a degree of control over Abyssinian affairs through its resident agent in Aden, was engaged simultaneously but independently in choosing and despatching presents of thanks to the emperor. With the recent Mutiny still much in mind, the Government of India was averse to giving arms to 'native rulers', and their choice was carpets, silver cups, and 'a sherbet service, richly gilt'. They were sent, so to speak, by parcel post, and owing to a further misunderstanding they arrived without either an envoy or a covering letter.

Cameron reached Gondar in June 1862, but the emperor being away, it was not until October that the new consul succeeded in getting an

[1] Lord John Russell (1792–1878), later the first Earl Russell, was the third son of the sixth Duke of Bedford. He was Foreign Secretary in Palmerston's government from 1859 to 1865, when he became Prime Minister. He was best known as the architect of the Reform Bill of 1832, but his patrician belief that that was as far as democracy should go later earned him the nickname of 'Finality Jack'. He was dimunitive and rickety in appearance, with a small, thin voice which often did less than justice to his incisive mind and biting wit.

audience. By then it was more than two and a half years since the emperor had seen a representative of the British Government. During that time his own position had become stronger. Cameron had already reported that Theodorus was now 'master of the sovereignties of Amhara, Tigre and Shoa—the late rulers of those kingdoms, with their nearer kindred, have either been killed or placed in a position to render them powerless. . . .' Cameron went on to say that the feudal system had been 'deprived of its more mischievous elements', and the whole country united under a military despotism. He also reported that Theodorus had tried to strengthen his position further by taking as his second wife Terunesh, a young girl of fair beauty and quiet charm, who was a daughter of his old rival Ras Ubye.[1] It was thus a self-confident and successful ruler who received the new emissary 'in a reclining posture, with a double-barrelled gun and two loaded pistols by his side'. Although Cameron naturally did his best in his official despatches to give the impression that he was received with the honour and respect he himself hoped for, it would seem from other sources that the emperor was in fact in an unreceptive mood.

He had, as was his custom, deliberately kept the newcomer waiting while his trusted agents observed and reported on his behaviour and temper. Theodorus soon came to the conclusion that, as far as he was concerned, Cameron was unlikely to fill the place of either Plowden or Bell. Although he was pleased with the Queen's presents and the inscription on the revolvers, he regarded the letter signed by Lord John Russell as an insult. 'Who,' he asked, 'is this *Ato* Russell who presumes to write to me?' (*Ato* being roughly the equivalent of Mister.) 'I wrote to Victoria . . .' Nor was he pleased with the arrival unaccompanied of the presents from India. 'He asked me,' Cameron reported, 'whether I came from the same people who sent these presents or from the Queen of England: and remarked rather strongly on presents being sent from one government to another without a friendly messenger or a letter of courtesy.'

Although he said that he would stop the slave trade 'not as a concession but because he hated it himself', Theodorus showed no interest in religious toleration, or indeed in any of the other matters raised by

[1] Also known as Tiruwerq or Teruwork. She and two of her brothers were kept as prisoners by Theodorus after he defeated Ras Ubye. Terunesh was taken straight from prison to the altar, so to speak, but her brothers remained prisoners for another eight years. The emperor's first wife died in 1858.

the new consul. All he was interested in was in evicting the Turks (which term included their subject Egyptians and Arabs) from the Red Sea coast of Africa, and from their encroachments in areas on the frontiers with the Egyptian Sudan which he claimed as belonging to Ethiopia by ancient right. He reiterated his dream of annexing the fertile lands along the banks of the Nile and of wresting Jerusalem from the hands of the infidel Turks. For this grand design he wanted arms and technicians from the European powers; as Christian nations he believed indeed that they had a positive obligation to help him.

With an impartial arrogance which one cannot but admire he now proceeded to address what amounted to a circular letter to the Queen of England, the Emperor of France, and the Tsar of Russia, asking for their assistance against the infidel Turks. To cover all eventualities, similar letters were also prepared or contemplated for the German powers, Austria, and Holland. Abyssinian standards of good manners and good tactics demanded that he should also offer in his letters to send envoys with presents of friendship, and prudence required that he should ask the recipients to ensure their safe passage through the lands under Turkish control with which Abyssinia was enclosed. For the same reason he sought suitable messengers to carry his letters to their destinations. Someone with contacts with the Russian Orthodox Church in Jerusalem was detailed for the approach to the Tsar; a French adventurer named Bardel was chosen to take the letter to France and given 500 silver thalers[1] for his expenses, while Cameron was given 1000 thalers to deliver the letter to the Queen. Whether the understanding was that Cameron would take the letter to London himself, or that he should take it as far as Massawa and wait there for a reply, is not clear from the evidence now available, but in the event he did neither. Instead he enclosed it with a covering despatch of his own dated 31 October 1862, and after travelling as far as Adowa he entrusted them both to a messenger. It was an error of judgement which he, and many others, were to regret.

Cameron never had any intention of going anywhere near Massawa. He hated its climate, its fevers, its people, and almost everything about it. 'Sun, dirt and desolation', was how one person described it, and Cameron himself reported that 'the island and all the coast around can be compared to nothing but a vast furnace where there is nothing to

[1] Each worth about four shillings: for explanation of thalers see p. 106.

enliven the eye, and where it is impossible to find rest either by day or night'. The buildings were not much better: '. . . a small stone house consisting of two miserable rooms which have been used lately as the Consulate of Her Britannic Majesty, a dirty bazaar, and a numerous collection of miserable straw huts inhabited by the Arab and small Turkish population.' As much as he hated Massawa Cameron loved the highlands of Bogos in the north of what is now called Eritrea. It was handsome, healthy country, and, as already mentioned, its inhabitants and not least its girls were handsome and healthy too. As Plowden confided to his private journal, one of its advantages was that 'a disease, that probably is as great a check to European lasciviousness as many precepts, is unknown. . . .' Cameron had also been captivated by Father Stella and the amiable hospitality of his Lazarist mission. Instead therefore of attending to the emperor's letter and to his routine consular duties at Massawa, he spent the best part of the next six months either up in the hills of Bogos, or down at Kassala and Metemma on the Egyptian side of the border, championing the causes of Father Stella's highland Catholics against their lowland Muslim neighbours. He employed a certain Captain Speedy, a huge and genial adventurer who was at a loose end, as a locum tenens at Massawa to attend to matters there during his absence.

It was not surprising that the Foreign Office found both Cameron's whereabouts and his activities inconsistent both with his own instructions and with the wishes of the ruler to whom he was accredited. Nor did the Foreign Office care for his frequent claims for expenses, or for his requests for money in advance. 'The rules of Her Majesty's Service,' he was primly informed, 'do not admit of sums being drawn in advance being allowed.' The result was that between April and October 1863 no less than five separate despatches were addressed to Consul Cameron by the Foreign Office telling him, in terms which became decreasingly diplomatic, that he should stop meddling in internal Abyssinian affairs, and taking sides in border disputes against H.M.G.'s allies like the Egyptians and the Turks, and that he should go back to Massawa and stay there, and concentrate on matters of trade. Although for his part Cameron continued to send reports to the Foreign Office during his perambulations, his arrangements for having his official mail sent on to him from Massawa turned out to be neither durable nor secure. Captain Speedy soon tired of Massawa and left, without telling Cameron, to seek his fortune in what were then known as the Antipodes; and at one point Cameron had to arrange for one of the emperor's own interpreters to go down to Massawa and bring up his letters. The result was that the Foreign Office despatches took even longer than usual to reach him, and that a few never reached him at all.

It was not until the summer of 1863, when it was very hot in the low-lands of Kassala and Metemma, that Cameron returned to the cool high-lands of Gondar, where the emperor still had his headquarters. But instead of going to Gondar he went to the Jews' Society mission at Jenda. His reasons for doing so are not clear, but Martin Flad, who had had some medical training, said later than Cameron had gone there for medical treatment.[1] Another likely explanation is that he was in no hurry to meet the emperor. He had heard that the newly appointed French consul, Lejean, had recently been put in irons for twenty-four hours for what were alleged to be insulting breaches of court etiquette, and was being held in polite but unmistakable captivity until such time as a reply was received to Theodorus' letter to Napoleon III. This somewhat unusual treatment of a foreign consul made Cameron anxious to avoid a meeting until he had in his hands a reply from London to the emperor's letter to the Queen. He had still had no answer to his cover-ing despatch of 31 October 1862, nor had he yet received any of the Foreign Office letters telling him to go back to Massawa.

Cameron reached Jenda in June. Three months later he and all the Europeans in the area were summoned by the emperor to Gondar to hear the reply which Bardel had at last brought from France. The opening words of the letter were in splendid Quai d'Orsay French. '*J'ai mis sous les yeux de l'Empereur mon auguste Souverain . . .*', but the Emperor of Abyssinia was not impressed. To start with the letter was signed by the French Foreign Minister, a mere servant, and it did not even bear Napoleon III's imperial seal. And 'Who is that Napoleon?' Theodorus fumed; 'Are not my ancestors greater than his?' The con-tents of the letter were no better. Instead of welcoming the idea of receiving an Abyssinian envoy, it rebuked 'Théodore'[2] for expelling the Catholics. Not only did it offer no help against the Turks, but it actually advised him against attacking their superior forces.

The emperor was angered and upset by this public rebuff, which

[1] According to Theodorus, syphilis was the cause of Cameron's ill-health.

[2] 'Théodore' was how the French rendered the Amharic *Tewodros*. As French was the language generally used in diplomatic circles in Egypt this version began to be used by the British consular officials there, until 'Theodore' eventually became the form most commonly used in English too.

served to confirm the suspicions of the French which he had had since they backed the rebellious Negusye. But thinking perhaps that he had gone too far in chaining and detaining Lejean and that it might invite retribution from the French government, he allowed the French consul to leave, only to find that as soon as he was safely out of reach, Lejean indulged in an orgy of abuse and invective. Although Theodorus continued to treat Cameron correctly, it soon became apparent that it was not only with the French that he was displeased. When assured by Cameron that a friendly reply to his letter to the Queen was bound to arrive soon, his sardonic answer was that he hoped it would not contain 'such friendship as was offered by France'. A few days later one of Cameron's messengers was stopped and stripped of his letters. They were eventually restored, but the emperor made it clear to Cameron that he should send no more letters out of the country without his permission.

The Jews' Society missionaries at Jenda had also noted a change in the emperor's attitude, and had indeed become so apprehensive that, as a precaution, they had decided temporarily to curtail their activities and expenditure in Abyssinia. On 13 October, two weeks after the public reading of the French reply, the Revd. Henry Stern, who had come out from England again on a brief visit of inspection, set off for the coast,

> and quitted, what I thought for ever, the capital of Abyssinia. . . . My people as well as myself were in the happiest mood, a feeling which our animals seemed to share, for they marched with ease along the dizzying precipices up to the plain of Woggera. Here to my surprise I saw the King's white tent glimmering in the sun's rays on one of the heights which dot the plateau. Duty, as well as courtesy, forbade me to advance without saluting His Majesty.

The emperor had been drinking with his soldiers and was in a bellicose mood. It is difficult to know what exactly was said or perhaps mistranslated, but Theodorus eventually lost his temper with something that Stern's interpreter said, and ordered him and another servant to be beaten by his soldiers so badly that they died. Horrified, Stern put his hand to his mouth, an act which was mistaken for an Abyssinian gesture of defiance known as 'biting the finger'. Angered by this gesture the emperor shouted, 'Give it to him too!' Stern escaped with his life, but was rendered senseless and made captive. Although Stern's gesture and his servants' behaviour were clearly the occasion for the emperor's outburst, it seems unlikely that they were the real cause. Theodorus had never liked Stern, and always referred to him contemptuously as '*cocab*', the Jew. He had heard from several sources that Stern had often cast aspersions on him and his antecedents, both in writing and in careless talk. He had also been upset both by reports he had heard of the Jenda missionaries behaving, in their style of living and in their religious observances, as if they were superior to everyone else, and by accusations of duress in their dealings with his subjects, the Falasha. It was said that, alarmed at stories of forcible conversion to Christianity, one body of the Falasha had set off in panic for the Promised Land; believing in miracles, and certain, for example, that the waters of the Red Sea would part for their safe passage, they had gone unprepared and unprovisioned, and had mostly perished on the way. Another influence was the attitude of the Swiss C.M.S. artisans whom the emperor affectionately called 'his Gaffat children'. Knowing that he disliked Stern, and fearing that this might eventually affect other Protestant missionaries, they had tried, without success, to persuade the emperor to refuse Stern permission to return to Abyssinia earlier that year. It was for this reason, no doubt, that Theodorus later told them, 'I have chained your enemy, and mine.'

Realizing that he had again gone too far Theodorus set about looking for evidence to support his suspicions. With the help of Bardel, who was often to be suspected of serving his own and his country's interest at other people's expense, he had Stern's belongings and indeed the whole mission searched, and eventually found what he wanted in diaries, letters, and books. These showed that Stern and his colleague Rosenthal had not only criticized and condemned him, but had frequently laughed and sneered at him too. What made this worse was that some of these opinions had been exposed for all the world to see in the book which Stern had published when he was in England.[1] One sentence in particular angered Theodorus. Speaking of the emperor's humble origins, Stern had written that 'the poor mother of Kasa, like numbers in that demoralized country where love is seldom hallowed by the religion that belongs to it, was, ere long, driven by want to eke out a miserable substance by the sale of *kosso*', *kosso* being explained in a footnote as 'a specific against tapeworm from which all Abyssinians suffer'.

As a result of these disclosures both Stern and Rosenthal had their hands and feet put in chains, and their Abyssinian servants were yoked

[1] See p. 34.

በስመ፡ አብ፡ ወወልድ፡ ወመንፈስ፡ ቅዱስ፡ ፩ አምላክ
ባንድነት፡ በሶስትነት፡ እግዚአብሔር፡ መርጦ፡ ያነ
ገሰው፡ ንጉሠ፡ ነገሥት፡ ቴዎድሮስ፡ ዘኢትዮጵ
ያ፡ ይድረስ። ከእንግሊዝ፡ ንግሥት፡ ቪክቶሪያ።
እንዴት፡ አሉ፡ እኔ፡ እግዚአብሔር፡ ይመስገን፡ ደኅ
ና፡ ነኝ። እስተ፡ ዛሬ፡ ድረስ፡ አባቶቼ፡ ነገሥታቱ፡ ፈጣሪ
አችንን፡ ቢበድሉት፡ መንግሥታቸውን፡ ለጋላና፡ ለቱር
ክ፡ አሣልፎ፡ ሰጥቶባቸው፡ ነበረ፡ ዛሬ፡ ግን፡ እኔ፡ ከተወ
ለድሁ፡ ፈጣሪዮ፡ ካመድ፡ አንስቶ፡ ኃይል፡ ሰጥቶ፡ ባባ
ቶቼ፡ መንግሥት፡ አቆመኝ፡ በእግዚአብሔር፡ ኃይል
፡ ጋሎችን፡ አስለቀቅኋቸው፡ ቱርኮች፡ ግን፡ ያባቴን፡
መሬት፡ ልቀቁ፡ ብላቸው፡ እምቢ፡ ብለውኝ፡ በእግዚ
አብሔር፡ ኃይል፡ ይኸው፡ ልታገል፡ ነኝ። እነእቶ፡ ቡ
ላዲን፡ እነሊቀመኳስ፡ ዮሐንስ፡ የክርስቲያን፡ ንጉሠ
፡ ታላቅ፡ ሰው፡ ክርስቲያን፡ የሚወዱ፡ አሉ፡ እናስተዋ
ውቅህ፡ አለን፡ እያሉኝ፡ እጅግ፡ እወዳቸው፡ ነበረ፡ የር
ስዎን፡ ወዳጅነት፡ ያገኘሁ፡ እየመሰለኝ። ሞት፡ አይቀ
ርምና፡ የጠሉኝ፡ ሰዎች፡ እኔን፡ ይክፋው፡ ሲሉ፡ ገደሉ
አቸው፡ እኔም፡ በእግዚአብሔር፡ ኃይል፡ ደመኞቼን፡
፩ ሳልተው፡ ፈጀኋቸው፡ የገዛ፡ ዘመዶቼን። በእግዚ
አብሔር፡ ኃይል፡ የርስዎን፡ ዝምድና፡ ሥፈልግ።
ቱርኮች፡ ከባህር፡ ላይ፡ ሁነው፡ መልክተኛየን፡ አናሳል
ፍም፡ ብለው፡ ቸግሮኝ፡ ሳለ፡ ቈንስል፡ ኪምሮን፡
መጣልኝ፡ ወረቀትና፡ የፍቅር፡ በረከት፡ ይዞ፡

The first page of Theodorus' letter to Queen Victoria, 29 October 1862

The emperor's seal

PUNCH, OR THE LONDON CHARIVARI.—August 10, 1867.

THE ABYSSINIAN QUESTION.

Britannia. "NOW, THEN, KING THEODORE! HOW ABOUT THOSE PRISONERS?"

to pieces of wood a foot in diameter and six feet long. Flad, with Brandeis and Staiger from the Scottish Jews' Mission, who had reached Jenda in 1862, seemed to have helped in the search and the translation of Stern and Rosenthal's papers, and were accordingly left free. So too were the European wives of Flad and Rosenthal, but their belongings were searched and sequestered, with the result that when Stern and Rosenthal were later deprived of their European clothes, their guards were able, for a consideration, to replace them with garments from these ladies' wardrobes.

Cameron kept what would now be described as a low profile while these events were taking place. He knew that the emperor was vexed with him for not taking his letter to the Queen as least as far as the coast, and for returning to Gondar without an answer. What had upset Theodorus even more, however, was that he had begun to suspect that Cameron's reason for going to Kassala and Metemma on the Egyptian side of the frontier was to make contact with the Egyptian authorities. He had been getting reports of Egyptian reinforcements being sent to the garrisons on the border. He knew too from his agents in Cairo and elsewhere that Britain and France were now on friendly terms with the Turks and Egyptians, and he began to fear that they were acting in concert and had designs on his territory. Another reason why he was suspicious of the British was that he had heard from Abyssinian pilgrims that the protection which had for years been given to them and to the representatives of the Abyssinian Church in Jerusalem by the British consul had noticeably diminished with the recent appointment of a new consul. But, as in the case of Stern, in the last resort it was seemingly small slights which appeared to rankle most with the proud and sensitive Theodorus. In Cameron's case it was a report that while entertaining the officers of the Egyptian garrison at Kassala Cameron had scornfully amused his guests by getting his servants to perform old Abyssinian war dances. Theodorus could suffer criticism better than scorn, and when he heard this he was moved to tell Flad, 'I hate all you Europeans; you are all, at heart, my enemies.'

When, therefore, Cameron's responsibilities as consul finally obliged him to plead the long friendship between Britain and Ethiopia as a reason for showing clemency to Stern, the immediate riposte of the emperor, who had still had no reply to his letter to the Queen, was, 'And where are the proofs of that friendship?' Despite the numerous despatches that had been sent to him, Cameron had received nothing from the Foreign Office for nearly a year, and he did not even know if the emperor's letter and his own covering despatch had arrived. As he told the consul-general in Egypt in a letter, 'It will give you an idea of the slowness with which my government correspondence is carried on, when I state that I do not know whether those letters have reached England or not.' When finally he did get a letter in December 1863 it merely reiterated the original instructions, which unknown to him had been sent on 22 April, that he should go back to the coast. He must have realized then that no reply, or at least no satisfactory reply to the emperor's letter, would be forthcoming, and, despite his hatred of the coast, it was perhaps a relief to read that his orders were to go to Massawa and stay there. Massawa might be hot and unhealthy, but it was probably better than the emperor's displeasure.

So, early in January 1864, Cameron wrote a formal letter to the emperor asking for permission to leave for the coast in accordance with his instructions from London. Theodorus summoned him to receive his answer in person. His answer was to put Cameron in chains.

CHAPTER VI

The letter

On 14 May 1864, seven months after Stern had been made captive, his English wife Charlotte wrote to Lord Shaftesbury, the veteran Evangelical whose concern for morals and social justice in the nineteenth century now seems so inappropriately commemorated by the statue of Eros in Piccadilly Circus. It was not the first letter she had written to him about her husband but in its consequences it was certainly the most important.

My Lord,

Yesterday I received a letter direct from Aden, giving me a copy of the slip of paper written by Captain Cameron to Mr. Speedy, with the addition of a few words which were omitted in my letter of last week; but as they seem to me so very important, nay, the very thing on which the release of the unfortunate prisoners depends, I take the liberty of sending them to your Lordship. They are as follows: 'No release until civil answer to King's letter arrives.' No doubt the Foreign Office have had a copy, and will, I earnestly pray, be guided aright in all they do in this unhappy affair.[1]

Shaftesbury sent this letter to his friend the Foreign Secretary with a covering note. 'Dear Russell,' it said, 'It may not be possible to do anything but this letter is worth looking into.' He added a p.s.: 'I had rather be the King of Abyssinia than the King of Prussia.'—meaning that however badly Theodorus may have behaved it was nothing compared with the wickedness of the King of Prussia who had recently invaded defenceless Denmark.

As Secretary of State for Foreign Affairs, Earl Russell, as he had now become, was a particularly busy man in the summer of 1864. Apart from Prussia's invasion of Denmark, the civil war in America presented many diplomatic problems and was having a disastrous effect on trade. There was an insurrection in Poland, General Garibaldi was soliciting British intervention on his behalf in Italy, and General Gordon had already involved himself in the domestic disputes of China. Her Majesty's Government was itself involved in wars with the natives in New Zealand and West Africa. There was, as usual, trouble in Ireland.

[1] The F.O. had received its copy on 7 May.

It was a situation disturbing and confusing enough as it was, especially for a good Liberal like Earl Russell. It was not surprising that he wearily took a well-worn pencil and scribbled a note to his officials on Mrs. Stern's letter. 'Is there', he wrote, 'any letter from the King of Abyssinia unanswered?'

This question was to be put in a variety of ways, and with varying degrees of heat, from many different quarters in the course of the next five years. The questions came first from Charlotte Stern and others acting on behalf of the two missionaries held by 'King Theodore'.[1] 'The whole affair of our imprisonment,' one of them wrote, 'turns around the government letter.' Captain Cameron's relations[2] and friends soon followed suit in their insistence that the emperor's displeasure at not receiving a reply to his letter to the Queen was the main reason why he had put the consul and the missionaries in chains; Cameron and Stern took the lead in propagating this theory, which had the merit of diverting attention from any contributory faults of their own. The questions and accusations and anxieties were taken up in an accelerating crescendo of clamour by those who claimed to have special knowledge of Abyssinia and its people, and by those in parliament and the Press who were on the look-out for any opportunity to discredit the Government. The Queen herself was moved to ask what it was about. Later, when the drama was hastening to its climax, the *Illustrated London News* compared the unanswered letter to Desdemona's mislaid handkerchief in its fateful and tragic consequences.

'The vexatious topic of the unfortunate letter', as it was described at the time, remained the subject of much argument and political recrimination for the remainder of the 1860s. The common opinion then was that the Foreign Office had mislaid the letter or carelessly forgotten it. The records of the Foreign Office themselves give a different impression.[3]

[1] Cameron and Stern and indeed almost everyone else during this period always referred to Emperor Theodorus as King Theodore.

[2] Cameron's sister was married to an M.P. called Captain Desborough.

[3] Ministers and officials of the Foreign Office at that time did not have anything like the generally solid and occasionally grandiose amenities of the present Foreign Office in Downing Street, which dates from 1868. They worked in a considerably older building in Whitehall which was described by Sir Horace Rumbold as 'dingy and shabby to a degree, made up of dark offices and labyrinthine passages—four houses at least tumbled into one, with floors at uneven levels and wearying cork-screw stairs that men cursed as they climbed—a thorough picture of disorder, penury and meanness'. It was no wonder that Earl Russell wrote most of his minutes in his own elegant house in Richmond Park.

The letter referred to was the one addressed to Queen Victoria by the Emperor Theodorus in 1862. The letter was not dated but it must have been written sometime in the last week of October. It was written in Amharic but an English translation was appended; the translation was done by the emperor's own interpreters and the whole was then sealed with the imperial seal. It was unsigned, but this was the custom with all royal letters coming from Abyssinia at that time. The letter, as explained in the previous chapter, had been handed to Cameron by Theodorus who gave him money for expenses, and clearly expected him to take it himself at least some of the way. As explained, Cameron took it as far as Adowa in the highlands of Tigrai, and there entrusted it with his own letter to a messenger to take to Massawa while he himself went on to Bogos. As few ships of any size called at Massawa then, Cameron's despatches and the emperor's letter would have been taken on by sailing dhow, or *buggalow*, to use the Indian equivalent, to Aden. The Political Agent at Aden, which came under the government of India, forwarded them by steamer to Bombay, and they eventually reached the Foreign Office on 12 February 1863, three and a half months later.[1]

By the time Cameron's despatch of 31 October reached the Foreign Office it had been joined by others he had written in November, with the result that when those concerned read the emperor's letter they had before them not only Cameron's covering despatch but several later despatches as well. The English text of the letter was not disclosed for some time, and until it was made public it was supposed to contain several fanciful demands and suggestions, including a proposal of marriage to the Queen. The actual text was as follows:

In the name of the Father, of the Son and of the Holy Ghost, one God in Trinity chosen by God, King of Kings, Theodorus of Ethiopia to Her Majesty Victoria Queen of England. I hope your Majesty is in good health. By the power of God I am well. My Fathers the Emperors having forgotten our Creator He handed over their kingdom to the Gallas and Turks. But God created me, lifted me out of the dust and restored this Empire to my rule. He endowed me with power, and enabled me to stand in the place of my Fathers. By His power I drove away the Gallas. But for the Turks I have told them to leave the land of my Ancestors. They refuse. I am now going to wrestle with them. Mr. Plowden, and my late Grand Chamberlain the Englishman Bell, used to tell me that there is a great Christian Queen, who loves all Christians.

[1] The route used for official mail and express letters was by sea from Bombay via Aden to Suez; thence overland to Alexandria, by sea to Marseilles, overland to Calais or Boulogne, and so on to London.

When they said to me this—'We are able to make you known to Her and establish friendship between you'—then in those times I was very glad. I gave them my love, thinking that I had found your Majesty's good will. All men are subject to death, and my Enemies, thinking to injure me, killed these my friends. But by the power of God I have exterminated these enemies, not leaving one alive, although they were of my own family, that I may get, by the power of God, your friendship.

I was prevented by the Turks occupying the sea coast from sending you an Embassy when I was in difficulty. Consul Cameron arrived with a Letter and presents of friendship. By the power of God, I was very glad hearing of your welfare, and being assured of your amity. I have received your presents, and thank you very much.

I fear that if I send ambassadors with presents of amity by Consul Cameron they may be arrested by the Turks.

And now I wish that you may arrange for the safe passage of my ambassadors everywhere on the road.

I wish to have an answer to this letter by Consul Cameron and that he may conduct my Embassy to England. See how Islam oppress the Christian.

Neither the style nor the contents of the emperor's letter presented any surprises to the Foreign Office. It was not, as has been explained, the first time that Theodorus or other Ethiopian rulers had addressed letters to the Queen, nor was it the first time that they had proposed sending envoys to Britain. What did surprise and even alarm the Foreign Office were Cameron's despatches. They left little doubt that closer relations with the Emperor of Abyssinia now were likely to involve Her Majesty's Government in some serious diplomatic complications and a number of embarrassing obligations. What Theodorus really wanted, or so it seemed to the cynical and sharp-minded officials of the Foreign Office, was British military and diplomatic protection against Egyptian incursions into his territory, and for the British Navy to keep the Turks from intervening while Theodorus himself raided or even occupied the more fertile lands of his Muslim neighbours on the convenient pretext of conducting a crusade against the infidel. It was suspected too that the emperor was seeking a continuation of the protection which British consuls had kindly but unwisely given in the past to an outpost of the Ethiopian Church on the roof of the Church of the Holy Sepulchre in Jerusalem. It was an assumption of responsibility which the Turkish authorities not surprisingly resented, and which threatened to sour Anglo-Turkish relations. The Foreign Office was also concerned at the amount of time which Cameron was spending in the healthy highlands of Bogos supporting local Abyssinian tribesmen in their interminable feuds with their Egyptian neighbours, when he should have been dealing with humdrum matters of official returns and trade, albeit in the hot and depressing climate of Massawa.

Another thing which disturbed the Foreign Office was the detail given in Cameron's despatches of the Emperor of Abyssinia's expectations in the way of professional and technical experts—civil engineers, artisans of various sorts, and doctors. There were also detailed lists of the presents which the empeorr would like—'Indian tents, silks, mortars, rockets, small cannon, grenades, fire-arms and ammunition'. Cameron had also suggested that the emperor should be invited to send to England 'a fixed number of lads who might receive a certain education and be afterwards instructed in some useful trade'.

These reports and Theodorus' letter were studied with care, and with increasing concern in the Foreign Office. 'I am afraid,' one official minuted, 'that if we accept Capt. Cameron's views our intercourse with Abyssinia will be both troublesome and expensive.' Another minute, the last of a series of minutes on these letters, sounded an ominous warning: 'If we do not take care we shall get into trouble in Abyssinia'.

On 22 April, after ten weeks of intermittent deliberation, a single omnibus reply was sent to all Cameron's recent despatches. He was left in no doubt that these included the one dated 31 October which had accompanied Theodorus' letter to the Queen. Considering that it was an answer to fourteen different despatches which contained a great deal of information and a great many questions, the reply was pointedly brief:

> I have received your despatches from no. 18 to no. 24 of last year and from no. 1 to 7 of the present year, and with reference to your no. 18 of 31 October last I have to state that it is not desirable for Her Majesty's Agents to meddle in the affairs of Abyssinia and you would have done better to return to your post at Massowah when the King told you to do so. This it will be right that you should do at once and you will remain at Massowah until further orders.
>
> You will of course keep Her Majesty's government fully and accurately informed of French proceedings in Abyssinia.

The specific reference to Cameron's covering despatch of 31 October was clearly intended to convey to the consul that the emperor's letter which had been enclosed with it had been received by the Foreign Office, and that it had been decided not to reply to it. In short the omission of a reply was deliberate and not accidental. It was felt presumably that less offence would be given by no reply than by one that was negative, however diplomatically it was worded. It seems unlikely, however, on the evidence, that Earl Russell or the officials of the Foreign Office were overmuch concerned with the susceptibilities either of a recently appointed minor consul or of a remote African potentate. The reply sent to Cameron was not only signed by Earl Russell, but he had himself initialled the draft and minuted in his own handwriting on Cameron's despatch. The reasoning behind the decision not to reply to the emperor's letter and to order Cameron back to Massawa is not disclosed in the Foreign Office records, but a later note, dated 12 June 1864, explains why. The note refers to a memorandum which had been prepared in the office on recent developments in Abyssinian affairs. It said: 'The appendix necessarily does not show why so little notice was taken of Capt. Cameron's suggestions because the decision to leave them unnoticed, except by ordering him back to Massowah, was come to after verbal discussion.'

The main reason is however not difficult to deduce from the memorandum and other papers on the files. The principal object of British policy in the Middle East at this time was the protection of communications with India. The Suez Canal, then under construction, was not due for completion until 1869, but for troops and trade the quickest route to India was still by sea to Alexandria, overland to Suez, and then by sea again to Aden and Bombay.[1] Egypt was still a Turkish province with a viceroy, and Turkey had also established outposts on both sides of the Red Sea. Good relations with Egypt and Turkey were therefore essential. The main object of Theodorus' letter being to seek help against the Turks and the Egyptians, any response to it by way of arms or technical assistance, or even by an exchange of envoys and presents, would be likely to prejudice British relations with Turkey and its provinces, without there being any prospect of compensating advantages to warrant deserting old allies. Cameron's activities in support of the people of Bogos against their Egyptian-protected neighbours were likely to have the same effect.

There was also another reason for not doing anything to upset the Turks. The American Civil War had started in 1861, and one result was a serious disruption of the supplies of cotton on which the Lancashire cotton industry depended, a disruption which, as *The Times* put it, had 'caused panic amongst the merchants and manufacturing classes'. Alternative cotton areas had to be found. They were soon discovered

[1] See note on p. 53.

in the valleys of the Nile and what is now the Sudan. Both were then part of the Turkish dominions. Another factor which the Foreign Office must have taken into account was their knowledge that, in addition to his letter to the Queen, Theodorus had written to the Emperor Napoleon III, the Tsar of Russia (to whom he had proposed a division of the declining Turkish empire), and, it was thought, to the King of Prussia, with none of whom, for various reasons, was Her Majesty's Government then on particularly good terms.

Soon after these decisions were taken and a reply had been sent to Cameron, Earl Russell took up his pencil again and marked Cameron's despatch of 31 October with the words 'India Office'. The despatch together with Theodorus' letter, both in original, were accordingly sent to the India Office on 5 May, with the bland request that they might be returned 'when done with'. There they remained for a year and six days. An investigation later revealed that they had gone to an official called Mr. Kaye. 'Lacking a pigeon-hole the letter had remained on his desk until F.O. came to collect;' Mr. Kaye 'took it for granted that it had been answered before it was sent to me'. The letter was returned to the Foreign Office on 11 May 1864, and was marked in pencil, 'To go by.'

In the light of this evidence it is surprising that Earl Russell had so far forgotten his involvement with Cameron's despatch and the emperor's letter that he should, not much more than a year later, blandly ask if there was any letter from the King of Abyssinia unanswered.[1] He

[1] In November 1867, when the handling of Theodorus' letter to the Queen became a considerable political issue, Layard, who had been the junior minister at the F.O. under Earl Russell, stated in the House of Commons, 'I never saw the King's letter . . . nor can Lord Russell, I believe, distinctly remember whether he saw it or not.' As a result of these statements the Conservative Government of the day ordered the F.O. to carry out a discreet investigation into the truth of them. The conclusion reached in December was that Russell and Layard had both seen all the despatches received from Cameron in February and March before Russell's despatch of 22 April 1863 was drafted, and that while it could not be said positively that Russell saw Theodorus' letter, 'he must have had under his eye or at all events in his mind the pp in Consul Cameron's despatch no. 18 (enclosing the letter from King Theodore).' In other words, the probability was that Russell and Layard both saw the letter and were parties to the decision taken to leave it unanswered. When this decision came in for heavy criticism and threatened to embarrass the Liberals, they tried to throw the blame on the permanent officials of the Foreign Office.

Henry, later Sir Henry Layard (1817–94), was aptly described in the *Dictionary of National Biography* as 'excavator of Nineveh and politician'. Although he entered politics in 1852, and became a junior minister in the Foreign Office in 1861 under Earl Russell, he deservedly remained better known for his excavations than for his public service. He was unmarried.

was 72, and it may be that with all his other preoccupations it had slipped his mind. If so, he was soon gently but firmly reminded by his officials that he had been a party to the decisions then come to. They were, however, very much at a loss to know what to suggest now as a means of securing the release of Cameron and the other Europeans. 'Force is, of course, out of the question. . . .' The best they could think of was to ask the India Office to find someone 'conversant with the native character who might be authorized to spend some money in effecting the object'. Neither the F.O. officials nor the minister wasted any time, and Earl Russell's answer was contained in a manuscript note from his home in Richmond Park on 19 May, only five days after he had received Mrs. Stern's letter.

I believe the best chance will be to send a letter of the Queen in very general terms, desiring friendship, and a letter from me saying we can hold no intercourse with the King, nor deliver the Queen's letter, unless he liberates Consul Cameron, Mr Stern and any other British subjects he has in custody. We must avoid promising any assistance against the Turks.

The Foreign Office officials did not think much of the Secretary of State's second suggestion, and politely but firmly set about superimposing their own ideas on his first. 'I am not sure', James Murray, the Permanent Under Secretary, minuted, 'that this sort of menace you propose yourself to address to the King might not make him more obstinate, and at all events neutralize the effect of the Queen's letter. I enclose the draft of a letter from the Queen which might perhaps tempt the savage to let our people go in the hope of gaining something from us.' The draft letter read:

VICTORIA, by the Grace of God, Queen of the United Kingdom of Great Britain and Ireland, Defender of the Faith, &c., &c., to Theodore, King of Abyssinia, sendeth greeting:

We have duly received the letter which your Majesty delivered to Our servant Cameron, and we have read with pleasure the friendly expressions which it conveys. We learn with satisfaction that your Majesty has successfully established your authority in the country over which you rule, and we trust that you may long continue to administer its affairs in peace and prosperity. We do not require from your Majesty the further evidence of your regard for ourselves which you propose to afford by sending a special Embassy to our Court. The distance which separates Abyssinia from England is great, and the difficulties and delays which would attend the journey of your Ambassadors might be hard to overcome, and much unavailing disappointment and regret might result from any accident which might befall your

Ambassadors on the road. Our servant Cameron will convey to us your wishes, and he will assure you of Our friendship and good-will, and we were glad to learn by your letter that he had been duly received by your Majesty.

Accounts have indeed reached us of late that your Majesty has withdrawn your favour from Our servant, and had subjected him and many others in whom we feel an interest to treatment which is inconsistent with your professions. We trust that these accounts have originated in false representations on the part of persons ill-disposed towards your Majesty, and who may desire to produce an alteration in Our feelings towards you. But your Majesty can give no better proof of the sincerity of the sentiments which you profess towards us, nor insure more effectually a continuance of Our friendship and good-will than by dismissing Our servant and any other Europeans who may desire it from your Court, and in affording them every assistance and protection on their journey to the destination to which they may desire to proceed.

Our servant Cameron will then be able personally to explain to us your wishes in regard to any matters which you may desire to represent to us. And not doubting that you will do this, we bid you farewell, and recommend you to the protection of God.

Given at our Court at Balmoral, the Twenty-Seventh year of our Reign

(L.S. The large signet.) Your good Friend,
(Countersigned) RUSSELL (Signed) VICTORIA R.

Superscribed: To our good friend, Theodore, King of Abyssinia.

This splendid example of calculated Victorian insincerity had its weaknesses, as became apparent later, but one suspects nevertheless that those who concocted it must have felt a certain satisfaction in passing over a delay of nineteen months by the use of the single word 'duly' at the beginning of the first paragraph, and in describing the emperor's actions in imprisoning and chaining a British consul as 'withdrawing your favour from our servant'. It was dated 24 May 1864.

No one thought it necessary to tell the Queen about the Emperor of Abyssinia's letter when it was received in February of 1863 or about the decision to send a belated reply in her name more than a year later. In due course the letter was naturally sent to her for signature but it seems unlikely that she took any interest in the matter then or asked any questions. She was still under stress as a result of the death of her husband in 1861, and Ministers had for some years not been exactly encouraged to bother her with matters of state. Some time later, however, Earl Russell was asked by the Queen's private secretary if he would kindly explain the circumstances of the Abyssinian captives' imprisonment and the steps being taken to secure their release. His surprisingly untruthful reply was that 'the King of Abyssinia wished to be invited to come to this country, and to be assisted against the French; and as these requests could not be complied with, he imprisoned the consul and the missionaries'. He went on to say however, that a memorandum was being drawn up in the Foreign Office, and concluded, 'Of course it would be useless to employ force but continued efforts will probably secure the release of the Consul.'

It having been decided in May 1864 to send a belated royal reply to Theodorus' letter in the hope of getting Cameron and the others released, the next question to be decided was how and by whom the letter should be delivered. Russell and the Foreign Office officials devoted themselves to these problems with machiavellian care. It was decided in the end that the best way would be to send the letter first to the British consul-general at Cairo, for reasons to be explained later, and thence by sea from Suez to Aden, where it would be carried by a special envoy to Massawa, there to await a favourable opportunity to be taken and delivered personally to the emperor in Abyssinia. As for the envoy, the emperor's temper was said to have deteriorated recently and there seemed to be a danger that whoever went might also be made captive. Ideally, therefore, what they wanted was someone who would be both effective and expendable; that is to say, a man of sufficient quality to get the letter delivered and the captives released, but not of sufficient importance or popular appeal to involve H.M.G. in any trouble or expense if he too were made captive. They first thought of a missionary with knowledge of the country and the natives, on the basis, perhaps, that missionaries were conditioned to accept a potentate's chains, like a cannibal's pot, as an occupational hazard. The redoubtable and resourceful Samuel Baker, who had a reputation for looking after himself, was also considered. He would have made a splendid foil for Theodorus' ruthless subtlety and charm, but, sadly for history, he was busy at the time looking for the source of the Nile and incommunicado. In the end the choice fell on Hormuzd Rassam.

At that time Rassam was on the staff of the Resident Agent at Aden, where he had risen from Arabic interpreter to the responsible post of First Assistant Secretary. He was born in 1826 at Mosul, where his father, an Armenian, was British vice-consul. The father was a Nestorian Christian and Hormuzd served for a time as an acolyte in a Roman Catholic church before becoming a Protestant. He attracted the attention of Henry Layard, who was excavating the ruins of Nineveh and Babylon, and was sent by him to Magdalen College, Oxford, for a time to study archaeology. Rassam was not everybody's choice. The view of the officials at the Foreign Office was that he 'lacked pluck', and that 'if he went to Gondar he would only make matters worse on account of his colour, nationality and want of confidence in himself'. Richard Burton 'knew him too well to believe that he would ever get up to Gondar'. But Layard was an M.P. and a junior minister, and it was he who recommended him for the task.

The third week of June 1864 must have been a busy week at the Foreign Office. Instructions for Rassam were drafted and sent to Aden, to be followed hurriedly by a postscript saying that he 'should be especially careful not to place himself in a position which may cause embarrassment to Her Majesty's government'. The India Office, in whose province Aden lay, was asked to co-operate, despite its frequently expressed desire 'to avoid all interference on the side of India with the States bordering on the Red Sea'. The Admiralty was asked to provide a naval vessel to convey the Queen's letter from Aden to Massawa 'in some state', and the letter itself was sent under cover of a despatch to the consul-general at Cairo for help on two matters before it was forwarded to Rassam. The first was to have a translation of the letter made into 'the language of Abyssinia'; the second was for a letter of commendation to be sought from the Patriarch of the Coptic Church, which, it was thought, might incline Theodore towards Christian forgivingness and mercy.

By bringing in the consul-general at Cairo the Foreign Office nearly overreached itself. The consul-general did not have any Amharic interpreters but had the letter done into Arabic, which, he was sure, would be understood at the Court of Abyssinia. The Patriarch was difficult too, and full of 'futile and unfriendly excuses', and in the end the Turkish viceroy in Egypt, who of course was a Muslim, had to be solicited in order to persuade a Christian Patriarch to write to a Christian king to intercede on behalf, *inter alia*, of a number of Christian missionaries. Having dealt thus with his instructions, the consul-general then sent a telegram to the Foreign Office by the new submarine telegraph from Alexandria:

> If it is not too presumptuous in me to do so I would suggest alteration in Royal letter. Well informed persons here think discouragement of embassy would give offence to Theodore and would be otherwise objectionable. Allusion to difficulties of journey would suggest idea of inability of British power. Despatch follows.

The despatch pointed out that Theodore was a ruler of energy, courage, and determination.

He probably is an utter barbarian but represents a race of kings who have reigned there since Solomon. I should not be surprised if, in his rage at the embassy being refused, he kills the captives and messenger. His proposed mission should be accepted and might do more good in opening up a fertile and productive country than any number of Livingstone and Speke expeditions. Let them see cannon cast, steam engines and ploughs at work and bring back a few of them. Theodore is a clever man and not without some good qualities but he cannot afford to be, as he considers he has been, affronted by any sovereign.

These arguments and forceful prose made a great impression on Earl Russell and the Foreign Office officials, and were a timely and persuasive reminder that theoretical reasoning and elegant prose in Whitehall did not always produce the best answers to practical problems in the field. It was agreed therefore that the Queen's letter should be amended, but in the end practical difficulties made this difficult, and Rassam was instructed to tell the emperor verbally that the Queen of England would be happy to receive his envoy if he did not mind the hazards of the journey. Another difficulty arose over the envoy's ship. The Admiralty said it could not provide a naval vessel, and in the end a steam transport, with some field guns hurriedly put on board to give her 'an appearance of armed equipment', was used to convey Hormuzd Rassam and the Queen's letter to Massawa. He arrived there on 23 July 1864.

In spite of the heat, the temperature only falling once below 93° Fahrenheit night and day, in the first four weeks, Rassam wasted no time. He had been warned that it would be difficult to find men willing to face both the hazards of the journey and the uncertainties of their reception when they reached the emperor's camp, but he managed nevertheless to send two copies of a letter to Theodore from himself by separate messengers the day after he arrived. He explained that he had brought a letter from the Queen and wished to present it in person. He had already heard enough at Massawa of Theodorus' unpredictability to hope that his journey might not in the end be necessary, and he added optimistically that if, for any reason, this was inconvenient, he would be happy to hand the letter to such envoy as the king might send to conduct Cameron and the other captives to Massawa.

Because of the rains and other hazards of the journey, Rassam's messengers expected to be away for a month. Five months later he was still waiting at Massawa for them to return with an answer, and he was becoming increasingly perplexed as conflicting reports reached him about the fate of his messengers and the situation of the captives. At the end of December he wrote a personal letter to Layard suggesting that Theodore was deliberately keeping him waiting in retaliation for the time he had to wait for a reply to his own letter. He added that he too did not care for the wording of the Queen's letter, partly because it had not been amended, as suggested by Cairo, so as to allow the king to send an envoy to England, and more especially because the letter made no reference to himself by name. 'His Majesty may take it into his head to treat me with contempt as he will find that I am not mentioned in the Queen's letter.'

During this period, the Foreign Office had been receiving many offers of help from other would-be emissaries to the emperor and suggestions about ways of making him amenable or bringing him to heel. As the months went by without progress, criticism of the choice of 'a mere Asiatic' as an envoy increased, and a Brigadier, Indian Army, retired, wrote to say that what was needed was a proper British officer and gentleman to accompany Rassam and give the mission status in the Emperor of Abyssinia's eyes. Another requirement, when one was dealing with native potentates, it was said, was a plentiful supply of presents. As a result of these and similar suggestions, and of mounting agitation in the Press and parliament over the failure of the government to get the captives freed, there were three important developments. The Resident at Aden was told to send one of his British officers to join Rassam. He chose Lieutenant Prideaux, a regular soldier who had worked with Rassam in Aden and also knew Dr. Henry Blanc, a British doctor from the Indian Army Medical Service who had been with Rassam at Massawa from the start. Orders were next issued to despatch 500 muskets, not of the latest model, to Massawa, for use as presents to the emperor. Lastly, the Queen's letter was at last amended and sent out to Rassam with such despatch that it reached him in less than a month. The amended letter, after mentioning 'Our servant Rassam' by name, concluded by saying that if, 'notwithstanding the long distance which separates Our dominions from those of your Majesty, you should, after having permitted Our servant Cameron and the other Europeans to take their leave and depart, desire to send an Embassy to this country, that Embassy will be well received by us'.

Although the new letter was signed by the Queen in February 1865 it still bore the date of the original letter, 24 May 1864.

With these new cards in his hand, Rassam continued his long wait in the heat and boredom of Massawa, periodically sending fresh messengers into the interior to bring him news of the captives and of Theodorus' temper and intentions. Not all of them returned, and those that did tended to bring reports that conflicted. They did, however, bring him two messages which had been smuggled out by Cameron. One, written on 17 March 1865, said, 'We are still lying here in dirt and chains. Another winter here and some of us must drop.' Another, dated 9 April urged Rassam 'to write strongly and to act if further waiting is of no use'; it ended with the warning, 'Don't come up here. He will cage you as sure as a gun.'

As the weeks and months went by, Rassam got more and more depressed, and more and more confused. He was in an agony of indecision. He had sent two further letters to Theodorus without getting any reply. His dilemma now was that if he went to Gondar without permission he risked the displeasure of the Emperor of Abyssinia, and if he stayed where he was or returned to Aden he risked the displeasure of the Foreign Office. He realized that Theodorus was playing cat-and-mouse with him, and when he did at last get an answer it only served to confirm this suspicion. The letter, as he told the F.O., was 'neither courteous nor becoming, and contrary to all etiquette'. Although it at last gave him permission to enter Abyssinia, it made no attempt to excuse or explain the long delay. To make matters worse the emperor told Rassam that, because of trouble in Tigrai, he should come up to Gondar by way of Kassala and Metemma. This meant a long and, at that time of year what Rassam described as a dangerously unhealthy journey through low-lying, fever-ridden country to the north and west of the Abyssinian highlands, and one which, because it traversed Egyptian territory, would require permissions and escorts from the Turkish authorities. In desperation Rassam took ship from Massawa to Suez, and made his way thence to Cairo for consultations and instructions, and, he added, to buy more presents for the king.

Rassam found the official atmosphere in Cairo both strained and stuffy. There were several reasons for this. He arrived there early in September, and was surprised, if that is not too mild a word, to discover that the Foreign Office had, without telling him, sent out William Palgrave to supersede him as an envoy to the emperor

Theodorus.[1] He also discovered, with no less surprise, that the consul-general, fearing as he put it that 'Mr. Rassam's mission may prove unsuccessful', had taken it upon himself, on behalf of His Royal Mistress the Queen, to write direct to Abuna Salama asking him to give an assurance to the emperor that if he now released the captives no action would be taken and no questions asked. To encourage the Abyssinian bishop to co-operate in this plea a number of presents accompanied this letter; they included 1 archbishop's black scarf, 2 pairs of red leather slippers, 2 jasmine pipes, 6 wires for cleaning pipes and tubes of mouth-pieces, and 1 bale of Latakia tobacco packed in canvas.

One can understand Rassam's vexation. Neither of these steps would be calculated to suggest to Theodorus that Rassam had his Government's full confidence. Nor was the atmosphere improved at that moment either in Cairo or in London by the discovery that the text of the Queen's belated letter to the Emperor of Abyssinia had been 'seen by persons unconnected with the government'. The Foreign Office naturally assumed that the leak had occurred in the lax ambience of Egypt, while the consul-general of Cairo as naturally insisted that it must have happened on the more corruptible verandahs of Aden or Bombay. Perhaps this atmosphere of irritation was one reason why, when Rassam telegraphed from Cairo asking for instructions in the light of Theodorus' last letter, he was told sharply that he should proceed to Gondar via Metemma as soon as possible, and that the delay in complying with the emperor's wishes was to be regretted. The unfortunate Palgrave was told to stay in Egypt, and was in due course informed that his services would not after all be required. The argument about compensation and expenses was to go on for months.

Rassam and his companions left Massawa on 15 October 1865, and arrived at Metemma on 21 November, which by all accounts was very

[1] William Palgrave (1826–88) equally fulfilled the Foreign Office private requirement that an envoy to Abyssinia at that juncture should be both effective and expendable (see p. 60). He was an accomplished Arabist, and was the son of Sir Francis Palgrave, deputy keeper of the public records. After Charterhouse and Trinity College, Oxford, he had served as a subaltern in the Indian Army. What made him seem expendable to the F.O., in spite of this eminently respectable background, was that his father had been born Cohen and had changed both his name and his religion when he married an English wife, and that William Palgrave himself had become a Catholic and had left the army to become a missionary. With his knowledge of Arabia and Arabic he had later joined the consular service, and as sometimes happens in the public service his specialized knowledge of the Middle East was rewarded with postings to the West Indies, Manila, Montevideo, and Bangkok. He was the younger brother of F. T. Palgrave of the *Golden Treasury*.

good going. They left for Gondar about a month later. Once across the border and in the Abyssinian highlands they gradually found themselves obliged by local custom and fear of giving offence to take on large numbers of extra retainers until they had over 1200, which, Rassam calculated, was 800 more than they needed. Their progress towards the emperor's camp was slow, and attended by frequent delays and changes in their orders which, they soon realized were deliberately designed to test their patience and good temper. Theodorus himself was travelling in the vicinity with a huge army of soldiers, court officials, and camp-followers of both sexes, and had, it appeared, to make frequent diversions to forage, or to deal with rebellious subjects. In these circumstances it was difficult to make firm arrangements for a meeting, and in the end it was 28 January 1866 before one took place.

Hormuzd Rassam, mounted on a mule, was on that day conducted by an irregular concourse of royal attendants to the foot of the small hill on which the Emperor of Abyssinia's tent of scarlet and yellow silk was pitched. The mule was a present from Theodorus himself, and although it was locally regarded as a mount of honour and dignity, it still contrasted poorly in appearance with the imperial bodyguard on their fine Abyssinian horses. After a further wait of three hours, Rassam, together with Blanc and Prideaux, was conducted on foot up the hill between two lines of musketeers who kept up their ceremonial firing until the emperor's tent was reached. The emperor, enveloped in a robe to his eyes as a mark of his superior status, received them reclining on a couch, with several of his ministers, and a bodyguard holding a double-barrelled pistol in each hand in attendance; and it was thus, soon after three o'clock in the afternoon of 28 January 1866, that the Emperor of Abyssinia was formally handed the Queen of England's reply to his letter. It was three years and three months, almost to the day, since he put that letter into Consul Cameron's hands.

CHAPTER VII

The hostages

During the frustrations and anxieties of their long wait at Massawa, Rassam, Blanc, and Prideaux had built up in their minds pictures of the emperor Theodorus as a barbaric and treacherous despot, given to acts of devilish cruelty and wanton destruction. Now, as the emperor welcomed them with quiet dignity, and politely asked them to be seated on the richly carpeted ground, they began to become aware of his compelling magnetism and charm, and of the disconcerting contrasts of his moods and his temper. 'The expression of his dark eyes', Blanc observed, 'was strange; if he was in good humour they were soft with a kind of gazelle-like timidity which made one love him; but when angry the fierce and bloodshot eyes seemed to shed fire.' Right from that first meeting, the emperor posed problems which tested Rassam's and his companions' wits and patience to the limit, and explored the strengths and weaknesses of their characters with subtle and ruthless penetration. Aware as he was, though the queen's letter lay unopened at his side, that Rassam had come to secure the release of the captives, Theodorus embarked at once on a recital of their misdeeds and a vindication of his own actions, and then invited Rassem to judge who was most at fault. The quick-witted Rassam saw the trap: accepting at this stage that the captives were to blame might prejudice their release almost as much as criticizing the emperor. He skilfully avoided the issue by saying that he had been sent by the queen not to pass judgment but to urge the emperor to forget the past in the interests of friendship in the future. Theodorus smiled his appreciation at the aptness of this response, and brought the first days audience to a close.

The following day, after he had seen a translation of the royal letter, and had satisfied himself that it had been both signed and sealed by the queen herself, he called Rassam and told him that 'for the sake of his friend the Queen', he had decided to pardon the captives, and to hand them all over to Rassam to be taken out of Abyssinia. He later confirmed this decision in a beautifully inscribed and as beautifully phrased letter in Amharic 'from the servant of our Lord, and his created Being, the son of David, the son of Solomon, the King of Kings, THEODORUS, to her whom God has exalted above all sovereigns and glorified above all princes and peoples, and made the Defender of the Christian faith, VICTORIA, the Queen of Great Britain . . .'.

Cameron and the missionaries, and the others imprisoned with them, had been moved from Gondar to the remote mountain fortress of Magdala at the end of 1864, and because of the distance and difficulties of communication it was some time before the emperor's promises to Rassam were translated into the actual removal of the prisoners' shackles. It was nearly a month before they reached the shores of Lake Tana, where Rassam and his companions had been comfortably encamped. Both Hormuzd Rassam and Dr. Blanc recorded their impressions of this happy period when they basked in the emperor's pleasure, and lived on the bounty of his hospitality in a fair countryside and an excellent climate. The emperor's hospitality took a variety of forms, and included numerous gifts. Presents of Abyssinian curiosities such as shields, spears, and saddles, and of pistols and old-fashioned muskets, were easy to accept and match with gifts of their own, but a pair of lion cubs presented certain problems, and so did a gift to Rassam of five thousand silver thalers 'to spend in any way you like except in a manner unpleasing to God'. Later the Swiss artisans from Gaffat were sent by the thoughtful Theodorus to provide Rassam and his fellows with European company, or to find out perhaps what they were saying in private. Blanc, who expected to see a party of simple evangelical missionaries, 'was never so taken aback as at the sight of these Europeans wearing the Abyssinian gala dress, silk shirts of gaudy colour, trousers of the same material, the shama thrown over the left shoulder, many with naked feet . . . '. A few days later, 'knowing that Europeans liked ladies' company', as the emperor delicately put it, he told the missionaries to send for their wives. The wives were even more surprising and colourful. Only three of them were wholly European. Two of the artisans had married the handsome daughters of John Bell and his Abyssinian wife, and two others had set up house with the local offspring of the German botanist Schimper. Most of the other members of this Church Missionary Society venture had been provided with local consorts by their royal patron.

The arrival of Cameron and the captive Jews' Society missionaries was more sombre. 'They all, more or less, bore traces of the sufferings they had endured,' Blanc noted, 'but Messrs. Stern and Cameron more than the others.' Theodorus particularly disliked Stern and Cameron, not only for what he believed they had said or done behind his back, but for their superior attitudes. He expressed his dislike and occasional wrath in ways which were positively medieval—ankle chains, hands tied to guards or fellow-prisoners, and on one occasion 'torture of the most cruel kind with ropes, our arms being lashed tightly from wrist to armpit, then brought together as close as possible by main force behind our backs, the ropes being wetted at intervals to produce the effect more completely . . .'. In some ways, however, they were perhaps no worse off than they would have been in many European prisons of that time. They were generally left to do much as they pleased during the day, and it was only at night that they were confined or guarded. They were allowed to maintain communications with the outside world, and to receive money and supplies. They were thus able, for a consideration, to persuade their guards to mitigate their circumstances, and allow them to introduce comforts and amenities of their own. They were all allowed one male and one female Abyssinian servant to attend to their needs, and at one stage Cameron had as many as fourteen servants in all to help him bear the rigours of imprisonment.

There were altogether thirteen European men in the party of released captives which came into Rassam's camp on 12 March 1866. Cameron had four European servants who had been imprisoned with him—Kerans and McKelvie who were Irish, a Frenchman named Makerer, and Pietro who was Italian. There were five missionaries of the Jews' Society: Stern, Rosenthal, Flad, Staiger, and Brandeis, who were all Germans, and Bardel, the French adventurer, whom many thought to be a spy planted among them by the emperor. There were, finally, two natural history collectors, one German and one Hungarian, who had somehow or other got caught up in the emperor's net, though he admitted himself later that he did not know who they were or why they were there. Both Flad and Rosenthal had European wives, and there were three small Flad children, making a total of eighteen in all. Of this number only Cameron, Mrs. Rosenthal, and Cameron's two Irish servants were British subjects.

Communications being what they were, it was some time before the news of Rassam's good reception and the release of the captives reached London. Meanwhile, and in ignorance of what had happened Cameron's relations and the relatives and influential supporters of the captive missionaries continued to agitate for more effective action to secure their release. Cameron's relations were already demanding the use of force, while the missionary elements suspected that the Government, for all its protestations to the contrary, was really only interested in its consul. One result of these activities was that a private Abyssinian Captives Liberation Fund was started in order to send an independent emissary to Abyssinia. The man chosen was Dr. Charles Beke, of Bekesbourne in Kent, the expert on Abyssinian affairs who had earlier sought the post of consul and who was later to be described in the House of Commons as a 'fussy, busy, mischievous, intriguing, meddling, troublesome person'. In the event, he did not get much further than Massawa, but he did send a plea to the emperor by a messenger who reached him in March, nearly two months after Theodorus had promised Rassam that he would release all the captives. This duplication both surprised and angered the emperor who, believing Rassam to have been sent to him by the Queen, could not understand how she would permit anyone else to make a separate approach, so to speak, behind her back. There were those in England too who were disturbed by Beke's mission, and believed it to be a serious mistake.

The arrival of the released captives at Rassam's camp on Lake Tana on 12 March seemed to be the vindication of Rassam's conciliatory approach, and of the policy which had been pursued by the British Government, but it also presented Rassam with a number of new problems. It was clear from the long discussions he had had with Theodorus during this amicable period, and from the many letters which they had exchanged, that the emperor still felt that Cameron, Stern, and Rosenthal had wronged him in deed and word, and that they should admit their offences publicly before they left. He told Rassam that 'he had received them well when they arrived and treated them as friends. Friends should be like a shield but instead of defending him when others spoke ill of him and his ancestors, they had repeated the calumnies and even put them in their books and letters'. Rassam had noticed how the released prisoners were avoided both by Abyssinians and by the missionary artisans from Gaffat, and he realized that if he were to keep the friendship and trust of the emperor, he and his companions would have to be careful not to appear too friendly with the captives or to be seen too much in their company. Another good reason for not seeing overmuch of them was to avoid having to take sides or adjudicate in the captives' frequent quarrels, and their tendency to blame one another for their misfortunes; as Cameron himself complained, 'All my people here are half mad and quarrelling like devils among themselves, and with me.' At the same time Rassam wanted to avoid any meeting between the emperor and the released captives. He feared that if they came face to face with one another in their present moods it might well upset the delicate balance that had been achieved. As an alternative he offered himself as an intermediary to put the emperor's charges of misconduct to Cameron and the others. When he had persuaded them that, as a matter of tactics, they should admit their faults and ask for forgiveness, he conveyed these results to the emperor. In due course his efforts were rewarded with a royal pardon, and confirmation that he could now leave and take all the released captives out of Abyssinia with him.

At last, on 13 April, after many changes of plan and several anxious moments, they all set out towards the frontier. After 27 months of captivity Cameron and the missionaries were understandably on edge with excitement. Stern, with his penchant for purple prose, expressed it thus:

> The following morning, which was to consummate our Abyssinian exodus, we hailed with joy and delight. Mr. Rassam, his companions and the European workmen, at sunrise embarked in a small fleet of bulrush boats for the royal camp, and about two hours afterwards the late Magdala captives . . . in high glee sprang into their saddles and trotted away. Our road lay across rough and uneven paths lined with stinging nettles and broken by dried-up canals and deep ruts. This however we did not notice; our excited imaginations tinted every object with lovely colours, and we stumbled over holes and ditches, brushed along weeds and bushes, in the delirium of a most ecstatic dream.

Rassam, still anxious to avoid a meeting between the emperor and the captives, had arranged that they should go overland to a rendezvous at the north-west corner of the lake while his party went across the lake to take their leave of the emperor at his camp on the other side. It was not only the released captives who were in good spirits. Rassam and his companions now felt that they had the success of their mission in their grasp.

The bulrush boats were far from watertight, and Rassam, Prideaux, and Blanc wore ordinary clothes for the journey, and changed into their full-dress uniforms and swords when they disembarked near the emperor's camp. They were received with the usual civilities and escorted to the pavilion tent which served, when the emperor was encamped, as a throne-room and hall of audience. As they made their way through the usual assembly of richly robed notables Rassam noticed that there was no one sitting on the emperor's throne. Their escort made an obeisance to the empty throne, and, as if this was a signal, armed men suddenly seized Rassam and his two companions, and took away their swords. Theodorus was hidden by a curtain behind the empty throne when this happened, and he remained there while a number of charges and accusations were levelled at Rassam through intermediaries. Eventually all their belongings were searched, and many confiscated, and they themselves were confined in an enclosure which appeared to have been especially made for this purpose in advance. The following day, Cameron and the missionaries, who had been arrested at the same time at the rendezvous, were brought into the emperor's camp in chains.

In the next few days Theodorus treated Rassam and the others with a bewildering mixture of harshness and kindness, and behaved in alternating moods of arrogance and humility. On the evening of the day of their arrest, Cameron and his party, though still in chains, were given a dinner by the emperor consisting of '11 cows, 11 baskets of bread, 11 jars of hydromel, 5 jars of butter and 3 jars of pepper'. He had earlier sent mules for Cameron, who was in his usual ill-health, and for the two missionary wives, and had with unusual consideration provided them with a separate tent. Rassam and his companions got ten jars of mead and the same number of sheep garnished with butter and red-pepper sauce. When, a few days later, they were subjected to the indignity of a public trial in the open, they were each given an umbrella to keep off the mid-day sun.

Theodorus sought at first to justify his actions by various criticisms of their conduct, and particularly by a claim that Rassam had tried to take the captives out before they had been publicly reconciled with him. It soon became clear, however, that he had for some time been debating with himself and his advisers the advantages and disadvantages of letting Rassam and the others go. 'How', he asked, 'can I trust any European now, after the ill-behaviour of those I have treated like brothers?' He still suspected that once they were beyond his reach Cameron and the missionaries would subject him to abuse and ridicule, as the French consul, Lejean, had done. When he said to Rassam, 'Is this your friendship that you wish to leave me and take away those who have abused me?' he was expressing his equally well-founded fears that once he let them go the British Government would send no more envoys and wash its hands of Abyssinia altogether. The core of his reasoning was contained in his answer to those of his own people who counselled him to let the captives go: 'If I let them go, what have I left in my hand?'

The crux of the matter was that Theodorus needed help. He had not yet abandoned his old ambition of recovering the lost lands of Ethiopia now occupied by the Turks and the Egyptians, or his hopes of freeing Christian Abyssinia from the menace of the Galla. Nor, despite the constant recurrence of domestic rebellions, had he by any means given up his determination to unify the country and to bring his people, whether they liked it or not, to accept the reforms and changes which he knew were essential if Abyssinia was to survive the pressures of the nineteenth century. For all these objects he knew that he needed the skills and equipment of the West. He needed them, he now realized, not merely to achieve his ambitions: he needed them in order to survive. As he saw it, his only hope of getting them, now that he had been rebuffed or ignored by all the major powers, was to hold Rassam and the other Europeans as hostages, and to make his needs their ransom.

Soon after he had arrested Rassam, he had the following letter addressed to the Queen: it began, as usual, with a flourish:

In the name of the Father, Son and Holy Ghost, One God.

From God's slave and His created being, the son of David, the son of Solomon, the King of Kings, THEODORUS.

To her whom God has exalted above all people, the Defender of the Christian Faith, the Protector of the poor and the oppressed, the Queen of England, VICTORIA.

Had your servant Hormuzd Rassam, whom you said you had sent in the affair of Mr. Cameron, been but the lowest of your slaves, I would have welcomed him. By the power of God, I have released Mr. Cameron and made him over to your servant Rassam; and by the power of God I have also released the other prisoners and all other Europeans who might wish to leave the country, and made them over to him; and I have kept your servant Rassam for the sake of consulting together upon the extension of friendship. We, the people of Ethiopia, are blind, and we beg of your Majesty that you should give light to our eyes, and so may you receive light in the Kingdom of Heaven.

He explained his needs more specificially in a separate letter to Rassam:

My desire is that you should send to Her Majesty and obtain for me a man who can make cannons and muskets, and one who can smelt iron, and an instructor of artillery. I want these people to come here with their implements and everything necessary for their work, and then they shall teach us and return. By the power of God, forward this request to England.

Remembering what had happened to the letter he asked Cameron to take to the queen in 1862, he told Rassam that he wished to see his covering despatch to the Foreign Office. He also told Rassam to select one of the other captives to take the letters to London in person and to wait there both for the queen's reply and for the men and the materials he had asked for. In the end it was the emperor himself who chose the messenger. He chose Martin Flad, the German missionary who had left his Pietist brethren at Gaffat and joined Stern's mission to the Jews at Jenda in 1864. The main reason why Flad was chosen was that he had a German wife and three young children with him in Abyssinia; Theodorus knew that he would not think of abandoning them to the fate which would await them if he did not return.

Mindful, perhaps, that it was over three years before he got a reply to his earlier letter, Theodorus wasted no time. Ten days after Rassam and the others had been arrested and made hostage, Flad was on his way to England.

CHAPTER VIII

The decision

The first reports of Rassam's good reception and the emperor's promise to release the captives arrived in London in April 1866. They were received with acclamation and particular satisfaction by those who had proposed and supported Rassam's mission. Although those who were closely concerned with what was becoming known as the 'Abyssinian Affair' or the 'Abyssinian Difficulty' soon began to feel twinges of apprehension at the strange lack of further news, the first indication that something was amiss did not reach London until 24 June. It was a brief telegraphic message from Cairo that Cameron had made an unsuccessful attempt to escape on his own, and that as a result he and Rassam and all the Europeans in the emperor's power had been imprisoned. This news was received with cautious incredulity at the Foreign Office partly because it came from a commercial source and partly because it seemed unlikely that even Captain Cameron could have behaved so foolishly. The report of Cameron's attempted escape did turn out to be untrue, but it was soon confirmed that Rassam and all the others had in fact been prevented from leaving Abyssinia. The source of these confirmatory reports was Flad himself, who had reached Alexandria after a difficult and roundabout journey of more than nine weeks.

Martin Flad arrived in London on 10 July. He had with him the emperor's letter to the queen together with Rassam's covering despatch to the Foreign Office. The latter seemed excessively mild in the light of the treatment accorded to a British envoy until Flad explained that it had more or less been dictated by the emperor himself. Flad also presented two long handwritten reports of his own which gave a first-hand account of recent events in Abyssinia. In these Flad paid a warm tribute to Rassam: '. . . the government could not have entrusted a man better fit for the mission of Mr. Rassam than himself. In all his business with the king he is calm, prudent, cautious and sincere. Not only the Abyssinians but even the Europeans did wonder at him. . . .' This eulogy must have provided food for thought for those who had written off Rassam as 'a mere Asiatic'.

There had just been a change of government in Britain with the Conservative Earl of Derby taking over as Prime Minister from the Liberal Earl Russell, and Derby's son, Lord Stanley, succeeding the Earl of Clarendon as Foreign Secretary. In an age when both political parties drew heavily, and in roughly equal measure, on the House of Lords to fill their cabinet posts, the effect of a change of government often meant a change of personalities rather than policies. This was especially so in the field of foreign affairs, and the staff of the Foreign Office seem to have had little difficulty in persuading the new Secretary of State to resist right-wing pressures for the use of force. Flad himself argued strongly in favour of continued conciliation or, as he put it, 'to finish with this man in peace'. Less than ten days after his arrival in London he was hurriedly writing to the emperor, in his distinctively Germanic English, that 'Your Majesty's letter, as well as myself, had by Her Majesty the Queen Victoria a kind and friendly reception', and that 'Her Majesty's Governors take every day great trouble to find the artisans Your Majesty wants'. Neither of these statements was strictly true, as the Queen had not then seen either the letter or Martin Flad, and the Foreign Office was under the impression that Flad was engaging the workmen himself. Flad was not an envoy by choice, and he was understandably more concerned with keeping the emperor happy, and his family safe, than with splitting the hairs of truth.

The emperor's needs had been set out with almost startling clarity in a separate letter which he gave to Flad. The technical details and the translation were probably the work of Waldmeier, whom Theodorus particularly trusted.

> I send Mr. Flad to Europe because I am in want of skilful artists. All those workmen who would like to come to my country rejoicing in their coming, I shall receive them with great honour, and give them good pay for their services. If they wish to remain in my country I shall make their abode most happy. But if they, after having teached my people their arts for some years, wish to return to their own country, I shall, through the power of God, give them a splendid pay, and with great honour I shall send them back to their country.
>
> Men and materials required by King Theodore from England and Her Majesty's Government.
>
> 1. Two gunsmiths.
> 2. An Artillery Officer.

3. An iron founder who is able to erect a foundry and furnace; all to be furnished with necessary tools and instruments.
4. One or two boat-builders.
5. A cart and wheel-wright.

His Majesty would also be pleased if Her Majesty's Government were to send the following articles:

1. A small blast steam-engine for foundry.
2. A turning bench, with necessary tools.
3. A distilling machine.
4. Machinery for manufacturing of gun-caps, with necessary copperplate etc.
5. A good telescope.
6. A gunpowder mill, with rollers.
7. A good supply of gunpowder and gun-caps.
8. Some handsome large square carpets, silks, tumblers and goblets.
9. Some double-barrel guns and pistols.
10 Two good regimental swords.
11. Some European curiosities.

Although Flad had said that he would find the artisans himself it was not as easy as he expected, and the Foreign Office soon came to the conclusion that he was 'useless'. In the end Colonel Merewether, the Government of India's resident agent at Aden, who was then in London, took matters in hand. He thought a sergeant and a pair of six-pounders from Aden would be better than an artillery officer, and he suggested that 'an enterprising and well-educated person' should be sent out to supervise the workmen and their equipment; 'It is better so', he observed, 'than to send out simple artisans by themselves who, being under no control, would quickly destroy themselves by excesses or fatally offend the King.' He soon had three volunteers for this supervisory post at a salary of £1000 a year, from which an Irish civil engineer named Talbot was eventually chosen. Merewether's estimate of what the operation would cost the government was £3500. One thing which substantially increased the cost was that the machinery had to be made so that it could be divided into porters' loads for the difficult overland journey from Massawa to the emperor's headquarters near Gondar. 'The sum may appear large,' Merewether concluded, 'but I submit that it is small compared to the cost of a campaign in such a country as Abyssinia.'

One more thing remained to be done. Flad had said that the first thing Theodorus would ask when he returned was whether he had actually seen the Queen. When this was put to the Queen in August she agreed to see him in the hope of being able to put an end to this sad captivity. Thus, by the time Flad sent off his next letter to the emperor on 1 September, he could truthfully say,

> The business Your Majesty had sent me to England for is, through the grace of Christ our Lord, accomplished. The artists your Majesty was anxious to get are found, and ready to come with me to your country. . . . Of Queen Victoria I have since I arrived here, nothing seen but friendship. For the necessity of life, I receive of Her Majesty every day five German crowns. Once I had a dinner together with Her Majesty's Minister Lord Stanley at Her Majesty's castle. On that occasion Her Majesty talked with me in a very friendly manner. Regarding Your Majesty, the Queen Victoria is a little grieved, saying why has the Emperor Theodore not sent over to me the prisoners whose relations are daily weeping before me? In reply to this I said, 'After having conveyed the artists to Your Majesty I shall come back and bring the released prisoners over with me to England.'

This indeed was the original plan. Although Lord Stanley had at first suggested that the presents should not be delivered until the prisoners were released, it was eventually decided that the presents—five hundred pounds' worth of arms, telescopes, field-glasses, carpets, silks, and 'ornamented tumblers, large size'—as well as the artisans and their equipment should be sent out with Flad, and to hope that the emperor would respond to this evidence of trust and goodwill by letting all the captives go. All seemed ready for this operation when, in the middle of September, reports started to reach London of alarming new developments in Abyssinia.

The news was that, after generally treating Rassam and the others with consideration, and occasional bursts of quixotic generosity, like providing a special feast on 24 June to celebrate Queen Victoria's birthday, the emperor suddenly summoned them all to another public trial, after which he imprisoned not only Cameron and the other former captives but Rassam and his party as well. A few days later they were all despatched to Magdala, where they were treated as prisoners rather than hostages. It seems probable that the real reason why he acted in this manner was that he wanted to move his hostages to a place of safety to prevent them escaping or falling into the hands of rebels. His main accusation at the trial, however, was that he could no longer trust the English as they had entered into an alliance with his enemies the Turks, and were building a railway from Suakin on the Red Sea coast to Kassala for the express purpose of transporting Egyptian troops to attack Abyssinia. Another argument he used was that once he released the captives, the English could with impunity send in her soldiers to exact retribution for the imprisonment of Cameron and Rassam.

When the news of the trial and the despatch of the captives to the fortress of Magdala reached the outside world, it caused a dramatic hardening of attitudes. Even Flad was sadly coming to the conclusion that 'as this mad man is going on his dishonourable way, once flattering, and a second time abusing and imprisoning those whom he had called his friends', it was time that the government took stronger measures. Colonel Merewether, whom the government was coming to accept as an authority on Abyssinian affairs, was one of the first to advocate the use of force, in a letter of sixteen closely written pages from his club at 14 St. James's Square[1] on 25 September. Not for the first time, however, it was the missionaries who adopted the most bellicose attitudes, urging for example, like Dr. Krapf of the Church Missionary Society, that 'it would be most desirable that Abyssinia . . . should be regulated, if not permanently occupied by an European power, for the Abyssinians will never be able to elevate themselves independently of Europe'. Liberal elements in both Press and parliament also demanded more vigorous action by Lord Derby's Conservative administration in much the same manner as the Conservatives would have done if the Liberals had been in office.

The Cabinet resisted these pressures, and decided on a middle course. Flad was to be sent back as soon as possible with a stiff letter from the queen expressing her displeasure at the latest developments, and asking once again for the immediate release of the captives. No threats were made but it was made clear that the arrangements for the despatch of the artisans were being temporarily suspended; the other things the emperor had asked for were being sent out to Massawa and would be kept there, like bait, to be handed over as soon as the prisoners reached there in safety. In actual fact both the artisans and their equipment, as well as the presents, were sent out with Colonel Merewether in charge, to await developments in Massawa. In a carefully phrased memorandum of instructions given to Flad by the Foreign Office he was also told to assure the emperor that nothing was further from H.M.G.'s mind than 'voluntarily to disturb, or encourage the Governor of Egypt to disturb

[1] The numbering of the houses in St. James's Square was changed in the late 1890s, with the result that the East India and Sports Club, as it is now called, is No. 16 and the London Library no. 14.

King Theodore in the peaceful possession of his dominions'. In short, while there could still be no question of helping Theodorus to attack the Egyptians, the British Government would make sure, if he released the captives, that the Egyptians did not attack him.

Martin Flad reached Massawa at the end of October 1866. When Merewether with his party of men and materials arrived there a month later poor Flad was still there. He had heard that both the direct route to Gondar through Tigrai, and the northern approaches from Metemma, were in a disturbed state, and that it would be dangerous for him to attempt either. All he had been able to do therefore was to send copies of the queen's letter by separate messengers, and hope that one at least might get through. In the end, Flad did not himself reach the emperor's camp and his own family until the following April; but one of his messengers did manage to reach the emperor and to return to Massawa, and in the middle of March 1867 reports of Theodorus' reaction to the letter arrived in London.

Theodorus had his agents in Massawa, and he knew that, despite what was said in the queen's letter, Colonel Merewether was waiting there with the workmen and their equipment as well as the presents. Not surprisingly his first reaction was satisfaction that by holding Rassam and the others to ransom he had persuaded the great Queen of England to send him what he had asked for, instead of provoking the hostile response which some of his advisers had warned him to expect. He was, however, disappointed that both the men and the goods were being withheld until the prisoners had been released and delivered. The difficulty was that neither side trusted the other to keep its promises. Theodorus was afraid that once he handed over the captives the British would find some excuse to continue withholding some or all of what he had asked for. As he put it, in a colourful local analogy, the Queen of England was like 'a certain woman who informed her guests that she was giving them in two covered vessels the *talak* and the *tamash* [the cuts of beef reserved for the most distinguished], but uncovering the vessels the guests found that they had been deceived, the one containing liver and the other the lungs'. Nor was he unmindful of the opportunities for trickery on his own part. In his self-confident moods he would boast that he could always outwit the English, whom he regarded as being generally too soft-hearted and squeamish to merit their claim to be defenders of the faith. Colonel Merewether was known throughout the Middle East as the Queen's representative in Aden, and if he could

George, Duke of Cambridge (1819–1904),
by F. Sargent

General Napier

The Derby Cabinet of 1867, by Henry Gales (1868); Lord Stanley seated, extreme left; Disraeli standing, holding opened paper; Sir Stafford Northcote, bearded, seated centre; the Earl of Derby standing at head of table.

be induced to bring up the gifts himself he would make a better hostage than any of the less important personages whom the emperor already had in his power. Although Tigrai was still in rebel hands, Theodorus had recently recovered control of the country north of Lake Tana, and he therefore suggested that Colonel Merewether should travel from Massawa to Kassala, and bring up the presents himself from Metemma.

For its part, the British Government, which was already being criticized both at home and abroad for being conciliatory to the point of gullibility, was determined not to be caught again, or to allow anyone or anything to be handed over until all the captives were safely out of the emperor's reach. Once it became clear therefore that Theodorus was insisting on getting everything before he handed over the captives, the chances of a peaceful solution diminished, and the arguments and pressures for the use of force became increasingly strong. But when Merewether wrote at considerable length in this strain in a letter dated 4 March 1867, the still reluctant Secretary of State passed his letter on to his officials with the comment, 'Merewether is back on fighting again.' The Permanent Under Secretary at the Foreign Office came to the rescue with a nicely balanced compromise between the rising tide of bellicose opinion in Press and parliament, and the Government's reluctance to go to war. After reminding those who advocated sterner measures that the recent punitive Persian war[1] had cost the taxpayer the sum of £2,195,728, he submitted the draft of a 'final letter' which skilfully managed to convey an atmosphere of ultimatum without once threatening the use of force. In stronger language than had been used before, it required the emperor, for the last time, to release the captives within three months, and expressed the hope that 'your Majesty will be sufficiently well-advised to comply with her demand, rather than forfeit the friendship which, notwithstanding all that has happened, the Queen is still disposed to entertain for you'. The letter was drafted for the Foreign Secretary's signature and ended, 'Having thus fulfilled the commands of my Queen my sovereign, I bid you heartily farewell.'

In case the language of this letter was too diplomatic for its message to be properly understood, it was proposed that 'a bazaar rumour' should be started that a military expedition was being prepared. With the letter went instructions that the presents should continue to be kept

[1] The Persians having, with Russian encouragement, occupied Herat in Afghanistan, three battalions under General Outram were despatched from India to evict them.

at Massawa in case the emperor responded to this final appeal, but the workmen, understandably disgruntled by this time and reduced in numbers by desertion and death, were to be sent home from Massawa, and the machinery and equipment sold in the hope of recouping some of the cost of this ill-fated operation. Undignified and parsimonious disputes over the sums due to these workmen or their dependants were to stain the pages of the Foreign Office files for years.

These proposals were made on 23 March, and in less than a month they had been approved by the Cabinet, and three copies of the letter dated 16 April 1867 were on their way to Massawa for despatch to the emperor Theodorus by three separate messengers in the hope that one at least might get through. Equally important was the fact that warning letters, which had been 'seen by Lord Derby and the Queen', were sent at the same time to the India Office and the War Office urging them to consider as a matter of urgency what further steps might now be necessary to secure the release of the captives.

While those concerned with Abyssinia by interest or duty were waiting with diminishing expectations to hear if there was any response from the emperor to this last attempt at a peaceful solution, the Foreign Office was beset by offers of help from numbers of would-be emissaries and captive-rescuers, and by helpful but often conflicting advice from those like Sir Samuel Baker who had had experience of eastern Africa, and from others whose qualifications were less impressive. One was a cavalry officer who had frequently made 'sudden dashes upon forts and walled places, invariably with success', and suggested carrying out a similar dash at Magdala. Another was a Captain Snow, who offered himself as an envoy to the emperor's court in the following terms:

> You are aware, My Lord, that all medicine-men, wizards, demented persons, skilful craftsmen etc. are, in a measure, held sacred in the East. I have found it so among all the many wild tribes visited by me in various parts of the world, and a reference to any of my works or to official reports will show that I have invariably succeeded even among the most savage races of mankind. I simply study them, and then adapt myself to their ways (without entirely losing my own self-respect) until I win their good-will and carry my point.
>
> It may appear absurd to relate how sometimes as an acrobat, then a medicine-man, next a grave reader of the stars, a laughing merry-andrew, but always kind and gentle as well as firm, I have got on. Playing with the children, admiring the women no matter how ugly, and humouring the men (who are often big babies) I have passed unscathed through wild people

who, before and afterwards (most remarkably in Australia and Tierra del Fuego), murdered the white men visiting them. A bold fierce dash with no show of timidity is however necessary, and they respect it. . . .

It says much for Lord Stanley's patience that when such letters were referred to him personally, as they often were, he would write in the margin in his own hand 'ack and thank' or 'ack and say we do not propose to act as suggested'. Even Merewether's copious reports and advice were now being viewed with a caution that grew into suspicion as it became apparent that he was beginning to see himself a possible commander of a military expedition. It came as a relief therefore when the Foreign Office received from Dr. Blanc at Magdala a memorandum which the Permanent Under Secretary described as 'the first paper on which I have felt that we may rely as giving us an intelligible history of the past and a truthful account of the actual state of affairs'. Blanc's memorandum seems to have dispelled any remaining doubts in the minds of the Government's civilian advisers that there was now no alternative to force.

But first the emperor had still to be given a reasonable time to reply to Lord Stanley's letter. The Cabinet had still to be convinced that war was in the national interest, and was likely to bring the party that sanctioned it more votes than would be lost.[1] A majority had still to be secured in parliament to vote the necessary funds. All this would take time; and those who were concerned with the practical rather than the political side of things knew that if there was to be a military expedition, it would, because of the rains in the highlands and the heat at the coast, have to take place between October and June. Some enquiries had therefore to be put in hand at once. The Foreign Office started the ball rolling on 25 June with a memorandum listing a number of points which needed to be considered without further delay. The Foreign Secretary knew that for every advocate of force there were still others who opposed it, and when he was shown the draft of this memorandum he cautiously minuted, 'I see no objection to the proposed enquiries being made on the understanding that we do not in any way pledge ourselves to send out an expedition.'

The time-limit laid down in Lord Stanley's letter to the emperor was the middle of August, that is to say three months after the despatch of

[1] On 11 May Stanley noted in his private journal: 'Cabinet at 3 . . . we decided not to send an expedition to Abyssinia.'

his letter from Massawa on 17 May 1867. On 13 August news reached London from Merewether that one of the three messengers had returned and had reported that 'he delivered the despatch into the king's own hand. The king took it and saluted by carrying it to his head. . . .' After ten days the messenger had been dismissed. 'No letter was delivered to him, and when he purposed asking the king about it he was prevented from doing so by the bystanders.' Merewether concluded that it was clear that Theodorus had 'no intention of sending any reply or of acting in accordance with the demand contained in your Lordship's letter'.

This is the only record of Stanley's final letter having reached the emperor, and of his reactions to it. With Rassam and his companions held captive at Magdala, first-hand information about the emperor's actions at this juncture depended largely on letters from the Gaffat workmen and the two European wives, and Rassam and Blanc were assiduous in sending Merewether news based on rumours and hearsay, and in speculating on their meaning. The general view thus propounded was that Theodorus' position inside the country had become so hopeless that he no longer cared, and that drink, dissipation, and disease had undermined his energy and his judgement. Mrs. Flad had, for example, reported that 'the King is since last week ill; he uses hot baths; and a good many of his concubines also have to use hot baths'. It is true that Theodorus had in his middle years of declining fortunes abandoned the abstemious, almost puritanical practices of his prime. He drank more frequently with his soldiers. His second marriage had not been a success, and he had taken to consorting with rough and boisterous women of the type once described by Samuel Pepys as 'a bad face but good bodied girle'. If, as Mrs. Flad implied and Colonel Merewether later claimed, Theodorus had a venereal disease, he was in good company. Both the Coptic bishop and the British consul were said to be fellow-sufferers from what was by most accounts a complaint as widespread in Abyssinia as the common cold in England.

According to Waldmeier, however, the emperor was still very much in command of the situation and of himself. If he did get a copy of Stanley's final letter and sent the messenger away without an answer, the most likely explanation is that he had come to the conclusion that his best course of action was deliberately to provoke the English into sending a military expedition. In almost every part of his dominions the people were in a state of revolt against the continual burden of providing supplies for the emperor's large standing armies; many of his unpaid and unfed soldiers were deserting, and the provincial barons and the restless Galla took advantage of his difficulties to flout his authority or rebel. In addition continual disagreements with the Church over its contributions to the royal coffers had led Theodorus to seize the rich contents of some of the churches and monasteries by force, and to hold the Coptic bishop in comfortable but unmistakable confinement at Magdala. In these circumstances Theodorus may have thought that a foreign invasion offered the best chance of rallying the dissident forces of the Church and State, particularly if it could be shown that the English were in league with Ethiopia's traditional enemies, the infidel Turks and Egyptians.[1] He seems to have believed too that if he concentrated all his remaining resources at Magdala, and reinforced its strong natural defences with artillery and fortifications, he would be in an almost impregnable position when the English army arrived, weakened by the difficult country and vulnerable to attack along the long, tenuous line of its communications with a coastal base. In such a situation he might even be able to persuade the British forces to help him overcome his domestic enemies and recover some of his lost lands as the price for being able to take out the captives they had come to rescue without a hazardous fight or a lengthy siege. It may be, therefore, that the failure of the emperor Theodorus to reply to Lord Stanley's final letter in the summer of 1867 was as deliberate and as calculated as the British Government's failure to reply to his own letter to the queen in the spring of 1863.

The consequences were certainly as momentous. On 19 August, less than a week after the receipt of Colonel Merewether's despatch in London, the decision was taken to send an expedition to secure the release of the Abyssinia captives.

The decision to send an expedition to Abyssinia was taken by the Cabinet. Parliament was temporarily in recess at the time during what were coming to be known as 'the sacred days of August',[2] and it was not until two days later, on 21 August, when members had returned for a brief formal meeting to prorogue parliament, that the decision was communicated to them and to the country in the Queen's Speech.

[1] A task made easier by a State visit to London that summer by the Sultan of Turkey and his Viceroy in Egypt.

[2] It was in the following year, 1868, that 12 August was fixed by law as the opening of the grouse season.

Although there were the customary complaints of decisions being taken when parliament was in recess, the decision to use force in Abyssinia was not a surprise to anyone. The matter had been ventilated at length in the House of Commons a month before. It was clear even then that the conclusion had been reached by both the Government and the Opposition that, if Lord Stanley's final letter evoked no response, there was no alternative but to issue an ultimatum backed by force, and to give orders for such force to be assembled and made ready. This conclusion had been reached with reluctance and regret by almost everyone in the House of Commons except perhaps for a handful of members who were acting as particular advocates of the captives or their causes. The attitude of both the Conservative Government and the Liberal Opposition was that whatever might have been done or left undone in the past, the inescapable fact remained that a British consul, a British envoy, and two British army officers on duty were being held captive and in chains in Abyssinia together with a number of missionaries who, while not British subjects, had been sent there by British missionary societies. Over a period of years several attempts at conciliation had been made without success. The question before the House on this occasion therefore was not who was to blame or how to prevent such a situation arising again, but what to do now; and was there any alternative left except the use of force? Payments of a ransom in cash had been suggested on the grounds that '£5000 would be better than an expedition costing £500,000', but this idea was rejected as it would provide a bad precedent, and might lead to 'semi-barbarous monarchs seizing Englishmen in all parts of the world and calculating their ransoms'. There were indeed few stratagems which had not been tried and discredited, and few ideas which had not been thought of but rejected. Yet even at this stage, if the necessity for using force could have been avoided by almost any more or less honourable alternative, almost everyone in Britain's pacific and parsimonious parliament would have been relieved.

The Government and Opposition in parliament might have to resign themselves to the unavoidable, but there was of course no reason why the Press should follow suit. Newspapers and weeklies were in the happy position of having power without responsibility, and could therefore praise or condemn, or pursue policies of their own, in the sure knowledge that they themselves would never have to decide the conduct of affairs or the expenditure of public money. This perhaps was barely true of *The Times*, which, under the long editorship of John Delane, had become almost part of the Victorian establishment. Where other organs of the Press, therefore, could and did openly praise or as openly condemn the use of force in Abyssinia, *The Times*, with its greater responsibilities, began by sitting on the fence. While conceding on the one hand that, in spite of errors of judgement and conduct, the confinement of the captives was arbitrary, illegal, and unjustifiable, it complained on the other that 'this Abyssinian business is almost the only blot upon the picture described in the Royal Speech'.

The Speech from the Throne had been delivered by the Lord Chancellor in what had become the familiar absence of the Queen. On this occasion the Press found the Queen's Speech very dull. After years of tiresome agitation and disturbing controversy, the Reform Bill had passed into law, and there were many who now looked forward to a period of undisturbed peace and prosperity. For readers of *The Times*, at least, the prospects looked pleasing. At home, the latest Fenian troubles, as they were then called, had been firmly dealt with. The conditions of the poor and the consciences of the rich had been eased by legislation—Factory Acts, improvements to the old Poor Laws, a new Master and Servants Act, while long-standing restrictions on workmen's combinations and trade associations were being gradually removed. Abroad, the picture seemed to warrant equally complacent satisfaction. The Emperors of France and Austria had had a meeting in Salzburg, and there were 'no grounds for apprehending war between France and Prussia at present'. Even the Luxembourg question had been settled.

Such prospects of calm and amity were good for the Funds and good for trade, and anything that threatened them was a nuisance. So it was that, after a week of reflection, a leading article in *The Times* sounded a warning by calling the Abyssinian expedition 'a leap in the dark'. It conceded that we had in recent years acquired considerable experience of military expeditions in out-of-the-way places—Persia, China, Kabool, Swat, Bhootan and Ashantee were named, and so spelt, as examples—but that in the case of Abyssinia 'there was hardly a country about which we knew less'. After a further week of indecision, which included a visit to Woolwich where new weapons 'hardly larger than toys' were being specially constructed at great public expense so that they could be carried on the backs of mules and men in Abyssinia, *The Times* at last came down, more or less, against the use of force. 'The gain must be nothing; the loss may be considerable, and the expense will necessarily be great.'

The correspondence columns of *The Times* reflected this unease in a spate of angry letters about the unnecessary cost of the proposed expedition, and an equal number of alarming but often contradictory letters about the hazards which it would encounter. A summary of the attitude of the British Press at that time said that it painted 'ghastly pictures of the malaria of the coast and the insalubrity of the country. At one time the expedition was to die of thirst, at one time to be destroyed by hippopotami. Every beast antagonistic to the life of man was, according to these writers, to be found in the jungles and swamps of that treacherous country. Animals were to perish by the flies, men by worms. . . .' Many of the letters to the papers were signed, after the manner of the time, with *noms-de-plume* designed to impress the reader with the writer's experience of foreign parts, like AN OFFICER WHO HAS SERVED BOTH IN INDIA AND IN NEW ZEALAND, and ONE WHO HAS SUFFERED SEVERELY FROM THE TSETSE FLY. But for everyone who stressed the dangers of the climate and the country, or complained about the cost, there were others who welcomed the plan 'to rescue Englishmen who are pining away in imprisonment in the midst of savages'. *Punch*'s spirited cartoon showed Britannia, calm and dignified, pointing her trident at a cowering black king with a funny hat and gaoler's keys. Many of those who wrote offered helpful ideas: 'Let me, as an old campaigner and sportsman, offer a few suggestions. . . .'

Radical opinion generally tended to oppose the war on the grounds that it would result in higher prices and increased taxation, and would divert resources that might otherwise be available to help the needy. The leaders of the Liberal Opposition in parliament were, however, not yet ready to reflect such views; with the bulk of the population still without a vote there was little political advantage to be gained from doing so. In foreign affairs, however, the position was different. The queen used to refer to the Liberal leaders Palmerston and Russell as 'those two dreadful old men' who kept supporting revolutionary movements against her numerous relatives sitting on the thrones of Europe. But supporting the causes of liberty and change abroad was one thing, and countenancing such things at home was another. In home affairs the Liberal party in 1867 was still at heart the party of the old Whig aristocracy, just as in the field of foreign affairs it was still the party of Lord Palmerston, who had rarely hesitated to use force, if need be, to uphold the rights of British subjects abroad. In parliament the leaders of the party were also well aware that any attempt on their part to criticize the use of force in Abyssinia would lay the Liberals in general, and Earl Russell in particular, open to the charge that it was a Liberal administration which was largely responsible for the situation in which the Conservative Government now found itself. The result, therefore, was that the Liberals tended to be more in favour of sending an expedition to rescue the captives than the Conservative Government. Lord Derby's Cabinet knew only too well that if anything went wrong they would get the blame, while they also had the unpopular task of finding the money to pay the bill.

Disraeli was then Chancellor of the Exchequer in Derby's Government, and it fell to him therefore to decide how the money should be raised, and how the matter should be presented to parliament and the public. His task had been eased by an assurance inserted in the Queen's Speech at the opening of the new session of parliament in November that the expedition was purely for the purpose of rescuing captives, and that the forces would not remain in Abyssinia any longer than was necessary for this purpose. It had also been helped by publication in a Blue Book of a large part of the official papers dealing with Abyssinia for the past twenty years. Although it did not include by any means all the letters that had passed or any of the confidential minutes, the Foreign Office officials who compiled it saw that it still ran to 495 closely printed pages, on the principle, it was said, that the larger the Blue Book the less likely it was to be read. What it did contain, however, was enough detail of what had and what had not been done by the previous Liberal administration to discourage criticism of Disraeli's proposals from the Opposition front bench.

Disraeli's aim was to get parliamentary approval for a credit of £2 million towards the cost of the expedition, and to pay for it by an increase of a penny in the standard rate of income tax, from fourpence, that is to say, to fivepence in the pound. His task was not made easier by the fact that his predecessor as Chancellor had been his rival, Gladstone, and that Gladstone had managed in the course of two peaceful and prosperous years to reduce income tax from sixpence to fourpence. Nor was Disraeli's task eased by the fact that both he and the prime minister were suffering from gout. Despite this Disraeli made a spirited speech. He was one of the first politicians of his time to sense that the small householders and skilled workmen who were enfranchised under the new Reform Act tended to be enthusiastic patriots who liked military expeditions and imperial expansion, and his speech was therefore freely laced with heady adjectives like 'scandalous', 'distressing', and 'intolerable'. For the benefit on the other hand of the middle classes, on whom the main burden of the increase of income tax would fall, he conceded that it was vexatious that we should have to have recourse to arms but there was 'a certain method in the King of Abyssinia's conduct which did not point to a very happy solution of the difficulty', and he likened Abyssinia to the classic cave: 'there were no signs whatever of returning footsteps (laughter).' Gladstone, for the Opposition, generally supported the Government's proposals in a speech that was lengthy, statesmanlike, and excruciatingly dull.

When the matter came to the less rhetorical scrutiny of the Committee of Ways and Means a few days later, the Government admitted that, although all they were asking for at this stage was a credit of £2 million, the cost of the expedition might rise to as much as £4 million. There were those on both sides of the House who suspected that the eventual cost would be considerably more. As an increase of a penny in the rate of income tax would only bring in £1,450,000 in a full year, this left a number of questions in the air. One of them was the contribution to be made by the Government of India.

When the India Office and the War Office had first been asked to consider the possibility of sending a military expedition to Abyssinia, it had been suggested by the Foreign Office and the Treasury that India should not only organize the expedition but pay half the cost as well. The Government of India, which at times appeared to conduct its relations with the home government as if it were an independent state, agreed to organize the expedition but firmly rejected any idea that the revenues of India 'should be subject to any portion of the expenditure which may be incurred for an object in which that country has no direct interest'. The argument continued for some time, and the Treasury, with that zest for savings in public expenditure which is often mistaken for occupational parsimony, proceeded to draw on a wide range of experience and intellectual ingenuity for ammunition to support its case. It argued, for example, that the chief beneficiary of an operation which was designed to show that British envoys could not be ill-treated with impunity would be the Government of India, which had representatives not only in places like 'Burmah, Nepaul and Cashmere but in even more distant outposts such as Aden, Zanzibar and

Muscat'. It was India too, the Treasury said, which had the most to gain and, with the recent memory of the Indian Mutiny in mind, the most to lose in the matter of prestige. There was also the beneficial effect which the rescue of the captives would have on the minds and behaviour of the thousands of Mohammedan Indians who travelled each year up the Red Sea to Mecca, and of those Indians who were trading in the outposts of Africa and the Middle East. Nor, it was added, should it be forgotten how much India depended on the maintenance of uninterrupted communications with Britain through the Red Sea, much of whose coast was claimed as Abyssinian territory. It was even suggested as an inducement that parts of the healthy highlands of Abyssinia could provide an admirable sanatorium for the Indian Army in the hot season, or 'a temporary gymnastic ground for its military exercises'. The weekly *Saturday Review* went further: it implied that the real reason for the expedition was to check Russian designs on India by showing that the British lion had claws as well as a tail for foreigners to twist. Russia it said, 'is slowly pushing her borders towards India; she is creeping up on us, bullying, bribing, conquering but always getting nearer . . .,' so 'in order to show that we are not afraid of a big power, we are to kick a little one'.

The Government of India was not impressed with these arguments. In the end the most it would concede was that the ordinary pay of officers and men of the Indian Army who were employed by the British Government in Abyssinia should continue to be paid out of Indian revenues. It was not surprising that when the exact composition of the expeditionary force became known, critics should insinuate that native Indian troops were being used in large numbers either to save the British taxpayers' pockets, or to avoid the use of home-based British troops in what was feared might turn out to be an unhealthy and hazardous operation.

In the end Disraeli got parliamentary approval for his credit of £2 million and for the increase of a penny in the rate of income tax, but on the clear understanding that as soon as the captives had been released 'we should retire for ever from Abyssinia, and that we shall never again mix ourselves up with the affairs of that or a similar country'. *The Times* quoted with approval an Opposition spokesman who had urged that 'those who were continually boring the Foreign Office with recommendations to open up commercial relations with this, or to send missionaries to that country, should in future be entirely disregarded'.

It concluded with the exhortation that 'our proper work in the world will be better done if we abstain from inviting wars with savages who wish nothing more than that we should leave them alone'. No wonder the historian Sir John Seely was moved to say in one of his lectures at Cambridge that 'we seem, as it were, to have conquered and peopled half the world in a fit of absence of mind'.

CHAPTER IX

Preparations

Although the decision to send an expedition to Abyssinia was not finally taken until August 1867, the possibility that it might be necessary to send one had been exercising several people's minds for some time. One of them of course was Colonel Merewether, who came to the conclusion as early as February that the last chance of conciliation had gone, and thereafter busied himself with getting information about possible landing-places and routes to the interior, and with working out what sort of force would be needed. No one had actually asked him to do this, but he made a point of reporting all his findings both to his superiors at Bombay and to the Foreign Office. Although the Foreign Office had sensed that Merewether was partly concerned with trying to make a case for the despatch of an expedition with himself at its head, it was still impressed with the quality and thoroughness of the information which he submitted. The information was in fact largely derived from a Swiss named Werner Munzinger who had been looking after British interests at Massawa since 1865, and whose knowledge and experience of Abyssinia and the Red Sea coast was probably greater than any other European's at that time.

Another collector of information was Major-General Sir William Coglan, who had also been Political Resident at Aden, and whose opinions about the Red Sea area were highly thought of in Whitehall.[1] He was the first to submit a detailed scheme for an expeditionary force

[1] According to Edward Hertslet it was largely on Coglan's advice that no reply was sent to Theodore's letter to Queen Victoria in 1863. Edward Hertslet (1824–1902), later Sir Edward, succeeded his father Lewis Hertslet (1787–1870) as Librarian and Keeper of the Papers at the Foreign Office in 1857, and stayed on well after normal retiring age to complete a family holding of this post of eight-six years. In addition to compiling a seemingly endless series of scholarly and elegantly written memoranda on the diplomatic issues of the century, including Abyssinia, the Hertslets also acted up to 1870 as agents in London for members of the diplomatic and consular services. When both Cameron and Rassam wanted money or news passed to friends or relations it was to Edward Hertslet that they wrote. Hertslet's famous *Treaties* comprised sixteen volumes, of which eleven were the work of the father and the last five of the son.

to Abyssinia. Both he and Merewether advocated a landing at Massawa or in Annesley Bay, and discarded alternatives like Tadjoura, or an overland approach through the Sudan and Metemma. Both also preferred an expedition based on Bombay, using forces drawn from the Indian Army, rather than one based on Malta with home-based troops, as was at one time suggested. One argument used was that, with the Suez Canal not yet finished, troops and especially artillery, which would only have to make a single sea voyage from Bombay to a Red Sea port, would have to be embarked and disembarked twice if they came from England or Malta. Another argument in favour of an operation mounted from India was that the Indian Army had its own familiar bands of the camp-followers which were considered necessary for such campaigns—bearers, porters, grooms, grass-cutters, and suchlike—whereas troops from Britain would have to recruit and then train such auxiliaries themselves. There was also the belief that, in the terrain and climate of Abyssinia, units from the Indian Army would have less to learn than soldiers fresh out from Britain. On such points both men agreed. Where they differed was that Colonel Merewether recommended a force of about 6000 men which could be commanded by a colonel with the acting rank of a brigadier, whereas Major-General Coglan envisaged a body of 10,000 men which would call for a commander of higher rank.

An even more important step in the process of preparation was taken at the end of June when, as explained in the previous chapter, James Murray, an Under Secretary at the Foreign Office, obtained Lord Stanley's cautious approval to ask the India Office and the War Office to 'make preliminary inquiries as to the precise steps to be taken in the event of its being found necessary to resort to force'. In this letter he posed seven specific questions:

1. What amount of force is considered needful; what should it consist of; and by whom should it be commanded?
2. Assuming Bombay to be the base of operations, how long, after receiving from England orders to prepare the force, would it take to insure its being ready for service?
3. What arrangements would be made for its transport?
4. At what point would it be proposed to land it, bearing in mind that it is essential, if possible, to avoid landing in Egyptian territory?
5. What commissariat arrangements would be required?
6. What reserve would be necessary to insure success, and how is it proposed to keep this supplied?

7. Whether any, and what, preliminary steps would have to be taken, and what time would be required for the purpose, in order to obtain answers to these questions?

This formidable list of Whitehall questions reached the Governor of Bombay on 10 July. The governor, Sir William Vesey Fitzgerald, was a former Conservative Member of Parliament of no particular distinction, and he passed it on to his military commander-in-chief, Lieutenant-General Sir Robert Napier. Napier in turn sent for his Quartermaster-General, Colonel Phayre, and told him to assemble all the available information about Abyssinia rapidly and in what soldiers call easily digestible form. Other staff officers were set to work at the same time, and in less than two weeks Napier had his answers ready. Within days telegraphic summaries of his conclusions were in London. The first arrived on 29 July, five weeks after Murray had drafted his questions in the Foreign Office.

The answer to Murray's second question was 3 to 4 months. Napier had also calculated that, if the expedition was to finish its task and be out of Abyssinia before the rains set in in June, it would have to be ready to begin operations not later than January. There was clearly no time to be lost, and the Foreign Office was told, almost too firmly for comfort, that ten thousand pack animals, for example, should be collected immediately. 'It would have been better', the telegram added, 'to have commenced earlier.' One suspects that it was Napier himself who drafted the signal.

Napier's answer to the third question, about the landing-place, was that, whatever the Foreign Office might stipulate, the best place was somewhere in the vicinity of Massawa which was claimed and occupied by the Egyptians. Travellers' tales and books by civilians were interesting but of limited value to a general, and Napier recommended that a detailed reconnaissance of the area should be carried out as soon as possible by a team of properly qualified naval and military experts; a similar reconnaissance should be made of the various routes into the interior. As he was to record later, 'the description of roads by a mere traveller, who did not travel with a view to observe military routes, and who probably has no idea of the power of movement of a properly equipped force, is of little value'. He preferred more practical advice, and it came as a relief to Napier, after reading the colourful and long-winded descriptions of travellers like Bruce, Salt, Dufton, and Beke to get a brief, matter-of-fact report from a Sapper major that a particular pass in Abyssinia was no worse than 'the passes between Bushire and Shiraz where mules regularly travelled 30 miles a day under loads of 300 lbs'.

The answer to Murray's first question reached London on 9 August. The size of the force, it said, should be 12,000 combatant troops. Napier was an experienced, careful, and thorough soldier, and he supported his case with good arguments. One was that the force must be large enough to ensure that it did not fail; an unsuccessful expedition would be worse than no expedition at all. Apart from the actual assault force of 5000 men, it would be necessary to establish and guard not only a base at or near the point of disembarkation but also a series of staging posts along the 400 miles of communications between the coast and the fortress of Magdala where the captives were held. It would also be necessary for the expedition to take its own reserves in case of unexpected casualties, from whatever cause, and in case the Emperor Theodorus decided to retreat to an even more remote part of his dominions and take the captives with him. In such a case the expedition might have to lie up during the rainy season until it could continue operations in the autumn. Napier's final argument was that while the help of some of the local population might be expected, it would be unwise to count on it; it would not be right in any case to accept such help from any Christian Abyssinian elements if they were likely to suffer for it after the British withdrew. Nor, as regards help from the non-Christian elements, 'would his humane and Christian feelings allow him to regard with indifference the prospect of British soldiers being the means of allowing the pagan Galla to overwhelm the representatives of a corrupt and vicious but still moribund Christianity'. Whatever may have been Napier's own expectations, his case for a larger force was impressive. All that the Governor of Bombay's telegram said about the question of command, however, was, 'Have you chosen Merewether for C. in C.? Most important I know this.'

A week later, on 16 August, London telegraphed its decision. The expedition, if there was to be one, would be organized in India. Its base of operations would be Bombay, and General Napier would command it. 'Her Majesty's Government, having great confidence in Sir Robert Napier, desire to place the whole conduct of the negotiations, as well as the military direction of the armed forces in his hands.'

Robert Napier had been a soldier since he was a boy. He had, so to speak, been born with a musket in his mouth. It was not by any means a silver musket. He did not belong to the aristocratic Napiers of Dorset, nor to the more famous Napiers of Merchiston in Scotland who had provided the empire with so many admirals and generals in the eighteenth and nineteenth centuries. His father, who was a major in the Royal Artillery, had died before his son was born, and Robert Napier was given the second name of Cornelis after the fort in Java where his father had been mortally wounded. He entered the old East India Company's military college at Addiscombe when he was 14, and was commissioned two years later into the Bengal Engineers. He went out to India in 1828 when he was 18 years old.

He took his duties as a Sapper very seriously. He built roads, bridges, and canals for civil purposes in the Punjab with the same zest and thoroughness that he applied to the construction of military defences and encampments, and when he came home on leave he sought out the great engineers of the day like Brunel and Stephenson, and travelled on the Continent to look at the work of French and German engineers. But he also believed that Sappers of all ranks should be able to fight. As a junior officer in the Sikh wars he was severely wounded, and had more horses shot under him than was usual in a captain of engineers.

Napier was on leave in England when the Mutiny broke out. On his return he was posted to Bengal, and for the next two years he managed to intersperse the cool and competent execution of large administrative responsibilities with the display of courage and resource in such operations as the relief of Lucknow, and the pursuit of the elusive Tantia Topi. He was later chosen to command a division in the China wars, and the care he took over such unfashionable things as ventilation and sanitation when he embarked his soldiers at Calcutta was reflected in the health and fighting condition of the men when they arrived at their destination. On his return to India he was made a military member of the governor-general's council, where he acquired useful knowledge of the operations and personalities of the central government in India, and of the workings of government in Whitehall and Westminster. In 1865 he was made commander-in-chief of the Bombay Army.

General Napier was so well fitted by experience, capabilities, and character to command the Abyssinian expedition that it should have reflected credit on the system and the people responsible for it. It is true that there had been important changes since the disastrous appointments to some of the higher commands in the Crimea in 1854

A separate Secretary of State responsible to parliament for the whole administration of the army had in fact been created in 1856, and the Duke of Cambridge had succeeded Lord Hardinge in the Duke of Wellington's old post of Field-Marshal commanding-in-chief, who, as a representative of the crown, still retained a measure of independence in matters of promotions and appointments. His Royal Highness the Duke of Cambridge, of whom it was said that 'his courage was high but he had not the imperturbability needed for war', was a grandson of George III and first cousin to the Queen, and was one of the few members of the royal family whom Queen Victoria permitted to perform a useful office. He was usually a conservative man, but at a time when appointments in cavalry and infantry regiments were still being auctioned in Charles Street, Mayfair,[1] he had the wit and the courage to appoint Napier, a relatively unknown and self-made General in the Indian Army, to the much-sought-after and lobbied-for post of commander-in-chief of the Abyssinian expedition. Perhaps the fact that the Duke of Cambridge was colonel-in-chief of the Royal Engineers was a contributory factor, and may have been one reason why the Duke maintained a particularly close interest in the progress of the campaign. He ended a private letter to Napier on 3 August 1867, 'I hope you will keep me informed of all the military arrangements you may have in mind and I remain, my dear Napier, yours most sincerely, George.' Napier kept the Duke informed in a series of personal letters, but he also took the opportunity to use the Duke of Cambridge's good offices to discourage and, if need be, eliminate interference from the political and military authorities both in London and in India. 'Your Royal Highness will, I am sure, perceive,' he wrote in a 26-page manuscript letter on 27 September, 'that however superior in judgement and experience those at a distance may be, yet they cannot judge the circumstances of the case as well as we can here, and that it wd be impossible to conduct an expedition of this kind on our hands under any interference from a distance.'

Once Napier had been appointed to command the expedition, and the decision to use force had finally been made, the control of events passed swiftly from London to Bombay. Although funds for the operation had to be approved by the authorities in London, Napier had shown on several occasions in the past that he did not care for financial

[1] The going rate for colonelcies in the cavalry at that time was £14,000, and for infantry regiments about half this figure.

controls exercised by faceless men in offices, and when he had first outlined his proposals for the expeditionary force he had added the rider that the best arrangements 'might be crippled by some misplaced economy'. General Mansfield, the senior military member of the governor-general's establishment at Simla, complained to the Duke of Cambridge in a private letter that Napier 'has the character of being too liberal and large in his notion with respect to public expenditure'. The civilian governor of Bombay and the Treasury in Whitehall both knew, however, that if they refused to provide the money for any particular item which Napier had asked for, they could and almost certainly would be blamed if anything went wrong. Napier knew this too, and was thus in a position of which he was never slow to take advantage.

With the stage so set, it only remained for London to comply with General Napier's request that he should be given precise directions about the objectives of the expedition, and what he could and could not do to achieve them. Napier had learnt from his own experience the wisdom of insisting on such directions, and of getting them in writing. The instructions which he eventually received from the Foreign Office through the Secretary of State for India were a conscientious armchair attempt to provide answers to all the questions which would arise in the field; but, like the instructions which used to be given to brides, they tended to cover all situations except the ones that actually occurred.

Although the direction of affairs had now passed into military hands, the Foreign Office still had one important matter to deal with. It had been hoped, by those in London whose geography was entirely derived from maps, that it might be possible to send an expedition to Abyssinia without passing through Egyptian territory. When it became clear that this was not the case, the Foreign Office set about getting the necessary permission. As there were doubts about who exactly was in legal possession of Massawa and the country in its vicinity, the request was addressed both to the Egyptian government and to the Turkish authorities at Constantinople, and in due course both countries gave their consent on the understanding that the expedition would leave Abyssinia as soon as its objectives had been achieved. The Egyptian government in particular gave its consent with an alacrity and enthusiasm which was positively alarming. It not only gave permission and offered every assistance on land and sea but it also sent reinforcements to its garrisons at Massawa and Suakin. Although the real reason for these reinforcements was probably to enable the Egyptian government to take advantage of any weakness in Theodorus' position to extend its own dominions at Abyssinia's expense, the reason given was that they were sent to provide assistance to the British expedition. This, of course, was the last thing that Britain wanted. It was bad enough having to ask the Egyptians for permission to pass through their territory. This alone was enough to make it appear that the British government was acting in concert with Abyssinia's traditional enemies; the presence of Egyptian reinforcements could be used by the emperor of Ethiopia to suggest a closer and more sinister alliance whose object was annexation, and forcible conversion of Abyssinia to Islam in the same way he claimed, as the British and the Turks had tried to do with Holy Russia in the Crimean War. The British government brought all its considerable influence to bear to dissuade the Egyptians from being so helpful, and in the end they withdrew some of their reinforcements.

The shift of the centre of operations from London to Bombay also meant a change of atmosphere. The special correspondent appointed by *The Times* to cover the expedition reported from Bombay that the Abyssinian war was as popular in India as it was unpopular at home. He was of course, referring to the British in India, but, encouraged perhaps by counter-rumours that Christian Abyssinia was secretly in league with Christian Russia to impose their hated religion on the Hindus and Muslims of India, native volunteers to serve with the expedition came forward from all parts of India. The advertised scales of pay and of rations may have been an inducement to some but for many of India's fighting men the attractions of a war were probably reason enough for offering their services.

As military adviser to the governor of Bombay, Napier had said that a force of 12,000 men would be needed, and as commander-in-chief he adhered to this in the face of pressures from different quarters to make it larger or smaller. He had more difficulty in reconciling conflicting views on other matters. One was the ratio of British and Indian troops in the composition of the expeditionary force. There was the argument on the one hand that, with the Mutiny only ten years past, at least a third of the troops should come from Britain; on the other hand there was the conviction that native Indian soldiers were better able to cope with the climate and the conditions likely to be found in Abyssinia. As on most questions, Napier had his own distinctive views. 'The mutiny', he wrote, 'exploded the theory that British soldiers could only be used in the field on special occasions. Properly dressed and properly used they were found to be as serviceable as native soldiers.' What went for the infantry applied with equal force to the cavalry. 'The 3rd Dragoons ride better than most native cavalry. They are better armed and fire better from the saddle.' He also made the practical point, missed by many who still thought that the war in Abyssinia would be fought in burning deserts or steaming jungles, that British troops would stand the cold of the Abyssinian highlands better than most native Indian forces. At the same time Napier knew from his own experience that Indian troops required less cosseting, less baggage, and fewer camp-followers than their British counterparts, and that properly led and properly treated they were in many cases as reliable and as loyal. In the end he made up his own mind, and took one British cavalry regiment to four of Indian cavalry, and four British infantry regiments to ten Indian.

The other controversial question was from which parts of India the native Indian troops should be drawn. It was one which was bedevilled by political considerations, provincial jealousies, and local pressures. India at this period was divided into three presidencies of Bengal, Bombay, and Madras, and Napier, with his considerable experience of all three, wanted to draw most of his forces from Bombay. In the case of Bengal his objection was not so much that many of its troops had been involved in the Mutiny as the purely practical one that caste rules in Bengal would not allow its soldiers to eat anything they had not cooked themselves or which had been contaminated by contact with leather. This meant, to quote Philip Woodruff, that 'it was necessary in the middle of the mornings to halt and to allow the men to remove their belts, boots and all their accoutrements, to light seven hundred separate little fires and cook fourteen hundred separate little cakes of wheat'. Napier, however, came under very strong pressure from the governor-general's establishments at Delhi and Simla to include some units from Bengal and Madras, and in the end he gave way to the extent of taking two regiments of Punjabi infantry and two regiments of Bengal Lancers, and three companies of Madras sappers and miners.

In operations conducted by the Indian Army there were usually more camp-followers than troops. The *Times* correspondent reported that the total number of men going on the expedition might be as much as 50,000. However, the difficulty and expense of transporting such numbers by sea, and of keeping them supplied in Abyssinia with what were regarded as the necessities of life, brought this figure down to 20,000, that is to say, 12,000 uniformed troops and 8000 civilian auxiliaries. Even in the English language the range and diversity of these auxiliaries made an impressive list—bearers, cooks, water-carriers, porters, grass-cutters, sanitary men, and a host of highly specialized men to look after the horses, the mules, the draught bullocks, the beef cattle, the camels, and the elephants. But the scene was now an unmistakably Indian scene, and the reports and memoranda which gradually found their way into the dry and dusty pigeon-holes of the Foreign Office and the India Office in London still gleam and chatter with the vernacular equivalents—*puckalees, bheesties, salootries, mutsuddies, moochies, jemadars* and *mahouts*. Though not listed in the official reports, there was also said by some eye-witnesses to have been a contingent of female corn-grinders from Bombay.

While Napier and his staff were busy composing the size and the shape of the expeditionary force and with bringing it into being, they were at the same time being pestered with requests, pleas, prayers, and sometimes with directives from London, to take on people some of whose qualifications or likely contributions to the objectives of the expedition must sometimes have seemed to Napier to be less than vital. Most of them were private volunteers and eccentrics, but there were also a growing number of foreign military observers who wished to accompany the force: the final total, with representatives from France, Prussia, Austria, Italy, Holland, and Spain, was twelve. The Foreign Office and the India Office were also beset by requests from travellers and retired military men who believed that they had indispensable knowledge or skills to contribute or who were anxious, for personal reasons, not to be left out. Most but by no means all of these pleas were turned down, but it was Napier himself who suggested that a surveyor, a botanist, a geologist, and a natural history expert should be attached to the expedition in order 'to add to our store of knowledge'. In the end the Royal Geographical Society and the Zoo sent representatives too. Napier was equally forthcoming in his response for facilities for the Press, an attitude which was not always shared by his staff or by his officers in the field. Several British daily papers like *The Times*, the *Morning Post*, the *Standard*, and the *Daily News*, and a number of weeklies like the *Illustrated London News* and the *Saturday Review* took advantage of these facilities to attach special correspondents to the expedition, one of whom, G. A. Henty, deservedly became better known as a writer of fiction than a reporter of news. The *New York Herald* sent an awkward, prickly, and ambitious young journalist named Henry Morton Stanley.[1]

To equip, supply, and transport an expeditionary force of 20,000 men required an immense amount of administration and unobtrusive hard work. But, as Dr. Austin, the *Times* correspondent remarked, 'it was difficult to give a tinge of romance or heroism to the manly sweat, albeit on military brows, which is induced by the exertion of auditing accounts, seeing that bullocks are branded, inspecting pack-saddles, or looking critically into the mouths of seedy ponies and venerable mules.' One administrative matter which did have a military complexion was the arming of the combatant troops. Up to that time British troops had been issued with muzzle-loading Enfield rifles whose ammunition consisted of a bullet and powder packed into a small paper cartridge,which had to be torn open with the teeth and the contents rammed down the muzzle of the rifle with a ramrod; a percussion cap had then to be fitted in position in the breech where it was fired by a hammer operated by a trigger. These operations took some time, especially when the barrel became hot from repeated use, and the rate of fire was only two or three rounds a minute. Breech-loading Snider rifles had been used both in the American Civil War and in the Austro-Prussian war of 1866, and experience there showed that they could fire two or three times faster. It was decided therefore to arm the British troops in the Abyssinian Expeditionary Force with these up-to-date weapons which, apart from the increased rate of fire, had the advantage of using a self-contained brass cartridge. Since the Mutiny Indian troops had, as a matter of policy, only been armed with smooth-bore guns of an obsolete and ineffective type.

[1] The full list of representatives of the Press and other bodies was as follows:

Viscount Adare	*Daily Telegraph*
Dr. C. Austin	*The Times*
G. A. Henty	*Standard* and *Pioneer*
Lieut. F. A. Shepherd	*Times of India*
C. Simpson	*Illustrated London News*
H. M. Stanley	*New York Herald*
Lieut. W. O. Whiteside	*Morning Post*
R. R. Holmes	British Museum
C. Markham	Royal Geographical Society
G. Rohlfs	German Medallist of the R.C.S.
Count Sayre	French Foreign Office

There were also a meteorologist, a geologist, and a zoologist.

Disregarding official policy, Napier sought and obtained permission to arm some of his Indian cavalry regiments with these new breech-loading rifles. He also sought authority to increase the fire-power of his Indian infantry by giving some of them the muzzle-loading Enfield rifles discarded by the British troops. Permission for this equally unorthodox step was more difficult to obtain, and in the end it did not arrive until the campaign was nearly over. Similar problems seem to have arisen over the arming of the auxiliaries: a telegram from Delhi to Poona in September said that 'government considers it objectionable to issue carbines to muleteers and think that swords ought to be arranged for'.

Most of the old files and records dealing with the Abyssinian expedition relate to less bellicose stores and equipment, and 13 pages of the official history of the campaign are taken up with a list of the items sent out from England, and another 10 pages with those shipped from Bombay and Kurrachee, as it was then spelt. There was a wide variety of clothing due to the fact that provision had to be made not only for a sea voyage in the hot season from India to the Red Sea and the sizzling conditions of the coastal plain, but also for the cold and the wet of the Abyssinian highlands. One comparatively novel item was khaki drill. The Indian Army had for some time been using tea or coffee, and even red ink from the orderly room to make their regulation white uniforms less conspicuous in the bare brown hills, but on this occasion khaki drill was manufactured and made an official issue. For the highlands, there were 4000 blue serge shirts, and the same number of neck comforters, nightcaps, and mittens; 18,659 Banians, flannel, 18,442 Cumblies, black, 11,730 Drawers, flannel, and similar quantities of dhoties, dhopatas, cholera belts, belly bands, and '150 Numdas or hairy mitchins'.

Among the foodstuffs there were 70,000 lbs of 'salt beef, Admiralty' and similar amounts of salt pork, large quantities of preserved potatoes, compressed vegetables, biscuits, and flour for the Europeans together with regulation issues of 'tea, black, 1st sort', 'sugar, Bengal, 2nd sort', and 'rice, Vergole, 1st sort'. To cook these rations there were also included 2,970,814 lbs of firewood. Among the extras were 34,000 lbs of cocoa and 30,000 gallons of rum in wood casks. 'Provisions for natives' concentrated on dhal, ghee, flour, and rice, enlivened with supplies of chillies, cocum, turmeric, betel-nut, cummin seed, salt fish, and tamarind. The list of medical stores included 150 'pots, chamber, zinc, round'; 3000 tins of condensed milk; 250 dozen of port wine; 100 of sherry; 5 dozen pints of 'Old Tom' gin; and some unusual items such as 21 lbs 8 oz. of cantharides and 800 leeches. One officer wrote in his notebook, 'A certain quantity of opium should be supplied in each ship for natives (especially Sikhs) to purchase. Some men died for want of it.'

As big and time-consuming a problem as arms and supplies was the question of transport. The whole expedition had first to be transported by sea from India to the vicinity of Massawa, and thereafter, while the troops marched towards Magdala, most of its supplies and equipment would have to be transported across a dry desert of coastal plain, up a series of steep, roadless passes to the highlands, and then across hills and mountains cut by a succession of the valleys and gorges of numerous rivers flowing westwards to the Nile. In regard to sea transport there were sharp disagreements over the respective merits of iron and wooden ships. If too many of the still comparatively new iron ships driven by steam were requisitioned there were complaints from the well-established owners of the old sailing ships made of wood, and arguments about the high cost of chartering the former had to be balanced against the longer time taken by the latter. But the problems of sea transport were small and straightforward compared with the problems of transport on land. In the end over 35,000 draught or pack animals had to be bought, requisitioned, or hired. The animals included horse, mules, bullocks, camels, and forty-four elephants. Of these the ones which caused the most trouble were the mules.

The Foreign Office files on Abyssinia for the latter part of 1867 are full of references to mules. Orders had gone out in August to Her Majesty's representatives in half the seaport towns of the Mediterranean and the Middle East to collect or to assist in the collection of mules. To give the matter a touch of consular distinction they were referred to in despatches as 'beasts of burden urgently required for the Abyssinian war'. In the following months between seven and eight thousand mules were collected in Gibraltar, Malta, Spain, Italy, Sicily, Tripoli, Syria, Turkey, and the shores of the Persian Gulf, and delivered with their own muleteers to staging-posts in Egypt. From the official despatches and personal letters exchanged on this subject the consuls and other officials concerned do not appear to have enjoyed their task, and their distaste and lack of interest was reflected in the quality both of the mules and the muleteers which they despatched. Nor, when they arrived at their destinations, did either the appalling heat of the Red Sea coast or the cold and wet of the Abyssinian highlands appeal to mules that were used to pulling carts over the cobbles of Alicante and Aleppo. They were landed in many cases without adequate supplies of food and water, and they ate through their tethering ropes and foraged with devastating pertinacity among the quartermasters' stores and the officers' tents. In the first few months more than five thousand of the mules died, and the muleteers, many of whom came from the back streets of seaport towns and were generally unresponsive to the disciplines of the Indian Army, soon became equally reduced in numbers through discharges and desertion. Mules were also collected at this stage from the west coast of India, together with muleteers who, according to one of the many reports later compiled on this matter, were mostly 'the off-scouring of the Bombay streets, broken-down native tradesmen, discharged Europeans and Eurasians from other departments and the class termed loafers'.

Another part played by the Foreign Office in the preparations for the expedition was in the matter of currency. By an oddity of history the only coin which was generally accepted in Abyssinia at that time was the Austrian Maria Theresa thaler of 1780. Its use dated from the long period when the trade in the Levant was centred on Venice, and from the shorter time between 1797 and 1866, when Venice was part of the Austrian dominions. It was an inconvenient coin; it was too large, too heavy, and, at an exchange rate with sterling of 4s. 3d., it was worth more than was needed for most everyday transactions in Abyssinia. To make matters worse it had no subdivisions in coinage form, so that for small change bricks of crystallized salt, seven inches long, two inches wide, and an inch thick were used at a variable rate of between twenty and thirty bricks to the thaler.

It was clear that the expeditionary force would need large sums of local currency, for supplies, for wages, for rewards, and for bribes. The estimate was for nearly a million thalers, or dollars as they were customarily called,[1] but enquiries through consular channels showed that the most that could be expected from the open market was about 15,000. Further enquiries revealed that the minting of Maria Theresa dollars had ceased in 1858, and that, although the dies were still held in Venice, the 'local financial authorities would not permit their use'. Pressure was then brought to bear at ambassadorial level on the Austrian govern-

[1] The word 'dollar' is in fact derived by sound from 'thaler'.

ment, who agreed to mint in Vienna 'any amount', ot Maria Theresa thalers of 1780 if the British supplied the silver. In the end 476 casks of 2000 thalers each were minted and delivered to the expeditionary force.

While this preparatory work was going on in India, in Britain, and elsewhere, the reconnaissance party had been carrying out detailed surveys on the spot to determine where exactly the expedition should land, the route it should follow, and where base camps and staging-posts should be established. It was a comprehensive team of experts chosen by Napier for their practical experience of the technical and logistical problems which were likely to arise—a naval officer, a colonel of the Royal Engineers, a doctor from the Indian Army Medical Service, and Napier's own resourceful Quartermaster-General, Colonel Phayre.

The area they selected for the landing was Annesley Bay,[1] an inlet about 50 miles south of Massawa. The inlet provided a good anchorage for the large numbers of ships which would arrive with men, stores, and livestock. It was not ideal; the most that could be said of it was that it was better than all the alternatives. The sea was so shallow that ocean-going ships had to anchor three-quarters of a mile offshore, and two 300 yard long piers had to be built to reach sufficient depth of water for the ships' boats and flat-bottomed lighters to tie up and discharge their cargoes at low tide. The horses and mules had to plunge into the sea after being confined in great heat between decks and face a swim of half a mile to the shore, a task which many were unable to accomplish.

The place chosen for building the piers was near a village called Mulkutto, but it was generally known as Zula, which was the more easily pronounceable name of a larger settlement in the vicinity. Antiquarians were gratified that Zula seemed to coincide more or less both in situation and in sound with the ancient Greek port of Adulis. It was, and still is, a singularly unappetizing place of pervasive and persistent heat, dust, and flies; not at all, as Austin told the readers of *The Times*, 'the sort of place I would choose for a picnic'. Its disadvantages were offset, as far as the expeditionary force was concerned, by the presence of fresh water, and the fact that the otherwise waterless and fiendishly hot coastal plain was at this point not much more than a dozen miles wide.

[1] Named after Sir George Annesley, who explored the Red Sea coast in 1805. He was described by David Mathew as an earnest, obscure, and eccentric nobleman who squandered his fortune, and so lost his disreputable aristocratic intimates and declined upon the middle classes.

The choice of a pass up the steep escarpment to the highland plateau presented similar difficulties. Most of the passes were little more than defiles carved by torrents of water that came down with great force during the rains. The escarpment was granite, and in places huge boulders torn from the sides or brought down from above were jammed in the defiles in masses up to fifty and, in one pass explored by Phayre, two hundred feet high. It was difficult for a layman to believe that an army of 20,000 men could possibly negotiate such passes with their baggage and their guns, or depend on them for their communications with their coastal base, but the army engineers in R Force, as the reconnaissance party was called, were not dismayed or discouraged. They noticed how the local people had made rough tracks with timber and stones over or round the boulders for their own heavily laden mules, and calculated that all that would be required to make a roadway 10–15 feet wide were '100 sappers and a few hundred pounds of gunpowder'. When supplies of water and forage on the various routes had been checked, and possible camp-sites examined, a route was chosen and the sappers put to work. The distance from the landing-place at Zula across the desert to Kumayli at the foot of the chosen pass was 14 miles, and work began at the same time on the track of a railway by which men and supplies would be transported in open wagons drawn by tall-funnelled steam-engines.

The first section of the pass itself was 13 miles long, and the upland staging-post at Suru was a pleasant place with plentiful grazing and water, and, to quote from *The Times* again, 'sweet scented shrubs like the English jasmine filled the air with fragrance; and juniper trees, mimosa and dense groups of evergreens completely hid the foot of the mountain, affording a tempting covert for the birds whose gorgeous plumage glittered among the boughs; and overhead the rocks, rising almost perpendicularly to the height of many hundreds of feet, admitted into the pass just enough of the sun's rays to make the air deliciously warm.' If it was warm by day it was, at an altitude of 1100 feet, pleasantly cool at night. But at Senafay,[1] 60 miles inland on the top of the highland plateau where the base camp for the advance brigade was being established, the altitude was over 7000 feet, and it became bitterly cold when the sun went down.

The advance party reached Zula at the end of October. It included fighting troops as well as sappers and men concerned with supplies.

[1] Also spelt Senafé, Senafè, Senafe and Senafee.

They worked hard and often frenetically to get things ready for the main body of the expedition. They were under the direction of Colonel Merewether, but here too he relied heavily on the composed and unassuming competence of Munzinger, 'the perfect polyglot', as Austin called him, 'gliding quietly from Arabic to Italian or French or German, and every now or then turning round to answer a message in some dialect of Abyssinia'. There were indeed a large number of things to be done—the landing jetties to be completed, the railway track to be laid, camps to be established at the foot of the pass and at a succession of staging-posts on the way to Senafay. There were roads to be blasted and formed and drained, depots to be set up with supplies for the men and compressed hay for the animals, water to be pumped or channelled from distant wells and springs, and water condensers to be built to transform sea-water into 120 gallons of fresh water every day.

Elements of the main body of the expedition started to arrive at the end of October, and all through November and December large numbers of iron and wooden ships of all shapes and sizes dropped anchor in Annesley Bay and debouched men, equipment, stores, and animals from all parts of the world in what were often bewildering quantities, illogical order, and frequent disarray. But out of a seeming chaos, which some observers had at first found disturbingly reminiscent of the Crimea, a form of workable order began to emerge. Although this was mainly due to the energy, resource, and cheerfulness of the Indian sappers and miners, a stimulating contribution was also made with the arrival in November of the 33rd Regiment of Foot. The English officers and largely Irish rank and file of what was better known as the Duke of Wellington's Regiment, came ashore in sun-helmets, khaki drill trousers, scarlet coats, and regulation hair-cuts. Under the unconventional and sometimes erratic command of a cavalry officer named Alexander Dunn, who had won a V.C. in the charge of the light brigade at Balaclava, they were soon bathing naked in the sea, shaving their heads bald, or growing wild-looking beards according to choice, and working cheerfully all through the hot afternoon while others complained or rested or slept. Another unusual thing about what was by repute a particularly tough, hard-drinking, hard-swearing, and hard-fighting regiment, was that it included a sizeable remnant of a British foreign legion of German volunteers which had originally been raised to fight in the Crimea. Nor did the regiment let the heat of the Red Sea interfere with its traditional Christmas dinner. Guinea-fowl, with half a dozen sitting birds carefully aligned for each shot to save cartridges, did passable duty for turkeys, and the regiment's Indian cooks pounded up rations of ship's biscuits to make plum pudding.

General Napier had stayed at his headquarters in India while these preparations were going on, and he remained there until the main body of the expeditionary force had been embarked. He finally left Bombay on 21 December 1867, and arrived at Annesley Bay on 3 January 1868 to take command on the spot of the expedition to release the British subjects and other Europeans held captive by the Emperor of Abyssinia.[1]

[1] A full list of the corps and units in the Abyssinian Expeditionary Force is given in Appendix A.

CHAPTER X

The captives wait and the emperor marches

While these preparations for their rescue were being made, the captives themselves waited in the fortress of Magdala where they had been since the summer of 1866. Magdala was new to Rassam, Blanc, and Prideaux, but Cameron and the others had of course experienced captivity there before.[1] It was therefore no great surprise to them when, three days after they arrived, the authorities at the fortress informed them with winning smiles and exquisitely phrased expressions of regret that, in the absence of European refinements like bars and prison walls, it was the custom at Magdala for prisoners to be chained. Whatever reasons there may have been for the practice, the process of putting the chains on was very unpleasant. Dr. Blanc described it in clinical detail:

> I was made to sit down on the ground, tuck up my trousers, and place my right leg on a large stone that had been brought for the purpose. One of the rings was then placed on my leg a couple of inches above the right ankle, and down came, upon the thick cold iron, a huge sledgehammer; every stroke vibrated through the whole limb and when the hammer fell not quite straight it pressed the iron ring against the bone, causing most acute pain. It took about ten minutes to fix on properly the first ring; it was then beaten down until a finger could just be introduced between the ring and the flesh, and then the two pieces, where they overlapped one another, were hammered down until they perfectly joined. The operation was then performed on the other leg. I was always afraid of the blacksmith missing and smashing the leg to pieces. All at once I felt as if the limb was being torn asunder; the ring had broken just when the operation was nearly completed. For the second time I had to submit to the hammering process, and this time the fetter was riveted to the entire satisfaction of the smith and the chief.

The chains consisted of two large rings joined by three smaller rings which left a gap of about nine inches between the two legs. The heaviness of the rings in each case was nicely graded according to the standing and culpability of the prisoner; in this, as in other things, Rassam and his companions were better treated than Cameron and Stern. Apart from the difficulty of walking and sleeping in chains, which took

[1] See p. 68.

some getting used to, there was the problem of trousers which the resourceful Blanc overcame by splitting his down the outside seam and sewing buttons up the side from waist to ankle. With these 'Magdala trousers', as he called them, he and his imitators were able to take off their trousers to bath and change into night-shirts at bedtime. Perhaps it was not coincidence that the tight cotton trousers generally worn by Abyssinian men were better suited to fetters, and could with practice be passed through the gap between the iron rings and the ankles.[1]

Abyssinian prisoners were expected to be fed and clothed by their relatives, and as Rassam and the European captives contrived in various ways to be rarely short of money, they were able to keep themselves in essentials from the weekly markets held in the vicinity. They complained about the lack of variety and the poor quality of the food—the chickens were 'stringy' and the sheep 'the size of a London cat', and the things they lacked were revealed in the letters and postscripts which they managed to send to Massawa, and to their friends and relations at home. Dr. Blanc wrote, 'Do not forget to send us a few stores; some tobacco, cheroots and anything to enliven the poor prisoners. . . . Books, letters and papers are what we most require.' Rassam was more specific: 'I shall feel obliged by your sending for the following articles: one dozen flannel shirts, two dozen snuff boxes, two dozen pencils, one dozen penknives of different sizes, about 100 reels of cotton, lots of needles of different sizes, and common enamelled buttons. It is very important that I should keep in favour, and any little present might save no end of trouble. . . . Farewell, and do not forget me.' Blanc, as a doctor, also had his needs for keeping in favour. 'We want medicines very much, not only for ourselves but for our native friends. As a rule I do not like to refuse any one now, it would not be prudent; and, if grateful for anything, the Abyssinian is sometimes so if he gets cured from old pox, or such like inveterate disease which has baffled the skill of all the blacksmiths and such reputed necromancers of the country. . . .[2] If possible,' he concluded, 'send some comforts with medicines.'

When Rassam and the others first arrived at Magdala they had all to share two huts. Although they were in the emperor's own compound,

[1] Mansfield Parkyns, the early Victorian traveller, always referred to these and other trousers as 'inexpressibles'.

[2] According to Blanc, 'it can be said that every Abyssinian, male and female, has been, is, or will be infected with syphilis.'

General Napier with officers of the Royal Engineers

Napier's camp at Zula

Unloading at Annesley Bay

and were as good as any in the fortress, they would, as Dr. Blanc put it, have been condemned by the R.S.P.C.A. Within a few months, however, the captives were able to take advantage of the kindness or the cupidity of their guards to improve and extend their accommodation considerably, and to install their own bedsteads, bedding, and household furniture, and lay down the carpets which Theodorus had given them earlier. With the help of flower and vegetable seeds sent to them by Merewether and Munzinger from Massawa, in order, as Rassam had asked, 'that we might have sweet odours as well as nice eatables', they made themselves trellises and gardens, and grew their own tomatoes, potatoes, peas, beans, mustard and cress, lettuces, radishes, cabbages, and turnips. 'We made our own bread, and always used table-cloths, and sometimes napkins, and never sat down to dinner, barring the first few days after our arrival, without beginning with soup which was occasionally followed by fish; then two or four entrées, then a joint, then a pudding or tart, winding up with anchovy toast, or cream-cheese—the latter made by our Indian servants.' This was how the honest and perhaps ingenuous Rassam described their diet. The Revd. Henry Stern, for the benefit perhaps of these who had contributed to the Abyssinian Captives Relief Fund, put it differently: 'Luckily, or rather providentially, we were seldom without money; or else we might have gnawed our lips in the grim agonies of starvation.'

There seems little doubt that most of the captives over-emphasized and exaggerated the pains and hardships of their condition in order to win sympathy and stir up support for efforts to secure their release. Cameron and Stern were the worst offenders in this respect. Blanc and Prideaux generally displayed the stiff upper lips, the resourcefulness, and the superior reserve expected of Victorian officers and gentlemen; but it was Hormuzd Rassam who had the sense of proportion and the moral courage to write that 'not one of the captives can justly complain that his imprisonment, during my time, was aggravated by privation'. He did not forget that they were chained, with all the restriction and discomfort and indignity which this entailed, but even that, he recalled, was put into perspective by the wives and daughters of the Abyssinian captives in the fortress who came to visit him with their 'sweet, soft voices' and their sad lack of cleanliness.[1] Much as they

[1] Rassam was not the only visitor to remark on the unwashedness as well as the charm of Abyssinian women, but the criticisms were not all on one side. One good Christian Abyssinian, after noting an Englishman's constant ablutions, scornfully

pitied his fetters—'O, may the Lord comfort you, Mr. Rassam!'—they reminded him how fortunate he was not to be chained by the hands as well, as most of their own menfolk were.

Their hardships were also mitigated for most of the time by the fact that they were able to communicate with Merewether and Munzinger at Massawa, and through them with their relatives and friends in England. They were also in touch with the European artisans who had remained behind at Debra Tabor with the emperor. They were thus able to make their needs and their news known to the outside world, and to get information both from England and from the emperor's camp.

They had to be careful what was said in both what they sent and what they received in case it became known to their guards; in practice however, it was rarely that their messengers or their own belongings were searched. Apart from devices like sewing messages into the lining of their messengers' clothing or the soles of their sandals, they used schoolboy French and simple mathematical ciphers and code-words like 'Bob' for Theodorus, and 'Shrimps' for Bardel, the Frenchman who was generally regarded as the emperor's spy. For some of them however, it was not so much the risk of discovery by their captors that made them so careful as the fear that any criticisms or complaints which might be made in private notes and letters might find their way into the newspapers, and be whipped up in ways which could upset and enrage the emperor; there seemed to be little which did not eventually come to his ears. Cameron and Stern, together with Rosenthal and his English wife were thought to be particularly indiscreet in what they wrote, and the letters of the more cautious Rassam and Blanc often contained postscripts like 'Kindly send me any bit of newspaper which does not contain abuse'.

Perhaps the hardest thing which the captives at Magdala had to bear was what Rassam called mental anxiety, the constant nagging uncertainty about what it was that their unpredictable captor had in store for them. This anxiety was not diminished by the harsh and sometimes horrific treatment meted out to some of the Abyssinians who were held as hostages or as prisoners at Magdala. Nor was it helped by the equally disturbing doubts and uncertainties about what the British civil and military authorities were, and were not, doing on their behalf.

---

asked, 'Is he a Mussulman that he washes so often?', while another said of the pale-faced Mansfield Parkyns that he was 'like a rather good-looking Abyssinian who had lost his skin'.

It was with a tremendous feeling of excitement and relief therefore that, after 17 months of confinement at Magdala, they received a message from Colonel Merewether on 19 December 1867 that an advance party of British troops had landed at Annesley Bay on 6 October, and was actively engaged in making preparations for the arrival of the main expedition. While it was an occasion for celebration, it was also a time for trepidation. If they themselves had got news of the landing, the emperor Theodorus would certainly have heard of it too. So, the first question the captives asked themselves was what will he do with us now? They had not seen the emperor since he had sent them to the fortress in the summer of 1866, and they had had no word from him for nearly a year. News of his whereabouts and moods and intentions was scanty and often contradictory. What they did learn, however, was that he had left his old headquarters at Debra Tabor in the first half of October 1867, and was said to be gradually making his way across country with his guns and his army, and a whole host of followers, towards the fortress of Magdala. It was a chilling thought as they celebrated their second Christmas at Magdala, and drank hopefully to rescue and freedom in the new year.

When the emperor Theodorus sent Rassam and the other captives to Magdala, he told Rassam, whom he still regarded as a friend and almost always treated with courtesy, that he did so for their safety and comfort during the rains. The real reason was probably that he was about to embark, despite the onset of what was generally regarded as the close season for fighting in Abyssinia, on a series of military operations designed to restore his authority in Begemder and Lasta. The last thing he wanted on the march was the encumbrance of looking after a party of difficult, quarrelsome, and, in the case of Cameron and Stern, physically unfit Europeans. There was also the danger that they might escape, or fall into the hands of his enemies. Theodorus looked on Magdala not only as a military fortress but also as a secure place of safety for his family, his wealth in cash and kind, his reserves of arms and ammunition, his stores of grain and liquor, and the superb collection of religious books and paintings which he had accumulated over the years through gift, purchase, or plunder.[1] It was the place where he

[1] The emperor had, in his time, also been a generous giver. The British Museum has a superb engraved chalice and paten from the palace at Gondar, inscribed with his name as donor.

kept his most treasured and valuable assets, and hostages, he knew from experience, could, if properly used, be as effective in achieving one's objectives as money or guns.

By no means all the Europeans who were in the emperor's power were sent to Magdala in that summer of 1866. There were at that time sixteen other European men under his control. Five of them, Waldmeier, Saalmüller, Bender, Zander, and Mayer were the remainder of the seven Swiss and German missionaries who had been sent out in the 1850s under the auspices of the Church Missionary Society, and who had, since 1860, been established at Gaffat, a few miles from Debra Tabor. Three others, Flad, Staiger, and Brandeis belonged, like Stern and Rosenthal, to the London Society for the Promotion of Christianity among the Jews. Flad was away at the time in London as the emperor's envoy, leaving his German wife and children behind as hostages, while Staiger and Brandeis had decided that their best chance of remaining at liberty was to dissociate themselves from Stern and Rosenthal and enter the emperor's service as artisans at Gaffat. In addition there were four adventurers of one sort and another who had also entered the emperor's employment, one of them being Bardel; the other three, Dr. Schimper, the German botanist who had been for many years in Abyssinia collecting plants, a Pole named Moritz Hall, and a French gunsmith called Bourgaud. There were also two men who had originally come to the country with the Duke of Saxe-Coburg in 1864 on a hunting and collecting expedition and had been there ever since—a Prussian named Schiller, and Essler, a Hungarian. To complete the picture, there were two of Cameron's European servants, the Irish McKelvie and the French Makerer, who had also decided that desertion was the better part of valour and had offered their services to Theodorus.

Whatever their motives, all these sixteen men had originally entered the emperor's service of their own free will, and, except in the case of the Swiss artisans who had believed that it would help their missionary work, they had done so for their own profit or advantage. Theodorus had on the whole a low opinion of Europeans, but he had to concede that, for reasons beyond his understanding, God had endowed them with technical skills denied to the otherwise superior people of his own kind. He needed these skills, and used all his considerable powers and means of persuasion to induce these Europeans to remain in his country and in his service. He hoped to persuade them not only by generous if irregular payments in cash but also by what are now called fringe benefits. There were only two European wives at Gaffat. Mrs. Flad, who was worthy and German, and Mrs. Rosenthal, who was English and plain, and had remained behind at Gaffat when her husband was despatched to Magdala. For the others at Gaffat Theodorus had, as already explained, gone out of his way to find local girls, whose home-making and other qualities would, he hoped, induce them to settle down and stay in Abyssinia. By the summer of 1866 Waldmeier and Saalmüller, his two most valued artisans, were still happily wedded to John Bell's half-caste daughters, while Bender was still domestically involved with one of Dr. Schimper's local offspring. Zander and Mayer had been married to Galla girls who had been converted to their own Pietist practices. Bourgaud had a wife who was classified as French, and Moritz Hall had married a girl who had both Abyssinian and Armenian parentage. These local wives were generally looked down on by the European wives, but contemporary photographs suggest that they compared favourably with Mrs. Flad and Mrs. Rosenthal in grace, dress, and deportment.

The emperor introduced conditions of employment for his 'Gaffat children' or 'European slaves', as he called them according to his mood, under which they were paid and fed strictly and sometimes ruthlessly by results. He also applied a system of deferred payments, which meant that wages due or bonuses promised were often withheld on a 'next week' or 'when I return' basis in order to discourage people from leaving. Even monies actually paid were sometimes liable to be taken back by their quixotic employer, and it was to circumvent this practice that the artisans sometimes sent their reserves of Maria Theresa thalers by trusted messengers to the captives at Magdala when the latter were in need of cash. Rassam gave them drafts on the Foreign Office in exchange, which were eventually honoured many months and in some cases years later by somewhat startled consular officials in different parts of Europe. In the last resort Theodorus discouraged the artisans from trying to leave by making it clear that the least of the consequences would be hand-chains and fetters.

For nine months after Rassam and his companions had been sent to Magdala, the Europeans at Gaffat worked in comparative peace and plenty on the various projects assigned to them by Theodorus. Although the projects were of a more military and secular nature than some of the missionaries might have wished, like casting small brass cannon and mortars, repairing muskets, making roads, and building gun-carriages, the Swiss and German artisans of the C.M.S. still had their Bibles and schools and workshops at Gaffat, with which they hoped to bring the Christians of the Abyssinian Church and the Muslim Galla to their own Protestant beliefs and practices. Life was not without its difficulties, however, particularly when the emperor came in person, as he often did, to examine their work. To those like Staiger and Brandeis, who were reluctant to work with their hands, despite the example which the emperor himself set, he was less than polite, but to those who worked, and especially to Waldmeier, whose skills, adaptability, and stolid willingness he much admired, he was generally generous and kind. Waldmeier recounted how one day Theodorus gave his cloak to a beggar-woman and asked him to lend him five thalers to give as alms. That evening he called Waldmeier and handed him a hundred thalers, saying, 'I always return and give like a king.' Another time he took the missionary's skilful hands and kissed them. 'Poor hands, for even these must one day be laid in the grave.' Mrs. Flad, however, who had a busy and often malevolent pen, painted a different picture, especially when she and Mrs. Rosenthal were handed large quantities of cloth and firmly told by the emperor to make them into shirts if they wanted to eat. 'Our present position', she wrote, 'is equal to that which the children of Israel were placed under Pharaoh. Read Exodus V.'

For most of the time the emperor was away. His visits to Begemder and Lasta took longer than he had hoped. He tried first to persuade the rulers and the people to increase their contributions to his revenues in cash and in kind. When persuasion and exhortation failed, he tried anger and threats. When these too proved ineffective, he resorted to coercion and plunder. Towards the end of the year, news reached him that a rebel had seized the rich town of Gondar and was refusing to pay the customary dues and taxes to the emperor. On 1 December 1866 he set out from Debra Tabor with a picked force of cavalry and light infantry. It was 80 miles to Gondar, across difficult country. He left Debra Tabor in the afternoon and was at the gates of Gondar at dawn, having done the distance overnight in sixteen hours. Despite this, the element of surprise was lacking, and the rebel and his soldiers were able to escape to the safety of the hills. Angered by what he believed was the complicity of some of the townsmen in the rebel's escape and their easy submission to his rule, Theodorus sent his soldiers in to search every building in the town for plunder—gold, silver, coins, silks, carpets, and above all grain. Gondar was an ancient town of 44 churches, and not one was spared. When the plunder was finished Theodorus told his troops to drive the ten thousand inhabitants of the town into the open country and set fire to the buildings. Of the 44 churches only four escaped destruction, and it was said that some of the priests were also consigned to the flames.

It is unlikely that Theodorus would have sacked and burnt the churches of Gondar had not his relations with the Ethiopian Church been already so bad that it made little difference to his position. The refusal of the ecclesiastical authorities to support many of his reforms, and to meet his increasing demands for taxes and tribute, had led the emperor in the end to send the head of the Church, Abuna Salama, to Magdala. Although he was never subjected to any physical restraint, other steps were taken to ensure that he did not leave. His worldly wants, which were varied, were provided for, but his spiritual influence was considerably curtailed. Salama was at Magdala during Cameron and Stern's first period of imprisonment, and he was still there when Rassam and his companions arrived. It was thought prudent on both sides that they should never meet, as Theodorus sometimes suspected that they were in collusion against him, but Salama did his best to alleviate the situation of the British prisoners by advancing them money, and interceding on their behalf with the fortress guards. In return they supplied him from the stores sent up to them from Massawa with some of the things he particularly fancied like cheroots, snuff, brandy, arak, and opium, and Blanc also offered him much needed medical advice through an intermediary. Bishop Salama died at Magdala, after what Blanc described as a long and painful illness, in October 1867. It was said that when a messenger brought the news to the emperor, Theodorus, noting the messenger's cautiously neutral attitude, said, 'Why did you not shout out "Good tidings"? I would have given you my best mule.' It was supposed by those close to the emperor, and firmly believed by those who relied on gossip, that one reason for the emperor's dislike of Abuna Salama was that not all the bishop's visits to the empress's quarters at Magdala were entirely concerned with spiritual matters. Some Catholic missionaries in Abyssinia, who thought that Salama had a Protestant bias, tended to attribute the ill-health which made him a frequent visitor to hot springs to similar proclivities, but his Protestant admirers preferred to attribute it to other tendencies on the principle, perhaps, that for a celibate bishop buggery was less of a sin than fornication.

In January 1867 five of the Europeans at Gaffat—the two Jews' Society missionaries Staiger and Brandeis, together with Schiller, Essler, and Makerer planned to escape. One of them confided the plan to Bardel, who, perhaps fearing the consequences for the rest of them if the escape succeeded, informed the emperor. Theodorus was both aggrieved and angry. He looked on attempts to escape as ingratitude as well as defection, and he assumed that in this case Staiger and the others must also have been in touch with the enemies and rebels who surrounded him. Although he dealt with the offenders, and their Abyssinian servants, in ways calculated to discourage others from following their example, this attempt was probably the reason why he suddenly descended on Gaffat on 17 April 1867, closed down the school and the workshops, and packed all the Europeans and their families off to his own encampment at Debra Tabor. Another reason may have been that the rebel forces were closing in on Gaffat from the north, and he feared that he might lose not only the prestige and the skills of his European artisans but all their valuable equipment.

It was at this awkward moment that Martin Flad finally reached the emperor's camp after an absence of nearly a year. Theodorus had already seen a copy of the letter from Queen Victoria which Flad had brought back with him and sent up in advance from Massawa, but when he arrived himself Flad had to break the news that the queen had charged him to convey a verbal message too. 'Well, what is it, what is it?' the emperor had asked.

Flad replied that the queen's message was, 'If you see the King tell him from me that if he does not at once send out of his country all those he has detained against their will, he has no right to expect any further friendship from me.'

After asking Flad to repeat this several times, Theodorus paused and said: 'I asked them for a sign of friendship which is refused to me. If they wish to come and fight, let them come. By the power of God I will meet them and call me a woman if I do not beat them.'

The emperor must have realized earlier, when he saw a copy of the queen's letter, that if he did not release the captives an expedition would eventually be sent against him. But it was probably at this point, when he heard what Martin Flad had to say in person, that he made up his mind to concentrate all his resources, including the European artisans, in the fortress of Magdala. He knew, however, that, with his heavy guns, and his large and slow-moving army of soldiers and followers, the journey of 90 miles would take him several months. The summer rains were due to start in June or July, and he dared not risk being caught by them on the march. This meant that he would have to wait at Debra Tabor until the autumn, when the rains would have ended, and the rivers would again be fordable. With all this time on his hands, Theodorus pondered how to use it to the best advantage. One day he called Waldmeier and said, 'You Europeans are very clever but you tend to conceal your capacities. Now I want you to make me a gun that will discharge a ball of a thousand pounds weight. If you say you cannot I will regard you as liars, and you know what I do with those that deceive me.'

Although Waldmeier and his fellows doubted whether they had the knowledge or the resources to make a weapon of this size and feared the consequences of failure, they feared the consequences of refusing even more. So Waldmeier did a drawing, and from the drawing they made a model. They then started to build two large furnaces nearby. Thousands of men were put at Waldmeier's disposal. Theodorus himself, when he was not away foraging or on punitive expeditions, came to see what they were doing and to ask numbers of very practical questions. Work went on all through the rains. The first attempt to cast the huge mortar was a failure, and it was the emperor himself who noticed that there was water on the ground where the mould had rested, and had trenches dug to drain the area. Waldmeier, who did not mention this first attempt in his memoirs, described the second attempt in his own special brand of biblical English:

> At last the day came for casting the great gun. The two furnaces were heated to melt the metal and thousands of people assembled. The King stood between the two furnaces and taking hold of my hand he said, 'Now tell me what is to be done and I will give orders to carry out thy will.' Wherever I went the King accompanied me, holding me fast by the hand. . . . I was afraid that if the gun failed we would all be put in the furnace. When I said that the metal was sufficiently heated, I asked the King to give orders to open the channel of the furnace and the heated brass ran like a fiery serpent into the mould that had been prepared for it. After twenty minutes it was finished and the King was glad and called the gun Sebastopol. It was opened after three days and found well cast.

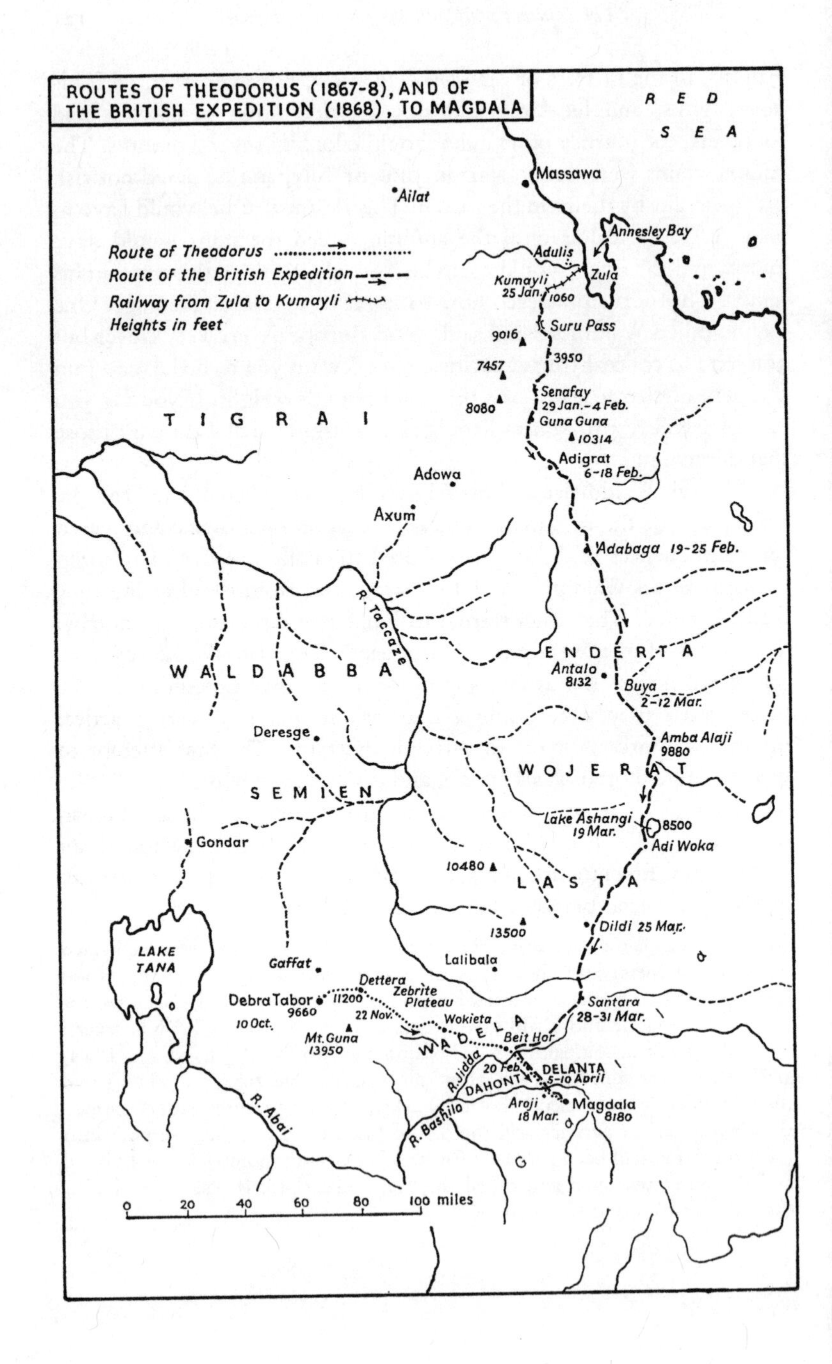
ROUTES OF THEODORUS (1867-8), AND OF THE BRITISH EXPEDITION (1868), TO MAGDALA
RED SEA
Route of Theodorus
Route of the British Expedition
Railway from Zula to Kumayli
Heights in feet
Massawa
Ailat
Annesley Bay
Adulis
Zula
Kumayli
25 Jan.
1060
Suru Pass
9016
3950
7457
Senafay
29 Jan.-4 Feb.
8080
Guna Guna
10314
TIGRAI
Adigrat
6-18 Feb.
Adowa
Axum
Adabaga 19-25 Feb.
R. Taccaze
ENDERTA
Antalo
8132
Buya
2-12 Mar.
WALDABBA
Deresge
Amba Alaji
9880
WOJERAT
SEMIEN
Lake Ashangi
19 Mar.
8500
Adi Woka
Gondar
10480
LASTA
13500
Dildi 25 Mar.
LAKE TANA
Gaffat
Lalibala
Dettera
Zebrite
Plateau
Debra Tabor
9660
11200
22 Nov.
Santara
28-31 Mar.
10 Oct.
Mt. Guna
13950
Wokieta
WADELA
Beit Hor
R. Jidda
20 Feb.
DELANTA
5-10 April
DAHONT
Aroji
18 Mar.
Magdala
8180
R. Abai
R. Bashilo
0 20 40 60 80 100 miles

Theodorus later claimed that that day was one of the happiest of his life. He rewarded Waldmeier and his helpers with presents of money, cattle, and sheep, and with garments of honour known as 'royal shirts'. He attributed his success, as he attributed his failures and his excesses, to the workings of Providence. 'God has given me in Mr. Waldmeier and Mr. Saalmüller workmen who can do every work for me.' When the gifts and the praise had been sufficiently lavished he set them all to work making wagons to carry the mortar and the other guns, and when these too were finished he directed the missionaries and their assistants to start improving the cross-country track from Debra Tabor to Magdala.

On 9 October 1867 the emperor destroyed his encampment at Debra Tabor and burnt the town. It was said that the only building which he spared was the church which he himself had built in atonement for destroying the churches of Gondar. The following day he set out for Magdala. He had with him an army which, though reputedly much depleted during the summer by desertions, consisted of about five thousand fighting troops. They were accompanied, as was the custom in Abyssinia, by camp-followers of both sexes who numbered between forty and fifty thousand. In addition to the 18 Europeans and their dependants, he had several hundred Abyssinian prisoners and hostages. And last, and by no means least in bulk and importance, were the wagons and gun-carriages loaded with his guns and mortars, of which the giant mortar Sebastopol weighed over seven tons. There were, according to Flad, fourteen wagon-loads of artillery and ten of ammunition. Although the army contained large numbers of horses and mules and bullocks, the guns and the ammunition were, because of the danger of mishap, all pushed and pulled across country by hand.

Every morning, half of the emperor's troops would set out with the guns and heavy baggage, and do a march of a mile or a mile and a half. This was as much as they could do in a day partly because of the difficulty of manhandling the heavily laden wagons, and partly because they often had to fight off rebellious forces or marauding bands on the way. When the camp-site was reached and guards had been posted, the remainder of the advance party retraced its steps and helped the rear party to carry and protect the people and the baggage that had been left behind. As Flad put it in one of his letters on the march, 'The King's baggage is very heavy and our progresses are very small.' Progress was slowest of all for the five Europeans who had tried to escape at Gaffat and who were chained both by the hands and the feet. It was fortunate for them that the emperor had provided mules for Mrs. Flad and Mrs. Rosenthal who were both pregnant, and who sent their mules back for these five men when they themselves had reached camp.

By 22 November the emperor had reached the escarpment which separated the fertile valleys of Begemder from the high plateau of Zebrite. Up to that point the going had been rough, but fairly level. Here for the first time he was faced by a seemingly impassable hazard for his guns, in the shape of an almost vertical wall of basalt. The only way up was by the steep zigzag track used by travellers and mules, which was too narrow and too sharp for the heavily laden wagons. It took Theodorus and the artisans and their thousands of workers three weeks to blast and make a road up which the guns and baggage-wagons could be dragged and pushed to the top. Theodorus drove everyone hard all day and sometimes into the night, and set an example with his own hands for all to see, moving rocks, carrying pans of earth, and filling hollows and holes with stones. Those who followed his example were rewarded with praise and with gifts. Those who were backward were subjected to a wide range of punishments. It was not only at work that the emperor set a stringent example. On the march he would pluck some ears of barley from the fields and rub them between his hands so that his soldiers and all the Europeans could see that a few dry grains and a drink of water from a stream were all that a man needed to sustain him in the field.

It was during this three-weeks enforced halt, while a road for the wagons was being made, that news reached the emperor that British troops had landed at Annesley Bay. Soon afterwards he saw a copy of a proclamation which General Napier had had sent out by Merewether from Massawa in October. It was addressed to 'the Governors, the Chiefs, the Religious Orders and the People of Abyssinia', and it declared that 'the sole object for which the British force has been sent to Abyssinia is the liberation of Her Majesty's servants and others unjustly detained as captives, and as soon as that object is effected it will be withdrawn'. It promised reward to those who helped the captives or assisted in their liberation, and severe punishment to those who harmed them. Some said that Theodorus went pale when he read the proclamation, but those who were actually with him at the time said that his only response was 'an inscrutable smile'. His reaction to the news of the landing of the troops was more practical. He sent for the Europeans and told them, 'Do not be afraid if I send for you in the night. We must be on the watch as I hear that some donkeys are come to steal my slaves.' He was as good as his word. That same night he called them and made them all sleep in a single tent next to his own, and there they remained, except when they were marching or working, for the rest of the journey.

By the end of the year, after further slow but steady progress across the plateau of Zebrite, Theodorus and his army had reached Beit Hor. Here again he was faced with a formidable obstacle—an immense gorge 3000 feet deep and 7 miles across, which the river Jidda[1] had carved through the hills on its twisting, turbulent way to the Nile. Here the emperor had to stay for another three weeks cajoling and driving the now ill and dispirited Waldmeier to mark out and make a track down the precipitous slope on one side and up the equally precipitous slope on the other. It was here at Beit Hor that Theodorus was still encamped while Rassam and the other captives at Magdala were celebrating that second Christmas of captivity, and while down on the coast General Napier was preparing to land and take command of the expeditionary force and begin his march to Magdala. Napier had a distance of about 400 miles to cover while Theodorus at Beit Hor was no more than 50 miles from his objective. It had already taken him three months to cover the first 40 miles from Debra Tabor, but with his encumbrances, and more precipitous river gorges to be crossed, he knew that it would take him another three months. And, as before, it was not only natural hazards that he had to face. He had been harassed by rebel forces and marauders all the way from Debra Tabor, but now that he was approaching Magdala he had more serious enemies to contend with. There was the powerful Wagshum Gobazey of Lasta to the north, the formidable Wallo Galla pressing from the east, and Menelik of Shoa coming up from the south. The captives waiting anxiously at Magdala were not the only ones to be wondering which of the approaching forces would get there first.

[1] Also spelt Chetta, Tshitta and Jiddah.

CHAPTER XI

The first hundred miles

General Napier had travelled in style from Bombay in H.M.S. *Octavia*, a naval frigate powered by steam, and he landed at Zula in similar state to take up his command in person on 7 January 1868. He had in fact been on board ship in Annesley Bay for several days with a temporary but inconvenient illness, but as the representatives of the Press had moved up into the hills to get away from the heat and the dust,Napier's indisposition escaped public notice. The situation on shore had been carefully groomed and whitewashed in readiness for the commander-in-chief's inspection, and, with the help perhaps of rose-coloured monocles and the shimmering heat, the staff officers and others who accompanied Napier were able to describe and depict a well-ordered scene of white canvas tents glistening in the midday sun while the troops went about their business in scarlet coats, and the white ensign floated serenely from a flagstaff above. Their picture showed boats and barges busy discharging their cargoes on to the new stone jetties, whence scores of workmen carried them to the precisely ordered depots and stores which had been established on shore; condensers at work pumping salt water from the sea, and delivering it as fresh water along tubes supported on trestles to the cisterns and neat lines of troughs where hundreds of animals from elephants to black-headed sheep patiently waited their turn to drink;[1] bands playing while the men worked, and others bathed, decently clad, in the lukewarm sea.

Henry Morton Stanley, born Rowlands and brought up in a workhouse in Wales, painted a somewhat different picture when he arrived soon afterwards as the correspondent for the *New York Herald*.[2]

> Thousands of half-naked coolies were shouting and chanting a barbaric song while they worked under as hot a sun as ever blazed in the tropics, and

[1] The distilled water, with coal at £6 a ton delivered at Zula, was alone costing the British taxpayer £4000 a day.

[2] It was three years before Stanley was sent to find Dr. Livingstone but it was already 'Mr. So-and-so, I presume?' each time he encountered his journalistic quarry in Abyssinia.

hundreds of uniformed superintendants, armed with long *courbaches*[1] were co-ercing the labourers under their charge to work. The braying of hundreds of donkeys, the neighing of horses, the whinneying of mules, and the lowing of thirsty kine, the shrill shriek of two anomalous locomotives, the noisy roll of rickety cars as they thundered to and fro, caused the scene to appear at first impression as if a whole nation had immigrated here, and were about to plant a great city on the fervid beach of Annesley Bay. The mountainous piles of stores covered with tarpaulins, the long warehouses with their roofs of brushwood, filled to the utmost with the *matériel* of war, the noble bay crowded with majestic transports, steamers, men-of-war, great sailing packets, tiny tug-boats, elegant little yachts and innumerable Turkish *kanjeahs* from Mocha, Jedda, Souakim and Massowah, flitting about with their swallow-tail sails, only served to heighten the illusion.

Napier was not a man to be impressed either by military whitewash or by a journalist's prose. He gave praise where he thought particular praise was due; for what had been achieved, for example, in getting the advance brigade into a good starting position at Senafay, but, as he tersely pointed out to the commissariat, it was not much use having advance forces in a good position if they had not got enough supplies of food and ammunition to advance. He politely but firmly reminded the authorities in London and Bombay of his repeated insistencies that six months supplies for the whole expeditionary force of 20,000 men and its animals should be landed at Zula by the time he arrived, and that he could not push on with an effective fighting force towards Magdala, as he was being repeatedly urged to do by armchair tacticians, until a similar amount of supplies for an advance force of 9500 men had been moved forward to the base at Senafay. A laconic statement in the margin of his official despatch was included to show how far his requirements had and had not been met:

At Senafe bread and flour for 1000 men for 36 days, with other rations in still smaller quantities.
In Koomayloo Pass, rations for 1000 men for six and a half days.
In Zoulla, and on board ships in the harbour, rations for 2000 Europeans for three months, and for 5000 Natives for six months.

[1] Usually spelt *kourbash*, from the Arabic word for the hippopotamus-hide whip then in common use in the Middle East and Africa as a means of increasing productivity. Labourers in these parts seem to have generally accepted its use as an occupational hazard, but among the civilians employed by the Abyssinian Expeditionary Force were a Frenchman and an Italian who objected, and submitted formal complaints through their governments afterwards when they got home.

It was not Napier's only complaint. Within a few days of his arrival he had sent to London for a further 15,000 pairs of ammunition, boots, 15,000 blankets, 15,000 pairs of woollen socks, 500,000 lbs of biscuits, 100,000 lbs of salt meat, and 30,000 gallons of rum. The case for each additional item was carefully argued: the socks from Britain were needed, for example, because the 'stockings procurable from Bombay were quite useless, having a seam which was certain to cause footsores.' Everything was to be sent overland through France for speed, and packed for transport by mule in loads not exceeding 80 lbs. Napier realized, as indeed he seems to have realized from the start, that the key to the success of the expedition lay in the matter of transport. In a 17-page handwritten letter to the Duke of Cambridge soon after he was appointed to command the expedition in August 1867, he had pointed out 'how necessary it is that we should not throw our troops beyond the means of feeding them. Our first point then and great difficulty is procuring carriage.' His own scheme for a special Land Transport Corps had been rejected as too expensive by the civilian Governor of Bombay (whose careful watch on public expenditure, as befitted a former member of the House of Commons, was frequently praised by Disraeli) in favour of what Napier described as 'a cheap irregular system which would never bear scrutiny'. This cheap irregular system turned out to be a disaster in terms both of expense and delay, and of animal suffering and wastage. The *Times* correspondent reported in January that baggage animals and horses were dying at the rate of two hundred a week, but found it difficult to say how much this was due to glanders, how much to lack of food and water, and how much to a transport corps which was in what he described as a state of utter confusion and disorganization. In the end his conclusion was that the radical cause was 'our English system of cheese-paring in military finance, and keeping an army in time of peace upon a footing costly enough to swell the budget but just short of the efficiency requisite to secure success in the commencement of a campaign'.

By the end of January, General Napier was able to report that transport arrangements had much improved. The improvements had been achieved in a variety of ways, mainly as a result of the findings of observers whom Napier had stationed at every staging-post on the route from Kumayli to Senafay. It was noted, for example, that many of the muleteers recruited in the Middle East were in the habit of riding one of the mules in their charge, instead of leading the mules on foot, which meant, to quote one report, 'that one thousand (1000) out of every three thousand (3000) were mere riding mules for these worthless men'. They were quickly replaced by less sybaritic muleteers from rural India. It was not only the muleteers who were replaced. Mules which were used to the 'long marches from Rawal Pindee in India to Kurachee in the Persian Gulf' were shipped to take the place of what were left of the tender-footed and temperamental Mediterranean mules, and arrangements were also made with a German firm to deliver 1000 mules at £5 a head, together with 200 German or Austrian drivers. As the road to Senafay was improved by the sappers, ox-carts, which could carry twice the load, were increasingly used instead of pack animals. Pressure on animal transport was further eased by reducing the amount of baggage, tents, and camp-followers which troops used to service in the physical and mental climate of India had come to regard as essential for their support and efficiency. It was not the first time, nor was it to be by any means the last, that Napier insisted on such reduction. The reports of newspaper correspondents, and the private letters and journals of military officers show that these reductions met with considerable opposition and complaint. But when it came to be written, the official history of the expedition was to gloss over the grumbling and say that

> things which in many campaigns would have been regarded as necessary were ungrudgingly thrown aside, and in the common cause every sacrifice was cheerfully made. By this reduction the necessary carriage (already considerably reduced in India) for an European regiment was decreased from 478 mules to 270; that for a Native regiment from 270 to 230.

The *Times* correspondent, who liked to work out his own statistics, calculated that a mule, with a carrying capacity of 150 lbs, ate 13 lbs of hay a day, which meant that, in the absence of forage on the 60-mile journey from the coast to Senafay, it could carry little more than its own food. The situation improved as local supplies of forage started to come in from the villagers, but Napier was still to complain in one of his despatches that mules were even more troublesome to feed than British troops.

Help with transport came from another quarter when the first batch of elephants arrived, and were spectacularly but safely hoisted ashore by the ship's derricks. The elephants were intended, and indeed destined, to carry heavy field guns and mortars across country, but to help with the general transport position they were first used to carry stores and supplies up the rugged pass to Senafay. Even these lighter duties presented problems as, to quote from an official report, 'the skin of an elephant is so tender that it easily becomes chafed, and serious galls and sores ensue from friction as well as from the pressure of the heavy weights.'

Another form of transport which engaged Napier's especial attention was the coastal railway. It was not the first time that a railway had been built for a military campaign in the field—7 miles of tram-line had been laid down in the Crimea—but it was the first time that steam locomotives were used. Like most innovations it evoked considerable criticism. G. A. Henty was particularly scathing about this railway from Zula to Kumayli which he described as 'without exception the most shaky and most dangerous piece of railway laid down'. Although it was beset with difficulties of supply and construction from the start, and was still three-quarters of a mile short of its planned ten and a half miles when the war ended, it carried a total of 24,000 men and 13,000 tons of goods across a particularly unpleasant stretch of coastal desert without a single accident, and its locomotives impressed and frightened the local inhabitants even more than the expedition's guns and the elephants. In all 8,000 rails, 35,000 sleepers, 100 wheelbarrows, 600 picks, 400 shovels, 4 station clocks, and 12 guard's watches were shipped out to Annesley Bay for the railway together with six locomotives (mostly second-hand for the sake of economy) and sixty trucks. The railway station at Zula had the distinction of being built entirely of old biscuit tins.

General Napier spent nearly three weeks in the heat and bustle of Zula dealing with matters of transport and supplies. His long stay at the coastal base, and the ungeneral-like attention he paid to logistics,evoked considerable criticism both at home and abroad. 'You must be wondering', even the patient *Times* correspondent wrote, 'what on earth we are all about, and how much longer the British public, which pays so dearly for the Abyssinian performance, is to wait until the curtain rises upon the second act.' In a more specific form the criticism took the shape of a demand for the despatch without more ado of a small body of fast-moving cavalry either to rescue the captives before the emperor reached Magdala, or to attack him from the flank as he approached. The captives themselves were strong proponents of this idea, and, led by the eloquent and persistent Dr. Blanc, supported and stirred it up with assurances that such a force of British cavalry would get help from the emperor's domestic enemies inside Abyssinia, and 'would be bound to meet with certain and easy success'. Blanc and his companions added the moving plea that if such action put their own lives at risk, that was better than a continuation of the indignities and uncertainties of their present condition. One can understand their wish to be rescued before Theodorus reached Magdala. Apart from his unpredictable moods and actions, there was the likelihood that, as soon as he had the Magdala captives under his hand again, he might try to use them as bargaining counters with the British, and if that failed, carry them off with him to an even more inaccessible part of Abyssinia like his native Kwara. The idea of 'a dash' or a 'flying column' had strong support too from armchair tacticians in parliament and the Press, and from former military men who in letters to *The Times* drew at length on their own experiences in other distant places. In the end even Napier's devoted supporter, the Duke of Cambridge, concerned and much criticized as commander-in-chief over the slow progress of the expedition and the mounting cost, and disturbed by reports that the emperor was steadily drawing closer to Magdala, told Napier in a personal letter that 'what is desired here is that a flying column or a succession of flying columns should be pushed forward and operate to the front so as to make a dash if possible and finish the business before the rains set in'.

Napier was not moved either by the arguments or the pressures. Nor did he give his critics the satisfaction of going on the defensive. He merely propounded the counter-argument that the news that Theodorus had left Debra Tabor early in October for Magdala did not reach him until 4 January. By then he calculated that the emperor would be within four or five hours ride of the fortress, and that if Napier had sent a flying column, therefore, to catch him on the march or to cut him off from the captives, Theodorus would hear of it in good time and would be able to push on without his guns and heavy baggage and be safely in the fortress long before anyone could reach him. Whatever the merits of these arguments and counter-arguments, the fact remained that, as Napier put it in one of his despatches to the India Office, 'other reasons made an attempt to surprise him on the march impossible'. The 'other reasons' were that experience had already shown that it would be foolish to rely on local resources and supplies in Abyssinia, and that not nearly enough reserves of imported stores had yet been built up at the advance base at Senafay to enable even a single raiding party to set out properly equipped for a return journey of over 700 miles across largely unknown country. Having made this practical point, Napier went over to the offensive in this secondary war of words, and politely but firmly made it clear that if there was to be any witch-hunting at this stage about slow progress, or his failure to send out a flying column, the blame would lie on the civil and military authorities in London and in India; that it was their dilatoriness, indecision, and parsimony which had delayed the accumulation of stores, and the establishment of a proper land transport corps which he had repeatedly asked for. His reply to the Duke of Cambridge's letter was less uncompromising, but the conclusion was equally clear. 'If' he wrote on 14 February, 'we could have sent out a light column to arrest him en route it would no doubt have been an admirable idea but under our circumstances it was simply impossible. The small force at Senafay was living from hand to mouth, and had they advanced for 10 days they would have been brought up for want of food. . . .' Napier must have realized that the Duke was being subjected to pressures and persuasions from many quarters, and that he was being torn between his obligations to them and his trust in Napier. It was this perhaps which led Napier to add a postscript: 'Your Royal Highness may be assured that nothing will be left undone, on my part, to bring the campaign to an early conclusion.'

The last word came in the end from the Duke himself. Conceding the vital importance of building up supplies and establishing good communications with one's base, he congratulated Napier with a nicely balanced blend of the old cavalry spirit which had proved so costly in the Crimea, and the new logistical approach which had contributed so signally to Moltke's recent victory in the Austro-Prussian war. 'You have resisted the dangerous temptation of neglecting these essentials for the more agreeable prospect of coming face to face with the enemy. This is a great and truly noble act of negation.'

On 25 January Napier left Kumayli for the expedition's advanced base at Senafay. The distance was 63 miles, and Napier, who had the reputation of being a hard rider, was expected to reach his destination in two or three days. When this did not happen the *Times* correspondent reported from Senafay that 'his not having arrived sooner can only be accounted for on the supposition that he is minutely inspecting every hole and corner in every depot along the pass'. The supposition was correct. Napier was a thorough man, and he liked to see things for himself. He was impressed with the work that had been done in the Suru pass to improve the almost impassable track and make it 'as good as any turnpike road in England'. But 'one or two luckless fellows got well wigged for neglect of sanitary precautions—one of the chief's pet hobbies'. It was 29 January before Napier had finished his close inspection of the pass and the staging-posts, and rode into Senafay with his very tired staff. One of these staff officers likened their arrival in the clean, fresh air and the wide plains of Senafay, after five days in the close claustrophobic atmosphere of the Suru pass, to Jonah's welcome to the open sea after the days and nights spent in the belly of a whale.

It was a busy time for everyone. A week before Napier left the coast the advanced brigade at Senafay had been ordered to send out a detachment to ensure that there was a passable road for the guns and the baggage to the next staging-post at Guna Guna, and to stand ready themselves for a general advance. Napier sent them forward two days after he arrived at Senafay, and, as they left, fresh troops were brought up from Kumayli to take their place. Their place at the coastal base was in turn quickly filled by new troops which Napier had already called forward from Bombay. It had at one time been proposed to use Aden as a place for holding reserves, but in the end it was decided that it was too hot and too lacking in fresh water to serve as a transit camp. In case of need two regiments of British troops were standing by at the ready in Malta. Napier did not believe in leaving anything to chance, or to Whitehall.

Once the expeditionary force had been thus engaged in gear, and had begun to move forward in carefully measured and carefully regulated order, General Napier started to apply himself more directly to some of the political problems which were in Colonel Merewether's province as his chief political adviser. As long as most of the British forces remained at the coastal base, such problems were few and mainly straightforward. Whatever the exact status of that area might be *de jure*, *de facto* it was under the control of the Egyptian governor and garrison at Massawa. As has already been explained, the acquiescence of the Turkish and Egyptian governments in the British expedition had already been obtained by diplomatic pressures in Constantinople and Cairo, and when the Governor of Massawa proved uncooperative Napier was able to have him simply removed and replaced by someone more agreeable. The indigenous inhabitants of this coastal area presented different problems. The Shoho, as they were known, were Hamitic people of itinerant habits and attractive appearance. At first they showed little inclination to help the British forces. The men were more interested in picking off stragglers or deserting mule-drivers as sources of genital items which they could display as trophies to impress their womenfolk, while the women themselves concentrated on the lengths of copper wire attached to telegraph poles, which they coveted as ornaments to attract the men. Eventually both sexes were persuaded to give up these pursuits for the more solid rewards of commerce and labour, a process which was facilitated by gifts to their headmen of what the scholarly Dr. Austin of *The Times* described as 'gorgeous red gowns something in the style of the Oxford D.C.L. gown'.

The situation at Senafay itself was different. Senafay, with most of the northern and eastern parts of Ethiopia as far south as the river Taccaze, were at that time the domain of Ras Kassai, the ruler of Tigrai.[1] The expedition's line of march to Magdala lay through his territory for a distance of about 150 miles. It was also the line along which the expedition would eventually have to return, even perhaps to retreat. It was essential therefore for Napier to secure and keep the power to pass through this territory. If need be, he would have to take and hold it by force, but he knew that it would much ease his situation if he could get what he needed by agreement, and better still if that agreement could be extended to the willing provision of local supplies of food and forage, and for the sale and hire of transport animals, and of cattle and sheep for meat.

Ras Kassai of Tigrai was at that time a man of about 30 years of age. He had only recently reached his present position. The way he had done so was not unlike that in which the brigand Kasa had become Theodorus, the Slave of Christ and the King of all the Kings of Ethiopia. He was related on his mother's side to Sabagardis, who, as ruler of Tigrai forty years before, had been one of the first in Abyssinia to welcome foreign travellers and traders, and to establish relations with European powers. Sabagardis was killed in battle in 1831, and eventually succeeded by Ras Ubye of Semien, who ruled over both areas until he in turn was defeated and deposed in 1855 by Kasa, the future emperor Theodorus. Theodorus found Tigrai especially difficult to master and absorb into his dominions. Its people spoke a different language and thought of themselves as different from the rest of Ethiopia, and were prepared to use force to assert their independence. Theodorus' hold on Tigrai remained tenuous, and in 1865 the Wagshum Gobazey of neighbouring Lasta took advantage of the situation to establish his own

[1] Also spelt Tigré, Tegre, Tigrah, and Tigre, as now, without any accent.

claim to Tigrai. Two years later it was wrested from him by Kassai, who at that time was one of his own lieutenants and who could and did claim a legitimate right to the province through his mother. By the time the British landed at Annesley Bay, Kassai had established his authority over the whole of Tigrai, and had not only asserted his independence of both Gobazey and of Theodorus but had gone as far as to lay a claim himself to the imperial title.

Ras Kassai was thus a person of great importance and power as far as the British expeditionary force was concerned. For this reason Colonel Merewether and Munzinger had made a special point of cultivating his friendship, and allaying his anxieties. They needed his permission in any case to prospect for routes, camp-sites, staging-posts, and local supplies of food and forage, and for messengers to pass through his lands in order to keep contact with the captives at Magdala. They had sought his goodwill by general assurances of friendship backed by more tangible proofs of amity, but when the main body of the British forces began to disembark at Zula, Ras Kassai thought it was time to find out more precisely what their intentions were, and whether they had the military strength to achieve them. Kassai had built up an extensive civil and military establishment at his headquarters at Adowa, including a Greek silversmith and a French armourer, and he sent two of his most trusted men to Napier's camp at Zula. One, described by Napier as 'the anglicized Abyssinian gentleman Mr. Woorkee' was a native of Tigrai named Murcha Werka, who had been educated at the Revd. Charles Wilson's Free Church of Scotland Mission school in Bombay, where he had learnt to speak good English and to understand something of European ways. The other was a cousin of Kassai, whose official title of *likamankuas* was quickly transposed by the British troops into liquor-my-goose. Realizing from his experience in India and China that the degree of Kassai's co-operation and help was likely to depend to a large extent on his estimate of Napier's military capabilities, General Napier went to some lengths to impress him. He succeeded beyond his intentions. Although Murcha Werka was too sophisticated to be unduly impressed with the locomotives and the elephants, and the conversion of sea-water into fresh which had so impressed other Abyssianian visitors, he was very impressed with the artillery and the discipline of the soldiers, and he found it difficult to reconcile Napier's large resources and huge preparations with his declared intention of coming merely to release the captives. As for Napier himself, it was one thing to impress Kassai's envoys, but what he really needed was to meet Ras Kassai face to face and let him see for himself the overwhelming military strength which was at Napier's disposal.

The next step therefore was to arrange a meeting. With this in mind, Napier sent one of his intelligence officers to Kassai's headquarters at Adowa. The man he chose was Major James Grant. Grant had never been to Abyssinia before, and spoke no Amharic; his qualifications for the assignment rested on his reputation as an explorer in other parts of Africa, where he had journeyed with Speke in search of the source of the Nile. Grant was a strong, reliable man, rated earlier by Speke as the perfect companion, and by General Gordon of Khartoum later as an insufferable bore. He was accompanied by Munzinger, who had the wit and the local knowledge that Grant lacked. They set off together on 21 January.

Grant's instructions were to arrange a meeting as soon as possible between Kassai and Napier.[1] On the first day he and Munzinger failed to see Kassai at all, despite the good offices of another Anglicized Abyssinian, named Gabro Werka, who was a brother and fellow-student in Bombay of Murcha Werka. On the second day, Grant had to report that 'we repeatedly made the attempt to get him to talk upon business but his reply was 'after the durbar he would be at leisure', or 'tomorrow he would find plenty of time'. To make a good impression Grant and Munzinger went to the Coptic church, as their failure to do so every day had led to enquiries whether they were Turks or Christians. Although the unsophisticated Grant had thought from their reception that they had at least made a good impression on the local ladies, the cynical Munzinger assured him that 'they cheer in this way only for those from whom they anticipate some good'.

On the third day the most that they could extract from Ras Kassai was a suggestion that the meeting with Napier should take place in a month's time and that meanwhile they should stay at Adowa as his guests. When pressed to commit himself to an earlier date the *ras* blandly declared that 'they had been drinking and that he would be able to give us a reply in the morning'. The following day, after an elaborate exchange of presents, which included a musical box for Kassai and 'a mule, a silk shirt, a sheet and a *lamd*, or skin collar' for

[1] Kassai was the form eventually adopted by Napier and most other persons connected with the expedition but earlier despatches and reports used Kassa and Kussa.

themselves, Kassai agreed to meet Napier in a fortnight, and meanwhile to allow the British forces to establish staging-posts on their route through his dominions.

There was method in Kassai's tardiness, and purpose in his procrastination. On the one hand he was impressed, from what his envoys and spies had told him, with the military strength and inventiveness of the British, and realized that it was possible, despite the difficult terrain and Theodorus' still formidable reputation, that Napier might succeed in his objective. The difficulty was that Napier kept insisting that this objective was simply to release the captives, and that the internal affairs of Abyssinia were no concern of his now or in the future. Kassai thus feared that if and when the captives were released, Theodorus might, as a result of negotiation or by a successful display of force, still be left with his political and military power unbroken. If Kassai helped the British forces he might therefore find himself branded by Theodorus and by others in Abyssinia not only as a private enemy but even perhaps as a national traitor. Another reason for procrastination was that he wanted to delay the advance of the British forces in the hope that this would give Theodorus the time and the freedom of action to attack and destroy the Wagshum Gobazey of Lasta, who was Kassai's immediate rival for control of Tigrai and its environs, and ultimately for succession to the imperial crown should Theodorus be defeated and deposed by the British. One way and another, Ras Kassai had good reasons both for sitting on the fence, and for trying meanwhile to play both ends against the middle.

Looking further ahead, Napier also began to solicit the help and goodwill of other rulers through whose territories he knew he would eventually have to pass. One was Kassai's arch-enemy and former master, the Wagshum Gobazey of Lasta.[1] To the south and east of the boundary of Kassai's own dominions near the town of Antalo lay the large amorphous areas which were peopled or controlled by the Galla. In its final stages the British expedition would also have to pass through the provinces of Delanta and Dahont, whose rulers owed a fluctuating allegiance to whichever of their neighbours was best able to protect them. General Napier not only wanted the co-operation of all these rulers in affording him passage and providing him with supplies, but he

[1] Wagshum, also spelt Wag-shum and Wakshum and meaning the Governor of the province of Wag, was the title usually given to Gobazey of Lasta, whose own name also appears as Gobazē, Gobazé, Gobazye, and Gobazyé.

also wished to encourage them to attack Theodorus and halt or delay his advance.

With Grant and Munzinger busy negotiating with the elusive Kassai at Adowa, and Colonel Merewether's usefulness in the interior limited by his ignorance of Amharic, Napier turned to a new arrival, Captain Charles Speedy, to help him in local political matters. The man originally sent out from London to undertake this task was the C.M.S. missionary, Dr. Krapf, whose connection with Abyssinia went back to 1837, but he had been forced by ill-health to resign and go back to England. Speedy was a different sort of man from the earnest and scholarly Dr. Krapf, but he too had had previous experience of Abyssinia and the emperor Theodorus. After early service as a soldier in India, he had gone to Abyssinia to shoot elephant, and had stayed there for several years in the emperor's entourage. He had later served for a short time as Cameron's vice-consul at Massawa.[1] He was a huge man of great strength; six foot six inches in height and with a large red beard, he had made a great impression on the emperor by his ability to split a sheep in two from tip to tail with one blow of his sword. He spoke fluent Amharic, derived, it was said, from intimate association with the people of the country. While he was with Napier's expedition, he always wore Abyssinian costume and carried a spear. The effect was a little spoilt by his short sight which obliged him to wear spectacles, but he was generally regarded by his fellow officers as 'a connecting link, in the fullest Darwinian sense of that word,' as one of them unkindly put it, 'between the Ethiopian and the Frank'.

It was Speedy who translated General Napier's letters to the Abyssinian rulers into Amharic when Munzinger was away, and who rendered the biblical language of their replies into the sort of pidgin English which was commonly used in the Victorian era to represent the communications of almost anyone who was not English by birth. Thus, one of the first letters received from Gobazey was translated,

> I am obstructing mine and your enemy that he cannot go to the *amba* [the flat-topped mountain fortress of Magdala] and destroy the prisoners. But do come now in great hurry, and if he [Kassai] tells you Tigre 'belong to me from my father', you must not take it for the truth.

Gobazey had in fact made no move to attack or obstruct Theodorus, and Napier was disappointed to find that, for all his boasting, and pro-

[1] See p. 45.

testations of friendship and alliance, Gobazey was much more interested in preserving his force of 30,000 troops to do battle with Kassai in the future than in risking them at that moment against the still formidable emperor. In the same way Napier was disillusioned by the cynical Speedy about the attitude of the chiefs and priests of the villages and communities they met with on the road. Napier only wanted unimpeded passage for his troops, and supplies for his commissariat, but Speedy knew Abyssinia well enough to realize that their bland assurances of friendship concealed a sharp eye for any sign of weakness which they could exploit, and an equally pointed intention that any help they gave Napier would be used as a bargaining counter to persuade him to attack their private enemies or right some ancient wrong.

While these civilian obfuscations were being attended to as a tiresome but necessary part of his duties as overall commander-in-chief of the British expedition, Napier as a general pushed his forces slowly but surely on towards his goal. By the end of January detachments had been established at intermediate points along the road as far as Adigrat, 37 miles south of Senafay. The going was easy for the most part, and presented few problems to the Indian sappers and miners who had been sent ahead to make the old caravan track fit for the heavily laden baggage animals and the carts. For much of the way it followed an ancient route along the crest of a watershed, with streams flowing westwards to join the Nile, while the rivulets on the other side trickled down the cool green slopes to lose themselves in the parched plains of the Rift Valley below. It was beautiful country, and Dr. Austin described it for his readers in terms which must have surprised those who had been led to believe from earlier letters to *The Times* that Abyssinia was a country of burning deserts and impenetrable jungle:

> At Goona-Goona or Goom-Gooma or Gunna-Kuma, whatever may be the scientific name, a rivulet, fringed with willows, runs through the valley, watering grassy slopes covered with cattle, and fields alternately green with barley and golden with corn, the softness and varied beauty of the scene being enhanced by its contrast with the bold masses of mountain and naked rock which shut it in.

The mountains and rocks had a dramatic and fantastic variety of shapes both round and square, some *ambas* with flat tops and precipitous sides, others sloping up to a point or pinnacle like a pyramid or ecclesiastical dome. Some of the rock masses ascended in tree-covered terraces until they were lost in the mist and the clouds, while others went up sheer in one dark mass of naked rock so that they stood like medieval castles keeping guard over the plain below. Soldiers' journals and diaries spoke of streams of water with roses and violets and cowslips along the banks, and of flowering shrubs, laburnum, lilac, oleander, and jasmine, sheltering vividly coloured starlings and scarlet humming-birds.

Dr. Austin found the country people equally agreeable—the men, tall and graceful, 'did the honours of their filthy mud hovels with courteous, almost dignified ease', while the women were 'very small, with delicate, and considerations of cleanliness apart, pleasing faces and figures'. Napier's orders for the behaviour of the troops on the march were very strict, and it was recorded in the official history that 'no plundering took place; and no swarthy damsel was subjected to any rude gallantry on the part of the red coats'.[1] Any supplies or services which were offered were paid for in silver thalers; the villagers took the money and inspected it with careful expertise to see if it was counterfeit. They were not used to armies paying for what they wanted, and they tended at first to regard these monetary transactions with suspicion. It was not long, however, before they learnt that, in the absence of smaller coins, they could charge the British, if not the Indian soldiers, a thaler, which was worth about four shillings, for every transaction however slight or small. The Press correspondents in particular soon began to complain that, because of this, living off the country was expensive.

The town of Adigrat was strategically placed at the junction of the road south to Antalo, Lasta, and Magdala, and the route that went westward to the ancient Ethiopian capitals of Adowa, Axum, and Gondar. It was also the centre of a fertile plain, and its occasional periods of wealth and importance were reflected in the use of stone in some of the buildings and larger houses. Many of these, however, were in ruins, and the generally dusty and dishevelled look of the town and its inhabitants came as a disappointmaet to those brought up on Samual Johnson's *Rasselas*. 'After reading of churches, princes, hierarchies and feudal aristocracies, it is staggering to be told that some little cowhouse under a cliff is a church, and that the very dirty person-

[1] The medical chapters of the official history of the expedition listed 'intermittent fevers' and 'bowel complaints' as the main causes of sickness; there was no mention of venereal diseases. Less publicized medical reports admitted that these were prevalent in Abyssinia, and attributed their small incidence among the troops to the siting of camps far from the villages.

age in a white turban who runs alongside your horse, clamouring for a dollar, is a high priest with full powers of absolution and excommunication.' It was equally difficult, poor Dr. Austin found, to accept that the single church, ruined palace, and mud-huts of Adigrat constituted one of Abysinnia's most important towns. Adigrat had been the capital of Sabagardis, the ruler of Tigrai mentioned on page 134. His son Sebat was captured and taken as a hostage by Wagshum Gobazey in 1866, leaving his widow and small son to mourn and wait for his return behind the walls of his crumbling palace. Clement Markham met Sebat's son at Adigrat: '. . . a little fellow about twelve years old, with a crimson fillet round his brow and lots of butter on his head, came out to walk with us, with a short double-barrelled gun slung on his back with one hammer off, and a broken stock spliced with cow-hide. He declared that when he grew up he would release his father. . . .'

Napier reached Adigrat on 6 February, and stayed there twelve days. He was now 100 miles from his coastal base at Zula. He had taken a long time to reach that point, and he still had 300 miles to go, but he was determined, with an undemonstrative but resolute determination, not to be persuaded into pushing his fighting troops forward until the route ahead had been carefully surveyed and prepared, and until he was sure that he had the means to keep them properly supplied. As his lines of communication grew longer, Napier had to use more and more troops to guard both the convoys of supplies coming up from the coast and the staging-posts along the way, and to ensure at the same time that his new advanced base at Adigrat was protected against any possible attack either from known enemies or from those who professed to be friends. Although he had several assurances of friendship and co-operation from Ras Kassai, Napier was too experienced in these sort of operations to take anything for granted, at least until his promised meeting with Kassai had actually taken place.

General Napier may have been painstaking and even cautious, but he was well aware that he could not afford to waste any time. First and foremost in his mind was the need to complete his mission and get his troops out of the country before the rains set in in June or July, and the heat of the Red Sea summer made the climate on the coast almost unbearable for Europeans. He was also engaged in a race for tactical and psychological advantage with the emperor Theodorus. If he could reach Magdala before Theodorus got there with his guns and heavy baggage, he might not only avoid a difficult and protracted siege but he might also be able to prevent the emperor from doing what he feared most, which was to decamp with his captives to a more distant and inaccessible part of his dominions. For all his thoroughness, therefore, Napier wasted no time and no opportunity to move forward.

Thus by the time Napier left Adigrat on 18 February he already had a substantial detachment of fighting troops and pioneers established at Antalo, eight marches or approximately eighty miles on. As usual, Colonel Phayre was already beyond that point surveying the country and chosing the best route. Communications between Adigrat and Antalo were being maintained by what were described in Napier's official despatch as '180 sabres of the Scinde Horse', who were distributed in small detachments along the road at convenient points. Napier's report from Adigrat went on to say that

> the telegraph is complete and open between Zoulla and Senafé, but I regret to say that it is not yet free from frequent interruptions. The road to Senafé has been for some time practicable for wheeled carriages, and today the road from Senafé to this place has also been made practicable, though with difficulty, for artillery. The road to the front between this place and Antalo is in some portions very bad but many working parties are employed upon it, and in a few days it also will be practicable for the passage of artillery.

By this time Napier had 12,650 animals[1] in his transport corps and 373 carts. It was still far from enough. Of the 12,000 combatant troops in Abyssinia, about 7000 were by this time in the highlands between Antalo and Senafay. In addition there were approximately 14,000 men officially described as 'public followers', the majority of whom were muleteers and drivers in the transport corps. Napier noted:

> At present, in round numbers, the troops and followers in the highlands may be said to consume 10,000 rations or 270 mule loads daily, and to be supplied for a fortnight; while the number of rations delivered daily at Senafé may be estimated at 20,000, so that at Senafé a daily surplus of 10,000 rations is collected. At this rate, it would require six months to collect six months provisions for the few troops at present on the highland but the long expected animals from Bombay and some camels from Berbera will considerably increase the supply.

[1] This did not include the 44 elephants, which were now engaged on their proper task of carrying the guns and mortars, which had been especially constructed to break down into elephant-loads of between 1324 and 1884 lbs.

He ended his report on a happier note.

The health and spirits of the troops continue excellent, notwithstanding the severe toll of working parties, and heavy marching to which they have been subjected. The climate is cool and agreeable. In the daytime, the thermometer averages from 70° to 80° Fahrenheit in the shade; at night it often sinks to freezing point, and sometimes even lower.

CHAPTER XII

The forces converge

While the British expeditionary force of 12,000 troops, 15,000 followers, and 12,000 transport animals was impelling its moving parts forward with slowly increasing tempo over the first hundred miles of its 400-mile journey, the emperor Theodorus was engaged in moving his own assemblage of guns, troops, and followers towards the fortress of Magdala. Although the fortress was only fifty miles away, progress was often so slow and so hard-won that it had to be measured in yards, and sometimes, it seemed, almost inch by inch.

Estimates by eye-witnesses of the number of his fighting men varied between 3000 and 8000. They were accompanied, like the British force, by an even larger band of camp-followers which, unlike Napier's, included almost as many women as men. The women were a recognized and integral part of an Abyssinian army.[1] In addition to their domestic duties, and the effective part they played in rewarding male bravery and discouraging cowardice, some of the rougher and tougher females were organized by Theodorus into special marauding bands which did not hesitate, if the need arose, to kill as well as plunder. But Theodorus was not only moving a traditional Abyssinian army. He was an itinerant who hated towns and liked camp life, and he was in effect moving his court and his capital too. This meant that he was burdened with large amounts of heavy baggage and equipment as well as his guns and mortars. Where Napier had elephants to carry his heavy artillery, and light guns that had been especially constructed to break down into portable loads, all Theodorus' guns and mortars were transported on carts made of wood which had to be manhandled up and down every slope; the largest mortar, Sebastopol, of seven tons, sometimes needed as many as 800 men to hold it back on steep inclines, and to drag it up the sharpest slopes.

On the day General Napier landed at Zula, Theodorus and his army

[1] The women did not do the cooking but they made the bread and the beer. One Abyssinian comment on the British forces was that the most remarkable things about them were the elephants and the fact that they had come without any women.

Ras Kassai,
by William Simpson

A Galla queen and her son

Sebastopol: an idealized representation from Rassam's *Narrative*

'The Elephant Train'

were still encamped at Beit Hor on the Wadela plateau. They still had to cross what Waldmeier had described as a gorge seven miles wide and three thousand feet deep, the gorge carved by the river Jidda on its way to join the Blue Nile. They had arrived there on Christmas Day, but it was two weeks before the missionary artisans and the thousands of labourers put at their disposal had blasted and dug and made a passable track down the side of the gorge, and the army and the guns could begin their perilous descent. It was hard work for everyone. On January 8 Mrs. Flad told Rassam in a letter that 'His Majesty seems to be in a great hurry to get that road down the bank this side of the Djiddah. From the earliest dawn of the morning until the dark of the evening sets in, my husband is away, as well as the other Europeans, and especially of late it would seem as if the Lord had forsaken us and given us over to perish.' She had not even been able to send any food to her husband at work, 'as the King was all day near them himself, fasting and working like——'. It was not often that this good German missionary wife let herself go to the point of an unprintable word, and the following day Flad himself added a postscript excusing himself for not writing because '. . . now I have to go down to His Majesty to assist the Europeans in boring and firing the rocks which are in His Majesty's way'.

The Europeans may have been near to exhaustion and despair but Theodorus himself was in excellent spirits. He had just received the submission of the chiefs of Delanta and Dahont on the high plateau between the Jidda and the valley of the river Bashilo, which still lay between him and Magdala. It was to these rebellious chiefs that Napier had written from Adigrat in January encouraging them to bar the emperor's advance, and they had also been promised protection by Wagshum Gobazey if they would refuse to provide the emperor's forces with food. But when they saw the emperor's slow but very sure advance with his guns across the seemingly impassable gorge of the river Jidda, they changed their minds. Napier's forces were still a long way away, and Gobazey's loud promises of protection seemed to consist largely of words. Theodorus knew well how to interpose offers of amnesty and peace with threats of horrific punishment, and it was not long before the chiefs of these two important areas which lay in his line of march were asking for forgiveness for their wavering loyalties, and promising Theodorus unhindered passage and all the supplies and labour that he needed to feed his armies and make his roads. Encouraged by this success, and the consequent diminished reputation both of his domestic rivals and of the foreign invaders, Theodorus countered Napier's recent proclamation by issuing one of his own which called on the people of Ethiopia to rally to his side in order to resist the British forces and their infidel Turkish and Egyptian allies.

Another reason for the emperor's good spirits was that, with Delanta and Dahont open to him, he was now within reach of his destination. Although there were still some very formidable natural obstacles to overcome as far as his guns and heavy baggage were concerned, he was now no more than a good day's ride from Magdala. It was for this reason perhaps that, after a lapse of nearly a year, he started to exchange messages and letters with Rassam again. 'How are you, how are you, my son? Thank God, I am well. Do not be afraid; we shall yet be happy. Do not grieve, I shall not be able to come to you as soon as I wished as I have some little work on hand.' In another message he spoke with pride of his giant mortar Sebastopol. 'I have had a very large mortar cast which has detained me so long on the road but when I reach Magdala and see you admire it, I shall forget all the trouble it had given me. . . .' Rassam reciprocated by addressing his reply, 'Most Gracious Sovereign . . .', and ending, 'May the Lord give Your Majesty perfect health and happiness, and show me the light of your countenance.'

Rassam kept all the emperor's letters in their beautiful Amharic script and copies of his own replies in Arabic, and reading the translations which he appended to them it is sometimes hard to believe that they were communications between a captive envoy who had recently been in chains and a monarch whose country was being invaded by a British army. The relationship between the Abyssinian emperor and the Kurdish envoy was a strange mixture of intimacy and formality, and of amity and reproach, and it was perhaps largely the traditional conventions of both their Semitic mother-tongues which made the relationship between them seem to Anglo-Saxon eyes to be one that verged on affection: 'How are you, my friend? The nearer I come towards you the happier I feel as I know that the pleasure of meeting you is drawing near. . . .'

While Rassam was carrying on this exchange of civilities with Theodorus, he was at the same time in regular communication with the emperor's principal enemies, the Wagshum Gobazey, the Galla queens and chiefs, and Ras Menelik of Shoa, both encouraging them to attack, and offering them inducements to try and set him and the other captives free. This may have been good diplomatic practice, but in the circumstances it was very rash. To add to the risks, he was also corresponding with Merewether and the advancing British forces, giving them a mixture of facts and rumours about the strength of the emperor's forces and about his intentions. His fellow prisoners at Magdala, Blanc, Cameron, and Stern, were also corresponding not only with Merewether but with their friends and relations in England. Their letters to Merewether were mostly about money, but they took the opportunity to ventilate their grievances and to complain about the emperor in terms which if intercepted, would have vexed him. They also joined the chorus of those who urged that Napier should send a flying column to intercept the emperor before he could reach the fortress. 'Quick, quick!' Blanc implored, 'Cut him off!'

It was a formidable operation for Theodorus to get his army and his guns down the steep and narrow zigzag track which Waldmeier had engineered down the side of the gorge of the river Jidda, with a sheer wall of rock one side and a vertical drop on the other. In the end it took them 18 days to reach the bed of the river. There Theodorus made camp, and without pause set everyone to work again marking and blasting and building a track for the equally steep and equally difficult way up. It was another three weeks before he completed the crossing of this huge natural obstacle and succeeded at last on 20 February in bringing the whole of his army and its equipment on to the top of the flat and fertile plateau of Delanta.

Like Napier, Theodorus always sent detachments of his troops on ahead to occupy key points, improve the road, and collect supplies. But, unlike Napier, he did not carry his own supplies of food or have them sent up regularly from a base. He was living off the country as he went. This naturally imposed a strain on local resources, and sometimes stretched them to the limit. As his forward detachments in this instance were collecting food and forage not only for his army's day-to-day needs but for a six months' reserve in case Magdala was subjected to a siege, the limit of the people's resistance in Delanta and Dahont was reached in the middle of February. When the people refused to part with any more of their stores of grain. Theodorus ordered his soldiers to take what was needed. Whatever promises he may have made to their chiefs when they offered their submission, the emperor had by no means forgotten that they had not only rebelled against his authority when he was absent but had been in touch with Gobazey and with the British.

Resorting to plunder may have provided Theodorus with food, but it made the people hostile, and from then on he had to use force to make his way across the plateau. Those who resisted were given the stark alternatives of being killed by the sword or burnt alive in their huts.

Faced with this situation Theodorus decided that the time had come to relieve himself of useless mouths. He first dismissed many of the more dispensable members of his entourage and told them to go back to their homes, and he then sent most of his Abyssinian prisoners and hostages on to the Magdala fortress. With them he sent Mrs. Rosenthal and her small child, and the five Europeans who had tried to escape. Although they had sometimes been harshly treated, when they arrived at Magdala Blanc reported to Merewether that they had spoken in high terms of the emperor's behaviour towards them. 'It is true that they were for a long time naked, in hand chains and a few of their servants killed, and that they made a few marches doubled-up but in other respects,' Blanc concluded, 'they were well treated.' And despite his own and his wife's almost biblical-sounding tribulations, Flad too spoke in admiration of the emperor's 'iron perseverance' in bringing his guns and mortars across the formidable gorge. It was noticeable that as Theodorus got closer to Magdala, the captives tended to refer to him more politely or perhaps more discreetly in their letters, and that as the British forces drew nearer to their objective, so the emperor for his part tended to treat his prisoners with more consideration and kindness. In a letter to Rassam, to whose custody he had consigned the five Europeans by word of mouth, Theodorus even apologized for not having done so by letter. 'I have lately been hard at work,' he explained, 'in making a good road for the gun carriages, and I hope that you will accept this as a valid excuse for my not writing to you to-day. I hope it will not be long now before I ascend to Dalanta when I trust to have the pleasure of meeting you, a joy which has been long deferred. . . .' He even asked how Cameron and Rosenthal and Stern had passed the time.

When General Napier left Adigrat on 18 February he expected to meet Kassai two days later at a place called Adabaga. 18 February was a Tuesday. There was no sign of Kassai at the meeting-place but a messenger arrived with a letter. It was addressed, in the name of the Trinity, to Sir Robert Napier, Commander-in-Chief of the English from Dejazmatch Kassai, Chief of the Governors of Ethiopia.

'May God bring us face to face,' ran the official translation. 'Your letter reached me. I am longing to see you. I am coming. I set out on Thursday. Written on day of Yekabit [19 February].'

Napier's reply, suggesting another day, also in the name of the Trinity, was equally laconic and equally unproductive. Several more attempts were made through envoys to fix a definite time and place but each suggestion was met, with exquisite politeness, by excuses and intangible alternatives. 'On Saturday the Prince cannot meet His Excellency; Sunday is a day of rest; but upon Monday the Prince will meet His Excellency at Mai Deeab.' When Napier offered presents in the hope that they might facilitate a meeting, they were refused with equal politeness: 'I want for nothing. God has been good to me, and I am happy with my wife and family;' but, just as he was taking his leave, Kassai's envoy did mention that his master had said that 'there were some troublesome rebels whom he wished us to punish with our artillery'. Napier was anxious to press on with his advance, and almost in desperation he wrote a final letter, this time in the name of the Father, the Son, and the Holy Ghost, proposing that the meeting should take place on the Saturday as he had to be on his way to Magdala on the Sunday as 'your Highness, as a soldier, must be aware that the movements of war will wait for no one'. Just as Napier was about to leave on the Sunday he received another letter. 'May the Almighty guard you', it said, 'till we meet for I have much to say.'

In the end Napier was persuaded to stay another two days, and the meeting finally took place on the following Tuesday at a place twelve miles off Napier's direct route. But the contest of appearances and advantage continued. The first round went to Kassai when Napier arrived at the rendezvous on time with an escort of 450 men, and had to wait until Kassai suddenly appeared out of the early morning mist with a force of 4000. The second round, however, was undoubtedly Napier's. They had arranged to meet at a stream, and Napier waited out of sight until Kassai set out from his tented encampment under a state umbrella of maroon-coloured plush riding on a gaily caparisoned mule. Napier then mounted an elephant decked in scarlet and, followed by a second elephant, rode down to the stream to meet the prince. The effect was slightly spoilt when the leading elephant refused to step into the running water, and Napier had to dismount and cross the stream on horseback, but it was still a splendid entrance, and made a great impression on all those, on both sides, who witnessed it.

Napier was not a drinking man, and the discussions which took place afterwards had to be consummated with toasts of port and brandy from the expedition's supply of medical comforts. Napier was more concerned with the impression made on his visitor by the appearance and armament of his small but carefully chosen supporting force: Bombay cavalry in light blue and silver, British infantry with their white helmets, scarlet coats, and new quick-firing Snider rifles, British gunners in dark blue and red facings standing to their equally new Armstrong guns, and a company of Indian infantry in scarlet coats and glistening white turbans. Kassai, no doubt, had the same object in mind, and, in their own way, his troops made an equally striking impression. Their arms—scimitar-like swords, percussion muskets, matchlock rifles, spears, and cowhide shields—may have been old-fashioned, and their clothing somewhat exotic—tunics of green, blue, or red silk embroidered with yellow flowers, mantles of velvet, leopard-skins, or lions' manes, and head-dresses, in the case of the commanders, of coloured bands and silver coronets; even the order and movements of the soldiers seemed to a British staff officer's eyes to lack 'recognizable formations', but a less hidebound observer noted that 'they stood or moved in a body compactly together, maintaining good order and perfect silence only broken by the sound of their drums'. The cavalry on their tough little mountain ponies were particularly impressive.

Whatever effect these exhibitions of military force and ceremonial advantage may have had, the private discussions which took place showed why both parties had gone to such elastic lengths to ensure that their meeting actually took place. Napier wanted reassurance from Kassai in person that the friendly co-operation he had obtained for his forces on their way to Magdala would continue, and would still be forthcoming when they returned. Apart from the benefits of getting local supplies of food,[1] Napier never forgot that Kassai could, if the need arose, call on an army of about 40,000 men. Nor did Napier forget that, while Ras Kassai frequently asserted that his predecessors in Tigrai had been friends of the British since the time of Henry Salt, in fact they had been much more friendly with the French, who were Britain's main competitors for advantage and influence in Ethiopia and the Middle East. Kassai, for his part, wanted to know what advantages he would get from such co-operation. Although Napier made it clear that he would not take sides, as Kassai had asked, in domestic Abys-

[1] Like Theodorus, Napier even offered free seed to the people in the hope of getting fresh vegetables on the way back.

sinian feuds and rivalries, he gave him an assurance that he would 'represent his friendship very favourably to Her Majesty the Queen of England and that I felt sure that Her Majesty would then acknowledge his friendship in the way most gratifying to him'. In his official report of the meeting Napier said that 'the promise thus implied was not lost upon the Prince'. Whether the implications were the same for both parties was less clear. The rewards that Kassai wanted most were the destruction of the emperor Theodorus, and his own succession to the imperial throne.

After this awkward but necessary delay Napier determined to push on as fast as possible. To facilitate this he ordered most of the remaining camp-followers—the officers' servants, the grooms, and the grass-cutters—back to the coastal base. It was not a popular measure, and the sharp and critical eyes of Henry Morton Stanley noted that in practice the order was not always followed. The same thing happened over Napier's instructions that the baggage allowances should be reduced to 75 lbs each for the officers and 25 lbs for the soldiers. This meant, on paper and in the official despatches to London, that a battalion of troops which in India would have had 600 camp-followers in the field and 1200 baggage mules, had now been reduced to 96 followers and 187 mules. In practice, as Stanley again noted, the train of followers and baggage animals still 'by its exceedingly encumbered length retarded any rapid advance'.

For the next five days Napier averaged 10 miles a day and advanced 51 miles. He himself and his staff were travelling in the van, with a force of about a thousand men. They set off each day at six in the morning to the music of a military band in a long, and often single-file, column of infantry, cavalry, artillery, and sappers, while the elephants and the long baggage train of patient and occasionally obstinate mules brought up the rear. On level ground the elephants, despite their heavy loads, were complete masters of the situation and drew admiring crowds of Abyssinian spectators to watch their steady progress, but on steep ascents the older elephants in particular felt their age and the altitude, and puffed and trumpeted their protest and distress.

On 2 March Napier reached Buya, which the *Times* correspondent spelt 'Booyeah' and which, as he told his bewildered readers as they plotted the army's progress with coloured pins on their highly inaccurate maps, 'opened a wide field for fancy spelling'. It was an important place for the expeditionary force in several ways. It was 183 miles from

Zula, and 192 from Magdala, according to official calculations made at the time, and it was therefore roughly half-way. It was also the southern limit of Dejazmatch Kassai's territory. Beyond it lay areas which belonged or paid tribute to the Wagshum Gobazey. General Napier needed the same assurances of present and future co-operation from Gobazey that he had obtained from Kassai, and with this in mind he sent Munzinger as his envoy to Gobazey's headquarters. His experience with Ras Kassai did not encourage him to press for a personal meeting, but his instructions to Munzinger were precise and in writing. He was to repeat to Gobazey what had been said to Kassai, that all General Napier wanted was peaceful passage for his troops and plentiful local supplies in exchange for cash, and that he would not interfere in any way in the internal affairs of Abyssinia. There was one small but significant change. Where Kassai had been told that the expedition had come solely for the purpose of releasing the captives, Munzinger was instructed to explain to Gobazey that the object was 'to effect the release of the captives unjustifiably detained by Theodore, and to resent the insult offered by the King to Her Majesty the Queen and the British Nation'.

The careful imprecision of the word 'resent' was evidence of the dilemma in which Napier was beginning to find himself. Unless he gave some hint that Theodorus would be deposed or at least humiliated beyond recovery, Gobazey and the others might continue to sit on the fence. If, on the other hand, he was too specific about his intentions, the emperor would be left no inducement to preserve the captives and treat them well. As Rassam put it in a letter to Merewether, 'Give him no hope, and he will kill us.' Although even the resourceful and persistent Munzinger did not manage to meet Gobazey face to face, he made particularly friendly contact with his uncle and deputy, Dejazmatch Mashasha, and the additional point about 'resenting' the emperor's behaviour would certainly not have been missed in translation or lost in the retelling. Gobazey absented himself during this critical period on the excuse of pressing military engagements, in much the same way as diplomats develop convenient colds. While he wanted to earn the gratitude of the British by giving them the clear passage and supplies which they sought, he did not want to be pressed to explain why he had not attacked Theodorus or even tried to hinder his advance, as he had repeatedly been asked and had as repeatedly promised. It was the general belief of Napier's political advisers and of the captives at Magdala that the reason for Gobazey's inaction was fear of Theodorus or cowardice, but a more likely explanation was that he thought that Napier could defeat Theodorus without any help from him, and that it would be wiser to keep his own forces fresh and undiminished for the struggle for power with Kassai and Menelik which he knew would develop as soon as the British had gone. While Munzinger sought him out to discuss the terms of a tactical alliance with General Napier, and the British forces marched steadily on towards Magdala, the astute and far-seeing, and far from cowardly, Wagshum Gobazey occupied himself, therefore, in the convenient remoteness of Begemder seeking allies and recruits to increase the strength of the 30,000 troops which he already had at his disposal.

General Napier remained at Buya for 10 days, reorganizing and replenishing his forces. He had now divided them into three groups, or, in military terms, into two divisions and one smaller coastal command based on Zula. One division comprised all the troops doing garrison and escort duties between Senafay and Antalo; the other, called the advance division, comprised all the troops from Antalo to the front. The fighting strength of this advance division, the spearhead of the expeditionary force, was about 5000 men, of which roughly half were British, and the other half Indian; there were also, to follow the order used in Sir Robert Napier's despatch to the Secretary of State for India, 1356 horses, 518 regimental mules, 33 elephants, and 1969 followers. The 5000-odd ordinary baggage mules and the 1800 muleteers were shown separately, like unfortunate afterthoughts, at the end of the list. One cannot but notice that, after all the efforts made by Napier to reduce personal baggage and followers, the commander-in-chief and his staff, numbering 36 in all, needed 120 followers and 130 mules for tents and baggage, whereas the whole of the 800 men of the 33rd Foot regiment had to make do with 132 followers and 221 mules.

With a reconnaisance and pioneer force under Colonel Phayre going on as usual two days in advance in order to pick and prepare the exact route, General Napier planned to set out on the second half of his journey on 8 March. The 192 miles ahead lay through high, hilly country broken by a series of steep river gorges. It was more difficult than any they had encountered before, but Napier still felt able to say in his despatch, 'Should no extraordinary difficulties occur, I may hope to be at Magdala by the end of the month.' At the same time as Napier was making this forecast, his intelligence officers were studying the letters and reports of the captives at Magdala and the scraps of news which came through from Flad in the emperor's camp, and had reported that Theodorus too was 'not likely to reach Magdala with his guns and mortars before the end of March'. Although the emperor's camp on the Delanta plateau was less than 20 miles from the fortress, he still had to cross the valley of the river Bashilo which was said to be even wider and more precipitous than the gorge of the Jidda. Everyone was now beginning to realize that it was going to be a very close thing. And it was not only the captives at Magdala who felt the tension as the opposing forces converged on the fortress. It was certainly felt by Napier and his expeditionary force, and it was, perhaps, felt most of all by the emperor himself and his concourse of followers as they contemplated the natural hazards of the Bashilo valley, and the human hazards posed not only by the approaching British forces but by the ruthless warriors and marauding bands of Gobazey and Menelik, and the encircling Galla.

These anxieties, on top of the cumulative strains and exhaustions of the long march from Debra Tabor, had the effect of sharpening the emperor's always sharp temper, and of sharpening the contrast too between his occasional good moods and his increasingly frequent bouts of anger or depression. He even quarreled with the loyal and almost indispensable Waldmeier. Hearing that Waldmeier had ventured to say that it would be better if the emperor now tried to come to terms with the English, Theodorus called all his European workmen to his tent, and berated Waldmeier with abuse, 'some of which', poor Mrs. Flad had to admit, 'our European ideas of propriety would even forbid me to mention'. Waldmeier was called, among other printable epithets, 'a dog, a donkey, a poor man from a far country who had come to be his slave, and who had been paid, clad, and fed by him for years'. 'What', Theodorus had demanded, 'do you know of my affairs, a beggar like you?' Waldmeier said in his memoirs afterwards that the emperor even threw a spear at him, which missed, and ordered him to sleep in a tent next to his own 'in case my people try to take you away to the rebels or the English'. Whatever exactly the emperor had in his mind, within a few days they were on good terms again, and Waldmeier was once more working from dawn to dusk, with the emperor working as hard by his side, as they plotted and blasted and dug a way down the side of the new gorge. By 3 March a passable track had been completed, and from the fortress of Magdala, now less than 10 miles distant, Rassam and

Blanc could with their telescope see Theodorus starting to make his way down the steep descent.

With the emperor so close, he and Rassam started to exchange messages almost every day. The emperor's followed the familiar friendly pattern: 'By the power of God, be of good cheer; the time of our meeting is approaching.' Rassam, for his part, continued as if Theodorus were his only friend, and his queen's closest ally: 'I hope also that you will cross the valley of the Bashilo without much trouble.' On 7 March the emperor sent Mrs. Flad, who was expecting a baby, on to the fortress so that she could be attended to by Dr. Blanc. This act of kindness was not extended to her husband, who had to stay behind and help with the road and the guns. A week later Flad wrote to Rassam:

> Yesterday we crossed, with the wagons, the river Bashilo. . . . From peasants we learned that yesterday our friends [the British forces] have reached Wadela, and will come by the road to Baet Hor.[1] It would be good if they would reach us before we reach the mountain [Magdala]. Two days ago His Majesty said to Mr. Waldmeier 'with love and friendship they, the English will overcome me; but if they come otherwise, I know that they will not spare me, and I shall make a blood bath and die. . . .'

On the same day Theodorus wrote to Rassam confirming that he had crossed the river-bed with all his guns. To celebrate the event a salute was fired from the fortress with the guns that were already there.

The emperor camped for the night of 14 March at a place on the Magdala side of the river in a valley called Worke Waha, and was only five or six miles from the fortress. But he still had to make a road up the valley and over the difficult approaches to the fortress gates, and drag all the guns up to the vantage-points which he had in mind for them. Dr. Blanc managed to send a letter to Colonel Merewether on the same day, and estimated that it would take the emperor another ten to fifteen days to complete the task. The emperor may have been close to his destination, but the race was still on.

[1] Another spelling of Beit Hor, which also appears in contemporary records as Bêt-Hor and Bethor.

CHAPTER XIII

The scene is set

It was on 8 March 1868, when he was encamped at Buya a few miles south of Antalo and 192 miles from his objective, that General Napier had reported to London that 'should no extraordinary difficulties occur, I may hope to be at Magdala by the end of the month'. In the end he did not leave Buya until 12 March. He had meant to leave several days earlier, and the delay came at a time when both he, as the commander-in-chief on the spot, and Her Majesty's Government in London were particularly anxious for the advance on Magdala to be resumed as quickly as possible. This may have been one of the reasons why the delay, and its causes, received such a brief and bare mention in Napier's despatches.

Colonel Phayre had as usual gone on ahead with a small force of soldiers and sappers to choose and prepare the road for the main body of the troops and their transport. On 7 March he sent back word that a pass with the fine Amharic name of Fulluk Eimuk Oonzool was, to use his own words, 'said to be, on the best native authority, more practicable in point of gradient and road surface than that on the direct line from Musgee to Attala by Alaji, and it was therefore adopted'. The route which Phayre adopted was not only six miles longer than the direct road, but it was judged by those who experienced it, including Phayre himself, to be the worst stretch of road they had met with in the whole of Abyssinia. One survey party reported that the 1600-foot descent from the top of the pass was

> covered from beginning to end with huge rocks, boulders and sharp stones so that it would be difficult for an elephant to find a single spot where it might place its foot in safety. Sometimes it goes through miniature defiles of rock originally formed by the descent of water from the heights above; at others it is little more than an edge overhanging precipices; while again the huge boulders spread along the path in wild confusion seem laid for the express purpose of obstructing all progress, the passage between them being in places so narrow that it seems impossible for a mule to squeeze through.

The ascent to the top of the pass, which was 10,000 feet above sea level, was almost as bad; the gradient was so severe in places that it rose like the steps of a giant staircase. The sappers said it would take them at least twelve days to make it into a passable road. Two days later, after much hard labour and as much bad language had been expended by the pioneers, and several horses had been lost, one of the officers who had been prospecting this difficult diversion decided out of curiosity to ride back by the rejected direct road over the Amba Alaji pass. He was astonished to find that it was not only shorter but easier too. By the time this news reached Napier at Buya, and the direct route had been surveyed, and then adopted and improved, between five and six precious days had been lost. Napier was not amused, but the only official reference he made to the matter, then or afterwards, was a brief, unobtrusive note in his own handwriting in the margin of the relevant part of Phayre's reconnaissance report: 'This information proved to be false; and on further examination the Alaji pass has been adopted. R. Napier.' Napier continued to use Colonel Phayre for reconnaissance,[1] but after this he always travelled with the leading party himself.

When the true explanation of this costly mistake emerged, it did little to ease Phayre's embarrassment or to diminish Napier's displeasure. The direct route by the Alaji pass went close to an isolated natural rock fastness nearly 1000 feet high, called Amba Alaji, which was the stronghold of a local chieftain named Wolde Jesus.[2] Wolde Jesus turned out to be 'the best native authority' referred to in Phayre's report, and it was he who had not only persuaded Phayre of the fictitious advantages of the longer roundabout route by Fulluk Eimuk Oonzool, but had also impressed him with equally imaginary stories of the dangers to be encountered on the Alaji pass from marauding Galla tribesmen. When both these deceptions were discovered, Wolde Jesus admitted that he was on bad terms with both Dejazmatch Kassai and Wagshum Gobazey, and that the last thing he wanted was any improvement to the direct road, which was close to his stronghold and

[1] One has only to read Colonel Phayre's very detailed and imaginative daily reports of his examination and assessment of the various routes open to the expedition to understand why Napier continued despite this incident to rely on him for reconnaissance right up to the end. In his concluding despatches Napier went out of his way to pay tribute to Phayre's 'most important services in the early examination of the country', and 'his very great energy and intelligence'.

[2] Also, and probably more correctly, spelt Walda Iyasus.

could therefore be used to facilitate a surprise attack by Kassai from the north or by Gobazey from the south.

Although Wolde Jesus was disappointed when he found that his misrepresentations had, in the end, failed to deceive the British, he appreciated, as a fighting man, that it was as necessary for Napier to take the best route as it had been for him to try and deceive Napier. And so, when the time came, he waited on the road below his stronghold to greet Napier, amiably but unrepentantly, as he went past. Wolde Jesus was a man in the prime of life, and he made a striking figure with his gold bangles, silver chain, and lion's mane tassel to his shield, surrounded by his band of supporters armed with sixteenth-century Portuguese muskets and modern double-barrelled shot-guns. Napier, to his credit, invited him to have a glass of wine, and presented him with, among other gifts, a telescope to help him keep a look-out for his enemies and thus offset any harm that might have been done to him by the improvements to the road. In exchange for these civilities Wolde Jesus undertook to protect Napier's troops and transports on their way through the territory of Wojerat which he controlled.

Napier described Wojerat, sandwiched between the expanding ambitions of two powerful neighbours, as the Belgium of Abyssinia. To look at, however, it was more like Switzerland. It was a rugged, mountainous country which encouraged, and got, much purple prose and many imaginative metaphors. 'Huge reddish pinnacles shot upward against the pale blue sky; slate-coloured reefs of granite rock piled one upon another; hills upon hills were tumbled into platoons, or were rolled into abrupt, serrated ridges.' It was tiresome and discouraging country for marching; each time a pass was reached after a steep and exhausting ascent, instead of a respite, all one got was the sight of an equally steep descent, and another even higher pass ahead. As the *Times* correspondent described it, 'the country heaved with mountains in every direction like a rough sea.' It had its compensations for the eye —forests and abundant valleys, gurgling streams rich with wild flowers and exotic birds—but it presented a series of challenging problems to those who had to choose the best route and then improve the track. On one cross-country stretch the Duke of Wellington's regiment, which prided itself on its physical fitness and durability, took 28 hours to cover 14 miles. The problems were correspondingly worse for those who had to lead the heavily laden elephants and mules up and down the precipitous ascents and descents, and to persuade the highly-strung cavalry horses to face the narrow ledges and dizzy heights. The transport animals, and even the marching troops, were often reduced to 8 or 9 miles a day, but Napier with his more lightly burdened advance force of 700 men was able to push on more quickly, and covered the 130 miles from Buya to Lat in 10 days. The only respite on this difficult mountain march was at Lake Ashangi, which reminded some of Napier's staff of Lake Ullswater, until they went shooting the wild duck and the gazelle on the fringes, and sank up to their armpits in mud.

From his camp on the shore of Lake Ashangi on 19 March Napier wrote another of his personal letters to the Duke of Cambridge, and told him that in a few days he hoped to receive information which would enable him to decide his onward route. 'I am looking out for a good place to concentrate my force and establish a secure depot, from whence I can march with a lightly equipped corps to invest Magdala where Theodore is endeavouring to improve his defences. I do not know if he will meet us outside.'

Beyond the mountains of Wojerat lay the province of Lasta. It was nominally part of the emperor's Abyssinian dominions, but it was by this time largely controlled by the rebellious Wagshum Gobazey. Up to this point Napier's forces had been travelling through Tigrai, whose rulers and people regarded themselves, as they still do, as kindred but separate from the rest of Abyssinia. In the province of Lasta the British army began to encounter the Amhara who, for their part, regarded themselves as the core, and their country as the heartland, of Ethiopia. To the surprise of the British forces and the newspaper correspondents, who had been led by travellers' tales and the complaints of the captives to expect something else, the Amhara were found to be generally honest, polite, dignified, and courteous, and as soldiers to be brave, disciplined, and better armed, according to Austin, than British infantry had been twenty years before. They were described as good-looking, with olive or light brown skins, thin lips, straight hair, and aquiline noses, and the men in particular as being careful and conventional in their dress. As some of them watched the British soldiers marching and working in the midday sun stripped to the waist with red faces and peeling backs, they were heard to remark that the English seem to have come into the world half-cooked and to have remained in it half-dressed. The good looks and charm of the Amhara women came in for more praise than their personal daintiness and decorum, and Dr. Austin felt obliged to tell the readers of *The Times* that, after the modest behaviour of the Muslim girls of the northern regions of Abyssinia, 'the morals of the country by no means improve as we get further on . . .', and that he regretted having to report 'the shamelessness and open disregard for decency' which was met with among the Christian Amhara of central Abyssinia.

The parts of the province of Lasta through which the British expeditionary force passed were its eastern extremities which bordered on the lands of the Galla. The Galla tribes tended to be Muslims or to have kept to the primitive usages and beliefs of their Hamitic ancestors. Napier therefore sent Mir Akbar Ali, a much valued Indian Muslim member of his staff of Intelligence officers, to accompany Grant on a mission to make contact with the Galla chiefs both here and in the areas to the east and south of Magdala. The Galla were the traditional enemies of the Christian Amhara, and the Galla tribes of these regions had in their time suffered military defeat and plunder at the hands of the emperor Theodorus, which they were anxious to reverse and revenge. They had a reputation as fierce and brave fighters, and they were disappointed but not discouraged when Mir Akbar Ali told them that all Napier wanted was unmolested passage and plentiful supplies. The Galla tribesmen were, however, inclined to independent action, and whatever their chiefs may have decided for reasons of politeness, policy, or self-interest, the British expeditionary force, with its slow-moving larder of cattle on the hoof and its occasional stragglers, offered temptations which the hungry and virile Galla warriors found it difficult to resist. This meant that Napier had to be on guard and to insist on precautions and practices against surprise attack at night which were far from popular with troops tired after marching and road-making all day.

General Napier reached the village of Lat with his advance party on 21 March. He had now got the further information from the captives and from Munzinger which he had hoped for, and on the basis of this information he decided to push on as quickly as possible with a lightly equipped and lightly burdened advance force. To facilitate this he ordered another drastic and even more unpopular reduction of baggage, camp-followers, and tents. This time his orders were more strictly enforced. Everyone was limited to what he, or his horse if he had one, could carry in the way of personal belongings, which in practice meant for most people a greatcoat, a blanket, and a groundsheet. No camp-beds were allowed, and all, including the commander-in-chief, had to sleep on the ground. The mules were fully laden with 15 days' basic rations. Everything else had to be left behind. Napier also took the opportunity to relieve his forces, and himself, of much of the paper work to which headquarters safely and comfortably established in towns always seem to attach more importance than those in the field. Napier's despatch informing the India Office in London of these decisions was laconic, but its meaning was quite clear.

I leave to-morrow with a light column, leaving all its baggage and the Headquarters establishments to follow at some distance in rear with the 2nd Brigade. This may make it difficult for the usual amount of correspondence to be maintained during the next few weeks. . . . My progress will depend to some extent on the obstacles which the country may present to our advance. But, as even our tents will now be left behind, excepting in proportion of one small bell tent for 12 officers, and a similar one for 20 men, every possible endeavour may be said to have been made to lighten the advance force of its encumbrances, and we may hope to be before Magdalla in the course of a week or ten days.

Three days later, on 25 March, he told London that he had reached Dildi. Since leaving Lat they had been advancing at the rate of 15 miles a day, and those who were following were expected to do the same. He was pushing his troops very hard, and although he admitted in his despatch that the country was becoming worse—'a continuous succession of mountainous tracts not less rugged and difficult than those of Garwal in the Himalayas'—and that the last days' march had been 'somewhat toilsome', there was one thing which he did not mention, and which again found no mention in the official history of the expedition. Stanley had likened the country to the teeth of a saw, but the mainly Irish rank and file of the Duke of Wellington's regiment used a number of more colourful expressions to describe the distances they had been made to cover, the sort of country they had had to traverse, the extra loads they had to carry, and the bloody mules laden with bloody rations which every soldier now had to lead. It was not only the rank and file who complained, and the complaints became so virulent that one of Napier's commanders, an artillery officer called Colonel Millward, felt obliged to make a written submission.

I have the honour with much regret to report that the swearing, grumbling and discontent of the men amounts to insubordination. . . . On yesterday's march, which was somewhat fatiguing, the openly expressed abuse of their superiors, given out in obscene and violent language, reached such a pitch that I had determined to bring the matter under the notice of His Excellency.

Napier had a great respect for the Duke of Wellington's regiment both as fighting soldiers and as workers, and because of this he, like others, was prepared to overlook their weaknesses. As one of their own English officers put it, they 'were addicted to drink and liked a good growl but they could work, none better.' But their behaviour on this occasion was too much. Napier had the regiment paraded in front of him at Dildi, and told them that they were no longer fit to have the honour of leading the expedition and that as a punishment they would be relegated to the rear. What made it worse was that their place in the van was taken by their great rivals, the 4th Regiment of Foot, the King's Own. This perhaps was one reason why Major Cooper, who had been commanding the 33rd since the death of Colonel Dunn, was, to quote from the private journal kept by Colonel Field, 'placed under arrest for refusing to retract some intemperate words which he addressed to Colonel Thesiger after the parade'.[1]

At Dildi Napier and his light column rested for a day to regroup and recover from the upsets and fatigues of their rapid advance. They were now 60 miles from Magdala. When Napier left Dildi on 27 March and continued his advance, the scene was set for the confrontation, and the last act was about to begin.

While General Napier was trying to make up for the delay caused by Colonel Phayre's mistake over the Amba Alaji pass, the emperor Theodorus was working his way steadily up the southern side of the gorge of the river Bashilo. By 18 March he was encamped with his artillery at Aroji,[2] an area of level ground below the last steep approach to the Magdala fortress. Although he still had to get his guns and mortars up to their planned firing positions on the heights above, Theodorus was now in a position to command the only practicable route into the fortress. He had thus successfully interposed himself and his troops between Napier's forces and their objective. He had also managed to collect, by way of tribute, gift, purchase, or plunder,

[1] Colonel the Hon. F. Thesiger, Deputy Adjutant-General, eldest son of the first Lord Chelmsford, one of the most handsome, eloquent, and imperturbable Victorian Lord Chancellors, with, to quote the *D.N.B.*, 'a pleasant if too frequent wit'. Colonel Thesiger, said by Napier to have great ability and untiring energy, went on to become a controversial figure when he was commanding British troops in the Zulu wars at the time of the disaster of Isandhlwana and the ultimate defeat of the great Cetewayo. Wilfred Thesiger, the distinguished Arabian explorer, is his grandson.

[2] Also spelt Aroge, Arogeh, Arogi, Arogie, Arogye, Arogee, and Aroje.

enough supplies of food to last him and his followers, if need be, for a six months' siege.

To reach this position, the emperor had not only had to overcome his many natural obstacles with the makeshift resources and skills at his disposal but, as has been explained, he also had to contend with widespread opposition from his own countrymen. The contending *rases* were, however, equally jealous of one another, and their behaviour in the early part of 1868 suggested that their mutual hatred was more potent than their opposition to the emperor.

Rivalry and mutual hostility were not the only reasons why the emperor's domestic enemies did not attack him. Theodorus knew that if his rivals in Abyssinia could be sure that the British forces would not only release the captives but defeat and destroy him, they would then feel able to attack him with impunity, and with probable profit from a grateful Napier. But they could not be sure on either count, and their uncertainty was increased by Napier's reluctance to say what exactly he intended to do with Theodorus if and when the captives were released. The emperor now deliberately added to this uncertainty by letting it be widely rumoured that the British were really coming as his friends to help him deal with his rebellious subjects. Flad reported him as saying, 'If I have once shaken hands with the English who are coming, my rebellious peasants will be afraid.' His rival barons might not have believed the exact letter of the rumours, but as rulers who knew from their own practice how hostages could be used, they may well have believed that helping Theodorus defeat his rebels was the price the British might be prepared to pay for the lives and liberties of the large number of European hostages their wily emperor had, over the years, managed to accumulate, in much the same way as others accumulated gold.

By these means, and by the leadership and determination which by the middle of March had brought him and his guns ahead of Napier to the gates of the almost impregnable fortress of Magdala, Theodorus must have felt that he was in a good position. He was still beset by his domestic enemies, and he knew that his weapons and equipment were inferior to the British, but he could nevertheless feel that he had now reached a position where he could negotiate and bargain with General Napier. With this in his mind perhaps, he sent Martin Flad and two of his own trusted men up to the fortress on 18 March with a conciliatory letter to Rassam:

> Oh, my friend, I have no quarrel with you, nor have I any rancour towards you. Formerly when I sent you to Magdala, I told my people to watch you only, but they sent me an answer that, out of precaution, they had put you in chains; but now when I, your friend, am brought by God near to you, your chains shall be opened; but until I see the object of your masters, we will watch you, but without chains.

With the letter came 2000 silver thalers in compensation for Rassam's stores which had got lost some months earlier, and a present of 100 sheep and 50 cows. Although Rassam acknowledged these purposeful gestures of recompense in his usual grateful and even obsequious fashion, he was embarrassed, though not deterred, by the fact that he was the only one of the captives to be freed of his chains. But when he wrote to the emperor asking for the release of the others, the emperor's reply evaded his question with polite and practised ease:

> A good day to you my friend. I am now so near that I can see the top of your house plainly; and if you come out and look down you will see my tent. Our meeting is at hand.

Theodorus' reluctance to release the others was not so much aimed at Dr. Blanc and Lieutenant Prideaux, whom, as he put it, he neither loved nor hated, as at Cameron and the two Jews Society missionaries Stern and Rosenthal whom he had long disliked and distrusted. Stern was still sending abusive and plum-coloured accounts of his condition and of the emperor's iniquities for publication by his sympathisers in England, and Cameron's attitude, and his lack of caution or concern for his fellow captives, are shown by the tone of a letter which he smuggled out to Colonel Merewether on 19 March, when the emperor was camped less than a mile from the fortress: 'But these black fellows', he wrote, 'are mere Bedlamites, and the King such a mixture of rogue and madman, that the sooner we are out of his hands the better . . .'

A few days later, on 21 March, Theodorus started to send his valuables into the security of the fortress, including a bar of gold 14 inches long and 41 inches square. By 25 March he had succeeded in dragging his guns to the foot of the flat-topped summit of Selassie while he himself camped on the open space of Salamji immediately below the main entrance of the fortress. He continued to send his valuables and personal belongings into the fortress, but he was at the same time bringing arms and ammunition from his arsenal in Magdala down to Salamji, and concentrating his military equipment there and on the twin heights of Selassie and Fala which overlooked and commanded the approaches to Magdala. Two days later, on 27 March, the emperor paid his first visit to the fortress, but he paid no attention to the captives except to say: 'Your brothers are coming to liberate you, and I, by the power of God, am ready to meet them. . . . As far as I am concerned, I am desirous of nothing but peace; and I pray God that your brothers are coming with the same good intention. . . .'

CHAPTER XIV

The battle

While the emperor Theodorus was already paying his first visit to Magdala, the speed of General Napier's advance was being reduced by the increasingly difficult country and the deteriorating weather to less than six miles a day. He left his camp at Dildi on 26 March, and the first day's march was especially hard going. It started with a climb of 3000 feet in the first five miles to a mountain pass 10,500 feet above sea-level. The path went along a ridge which fell away steeply on both sides, and the track was so narrow that the whole column had to march in single file. Heavy rain and strong winds set in in the evening, and it was very cold; the path became very slippery and treacherous, and conditions got so bad that it was after midnight when the last of the troops reached camp. The descent from the pass was easier, but the weather continued to be bad; squalls of rain and hail, and storms of stupendous thunder and spectacular lightning hampered progress during the day, and at night and in the early morning the ground was covered in frost, the water froze, and the hilltops were seen to be dusted with snow. When the sun came out it became hot and sticky, and both the British and the Indian soldiers sweated and swore under their extra burdens of greatcoats, blankets, and groundsheets, which they needed in the wet and cold of the night. To make matters worse, a hitch in the transport arrangements meant that there was no rum or sugar to cheer their basic rations.

On the third day of the march from Dildi the British troops had their first sight of the formidable gorges which the rivers in central and northern Abyssinia had carved on their way to join the Atbara and the Blue Nile. The first one encountered was the river Taccaze. The northern slopes were gradual and presented few difficulties, but the southern side looked from a distance like a precipitous wall of rock between 2000 and 3000 feet high. On closer viewing it turned out to be zigzagged with a narrow, hair-raising mule-track with sheer rock above, and almost sheer rock below. The sappers had already been working on it with explosives to make it easier for the marching troops and the transport animals, as well as the cattle and sheep which accompanied the expeditionary force to provide fresh meat. As a result of the sappers' efforts, the whole of Napier's force was able to cross the gorge that day, and to camp for the night on the Wadela plateau.

Napier was very relieved to reach the plateau. He had recently received a report that the emperor had retraced his steps and crossed to the north bank of the Bashilo, and Napier was not the only member of the expedition to realize how vulnerable they had been as the long thin line of tired and breathless troops and transports made their way up that zigzag track from the bed of the Taccaze to the plateau above. The alarming report about the emperor's movements turned out to be false, but it underlined the importance of gaining a foothold on the high ground as soon as possible. Napier also had another reason for hastening the pace of his advance. The rain they had had since they left Dildi, and the slippery conditions it had created on the steep ups and downs of the route, were chilling reminders that the expedition had not only to achieve its objectives before the summer rains set in, but to get back to the coast as well. When they crossed the river Taccaze itself the stream had been a trickle; once the rains began in earnest, it, and the other rivers ahead of them, could quickly become impassable torrents.

With the emperor's fast-moving cavalry so close, and two more precipitous river gorges to cross, the risk of a surprise attack had become very real, and Napier decided to halt at Santara on the Wadela plateau for two days to give time for the rest of his advance force to catch up, and allow him to reform and concentrate his spearhead troops. He himself and his headquarters staff were in the van, with the first of the three brigades which made up the advance division; the second brigade followed one march behind, with the third brigade bringing up the rear the following day. At this point the division comprised approximately 4000 men. It was not a large force, but it was well balanced and well equipped. The infantry and the artillery were mainly British, the cavalry and the engineers mainly Indian.[1]

Another reason for the halt at Santara was that Napier wanted to collect and assess the latest information available about the approaches to the fortress and its defences, and about the emperor's dispositions and intentions. He had already come to the conclusion that any facts or opinions which emanated from the captives or from the Europeans in the emperor's camp were of limited military value. 'If', he once said

[1] For composition of the advanced division see Appendix B.

'any of the Europeans within the fortress has ever furnished us with an intelligent description of its military features I have not seen such a description.' It was not that they were backward in putting forward either facts or opinions on such matters, but Napier had realized by now that what they said was tinted and often over-coloured by their desire to be rescued whatever the cost. Napier preferred therefore to rely for his information and advice on his own intelligence staff, particularly on Munzinger, who was operating in Lasta and in the country to the north and west of Magdala, and on Grant and Mir Akbar Ali, who, as explained, had been sent to keep in touch with the Galla on the eastern and southern approaches to the fortress.

Wagshum Gobazey had continued to absent himself, but Munzinger maintained his friendly relationship with the deputy Mashasha. This, and the good impression which Mashasha himself made when he met Napier on 29 March at Santara, were to bring great advantage to both sides. Napier, and indeed all who witnessed their meeting, were equally impressed with Mashasha's escort of 400 or 500 horsemen, whose dramatic appearance was thus vividly described by Stanley:

> At the end of about half an hour a long line of cavalry crested the ridge. After a pause, during which it may be supposed that they examined the strange camp below with its thousands of men and animals, the whole of the cavalry marched down the steep sides of the bluff as coolly and as deliberately as if they were on a level plain. There was no appearance of commotion or jostling, though the precipitous faces of the elevation were uneven enough with rough boulders and toppling stones. No European cavalry could have done so without being huddled in groups, and in stumbling and sprawling masses.

About half of the horsemen were armed with flintlock muskets, the others with spears and swords. Not one of the horses was shod. Theodorus was reputed to have even larger and better armed bodies of cavalry, to take full advantage of the difficult river gorges and narrow, wooded valleys which still lay ahead. Napier was particularly glad therefore to get assurances from Mashasha that he would be accorded safe passage through the provinces of Wadela and Delanta, and plentiful supplies of local produce. Mashasha, for his part, gracefully accepted a present of a horse, a double-barrelled shot-gun and a carpet, while making it clear that he did not look on them as substitutes, for the more substantial benefits which he and his master, Gobazey, expected later on in return for the assurances which they had given. Napier's official report of his meeting with Dejazmatch Mashasha showed how the alleged fears of the Galla were used to indicate obliquely what Gobazey's own expectations were:

> The attendants having been dismissed to a little distance, the Dejaj begged me to be on my guard against sudden attacks on the part of Theodore who, he observed, is a man of whom no one can say what he may do. . . . He then stated that Theodore had given out that the coming of the British was entirely in friendship, and that the Gallas who were opposing him were rather alarmed at the report, fearing that the King would become more powerful than before. Dejaz Mashashah intimated that it would reassure the Galla if we were to say that no peace would be made with Theodore. To this I replied that it would not be expedient to give any indication at present of the course which I intended to pursue, as a short time would show.

Nor were Napier's obligations to Gobazey and his deputy diminished by an unfortunate incident which took place a few days later when an outpost of British soldiers fired by mistake in the dusk on a party of Mashasha's cavalry. Although Napier had generous compensation paid to the relatives of the one man who was killed and another who was wounded, it was Mashasha's ready acceptance of the happening as an accident, and his refusal to make an issue of it, which made the deepest impression and which, in the end, gained the greater advantage.

When Napier came to deal with the Galla themselves, however, they did not complicate matters by making any pretence of acting on anybody's behalf but their own. The negotiations with the Galla queen Mastiat and her adolescent son were conducted by Mir Akbar Ali, who explained that what was required of them now was that their forces should close in on Magdala from the south and the east so as to make it impossible for Theodorus to escape or to retreat in those directions. Queen Mastiat and her son agreed to do this, but they made it clear that in return they wanted a firm promise that the British would not merely make Theodorus release his European captives but destroy his power completely. Napier's need of the Galla's help to prevent the emperor from eluding him was so great that in the end he gave them what he had not given anyone before, an assurance in writing that his purpose was not only to release the captives but to punish the emperor for his misdeeds.

Although the plateau of Wadela was only a few miles wide, Napier's force had to march its full length of nearly forty miles from east to west to reach a place where they could cross the river Jidda. It was, for a change, four days of easy and pleasant marching. The country, which Stanley likened to Nebraska, was open grassland with gentle undulations, dotted with crops, ploughed fields, and stubble. The people were friendly, and supplies of grain and fodder plentiful. But the sight which greeted them when they camped at the western extremity of the plateau was an alarming contrast. They camped at Beit Hor, at the same place where the emperor and his army had camped two months before. The gorge of the river Jidda, 3500 feet deep and nearly eight miles wide, according to the expedition's calculations, made a great impression on the British troops when they 'came to the brink of a vast and at first sight impassable gulf so suddenly that it seemed to have opened in the earth's surface at our feet', as one of them described the event for the readers of *Blackwood's*. Even Napier, who was not given to exaggeration, described the descent as being 'down the face of almost a sheer precipice', and the difficulties and hazards of the other side such that 'had Theodore taken up a position on the opposite bank, we could only have forced the ascent at some loss'. This was said with feeling as Napier had just received another report that the emperor was on the move, and he had in consequence ordered a forced march of 18 miles in order to gain the high ground on the Delanta plateau on the south side of the gorge with the least possible delay. Conditions were so bad, however, and progress in single file so slow, that the end of the column did not arrive until 24 hours after the leading troops had made camp. There was no lack of complaints about the long day's march, but Napier knew that where the British expeditionary force had found a ready-made track across the gorge, Theodorus and his army had had to spend three weeks carving their own way across it.

Napier stayed on the Delanta plateau for five days. Once again his object was, as he put it, 'to concentrate the force and gain information regarding the state of affairs to my front and generally around me'. The emperor's achievement in making a way across the formidable obstacle of the Jidda gorge with his guns, and the sight of Mashasha'a Abyssinian cavalry, had given Napier much food for thought. He was soon to have more. On the final day of his stay on the plateau, 9 April, he went forward to the edge of the gorge of the Bashilo, the next and last river which lay between him and his destination. Here, twelve miles in a direct line from the emperor's fortress, he had his first view of the position and its approaches. Magdala itself was concealed by the spurs of Selassie and Fala, but Napier and those with him could see enough to realize how strong the position was. He wrote:

I was able with a good telescope to appreciate the formidable character of the whole position, and became aware that I should require all the infantry I could possibly collect to make the attack effective, and that every cavalry soldier that I could bring forward would be necessary for the investment.

He knew that he had not got enough troops in hand to encircle the fortress completely, and another reason for his decision to stay on the plateau for a few days was to make sure that Mastiat and her Galla horsemen were in position to the south of Magdala before he himself made an attack from the north. He also needed once again to build up his reserves of food and ammunition. The transport mules and their escorts were bringing up supplies every day over the difficult country, but the concentration of so many of the fighting troops at the front meant that Napier's lines of communication and his supply trains had become more vulnerable to interference from bandits and minor chiefs, who often saw no reason to respect the promises given to Napier by their nominal overlords in return for benefits which they themselves were not always invited to share.

From Beit Hor on the river Jidda, the shortest and easiest way to Magdala was to follow in the emperor's footstsps. While there were clear advantages for Napier in following the route and using the roads made by Theodorus, there were also disadvantages. It meant, in particular, that the country had already been ransacked for supplies by the emperor's troops, although in practice the reports of wholesale devastation and pillage which the captives and artisans had been sending were not always borne out by the plentiful supplies of food, forage, and firewood which still came forward once it was known that the British paid, and paid well, for what they needed. But if the British forces gained from this generosity in terms of local produce, they lost, it seemed, in terms of the awe and respect they commanded from the local population. The *Times* correspondent reported, for example, that when the people of Delanta saw that the British paid the equivalent of 5d. each for eggs, they immediately came to the conclusion that Napier would be no match for Theodorus. 'He', they said with barely concealed admiration, 'would just take the good ones, and by way of payment pelt us with the rotten ones!'

While Napier was building up his forces and his supplies, he was also planning ahead in other ways. He had already sent a letter to the emperor with the object, as Napier himself put it, 'neither to exasperate him or render him desperate on the one hand, nor give him grounds for misconstruing our intentions with respect to him on the other'. It was a short letter in Napier's own characteristically matter of fact and laconic style:

By command of the Queen of England I am approaching Magdala with my army, in order to recover from your hands Envoy Rassam, Consul Cameron, Dr. Blanc, Lieutenant Prideaux, and the other Europeans now in your Majesty's power. I request your Majesty to send them to my camp, as soon as it is sufficiently near to admit of their coming in safety.

At the same time, in case he got no response to this appeal, he was assessing the strength of the emperor's military position, and making his plans to assail it. He reported his conclusions in the following terms:

The centre of the position is the rock of Selassie, elevated more than 9000 feet above the sea, and standing on a plateau called Islamgie, which is divided into several extensive terraces, with perpendicular scarps of basalt. A saddle connects these terraces with the hill called Fahla. It domineers completely all approaches to Islamgie; the sides appear precipitous, and the summit surrounded by a natural scarp of rock, accessible only in a few places, and from 18 to 20 feet in height. . . . The road to Magdalla winds up the steep side of Fahla, subject to its fire, and to the descent of rocks and stones. One part of the road is so steep that few horses, except those bred in the country, could carry their riders up and down it. The whole road is flanked by the end of Selassie and the broad scarp side of Islamgie. Altogether, without taking into account Magdalla itself, the formidable character of its outworks exceeded anything which we could possibly have anticipated from the faint description of the position which had reached us.[1]

Napier's judgement was that the point to aim at was Salamji, where Theodorus had concentrated most of his forces, and that Fala, where he had positioned most of his guns, was the key to the whole position. The ridge of Fala thus became his first objective, with the flat ground of Aroji as the place in which to assemble his forces for the attack.

[1] In the text the three main features of the Magdala position mentioned in Napier's report are spelt Selassie, Salamji, and Fala. In contemporary records and maps they appear variously as Selasse and Selassyè; Islamgee, Islamgie, and Islamgye; and Fâla, Fahla, Falla, and Falah.

By the evening of 9 April there had still been no reply to Napier's letter, and no sign of the captives having been released. On the morning of 10 April 1868, Napier and his advance division of four thousand troops moved in to attack.

Theodorus had paid his first visit to Magdala on 27 March. Two days later he paid another visit, and this time he summoned Rassam and received him with his customary disconcerting mixture of formality and amity. Rassam had been told to put on his official blue uniform, and two thousand square yards of ground had been covered with carpets as a setting for the scarlet tent in which he was received. It was the first time the two had met since Rassam and his companions had been sent to Magdala from Debra Tabor in June 1866, and Rassam noticed how much the emperor had changed, and how his hair had gone grey. Theodorus was, however, in a jovial mood, though it must have needed a strong sense of humour to appreciate some of his banter. 'It is true', he told Rassam, 'that I put you in fetters, after the barbarous custom of my country, which I admit is a bad custom, but have you seen a hand chain? That, I assure you, is far worse.' In the afternoon, he had Blanc and Prideaux released from their fetters. This was done at Rassam's request, but it must have been galling for the two officers to hear the emperor's bland explanation that he did not really know who they were or what they had come for. 'I chained you because I chained Mr. Rassam; now I open your chains because he promised to be your security.'

Three days later they were all invited to watch the big guns and mortars being dragged to the heights of Salamji and Selassie. Theodorus had had a road made to bring the guns up from the valley of the Bashilo. The road, quickly to become known as the 'King's Road' by the British troops, was very steep in its final stages, with a gradient of 1 in 3, and one very sharp and angular bend. The emperor directed the last and most difficult part of the operation himself from a commanding but precarious position on a crag. Between 500 and 600 men were needed to haul the huge mortar Sebastopol on its wooden carriage with leather ropes up the steep slope, while others were required to risk their limbs by crawling up behind the carriage and putting stones behind the wheels to stop it slipping back. In all several thousand men were involved in the operation. The noise was considerable, but Blanc noticed that the emperor had only to raise his hand 'and not a sound would arise from the thousands engaged in the work and the clear voice of Theodore would alone be heard in the deep silence that his simple gesture had produced'.

That same afternoon, and again at Rassam's special request, the emperor had Cameron and the other Magdala captives released from their chains. Knowing how much Theodorus disliked the consul and the two missionaries, it must have seemed a risky request to make, but Rassam had judged his moment well. For all his euphoria at getting his artillery up the slope and into position, the emperor was in a conciliatory mood. He kept asking Rassam and his companions what Europeans did when they made war, by what means exactly the King of Prussia had overcome the opposition in the recent Austro-Prussian war, and whether the defeated Emperor of Austria had been imprisoned and made to lose his country. And, looking at his own tattered and ill-clad soldiers going about their business, he turned to Rassam and said, 'How can I show these ragged soldiers to your well-dressed troops?'

During the next few days the emperor began to show other signs of anxiety. He spent much of his time on Salamji with his telescope watching the British troops on the plateau beyond the gorge of the Bashilo slowly and methodically building up their strength and their supplies. He kept asking impatiently when Napier would resume his advance, and what his military and political intentions were. He had had no official communication from the British since they had landed, no demands or promises or threats, not even a formal ultimatum. (The letter which Napier had written to him on 3 April asking him to release his captives had not reached him because, it was said, no male messenger could be found who was willing to risk the emperor's displeasure when he read it; in the end, females being safer on such occasions, it was a woman who took the letter from a messenger and handed it to Theodorus on 10 April.) The emperor's mood at this time was vividly described by Waldmeier: 'Take this telescope,' Theodorus had said to him, 'and look over the gulf of the river Bashilo. There thou wilt see thy brethren who have come from England to kill me. I am pleased to see those red jackets. I am glad that I have moved England to bring me the answer which Consul Cameron, the liar, promised to bring.' After this, Waldmeier went on, 'the King became gloomy and dark as night, restless and angry as Saul, and I trembled with fear. . . .'

Theodorus was busy during the day putting his guns and mortars into their firing positions, improving the fortifications and defences, and encouraging his troops with gusts of rumbustious, boastful recapitulation of past martial exploits and anticipations of the braveries and slaughter and rich looting in the battles to come. It was at night that the dark moments of doubt returned to oppress him, and he took again to drinking with his soldiers for a temporary relief from his anxieties. It was during this difficult period of alternating moods of elation and depression that he started to release some of the hundreds of his subjects who were held as prisoners or hostages in the fortress. Some had been at Magdala for years, dependent on their relatives or the exiguous charity of strangers for their food and clothing. Men of rank and political hostages were often well treated, but others were chained by hand and foot, and had to crawl, dragging emaciated bodies covered in the sores of disease and deprivation in search of sustenance and shelter. They were not a pleasant sight, but conditions of survival in Ethiopia, then as now, were such that rulers could rarely allow themselves the luxury of kindness. On the first day, according to Rassam, 186 women and children were released, together with 37 chiefs and other notables; seven men were executed. On the following day, 9 April, Theodorus ordered the release of the rest except for a few, who would now be described as political prisoners. Some of these released prisoners became impatient at the time taken to free them from their shackles, and others complained, according to Waldmeier, at the lack of food and water. In a sudden but characteristic blaze of anger, and some said, drink, the emperor seized his spear, and shouting, 'I will teach them to ask for food when my faithful soldiers are starving!' he started to attack the complainers. His soldiers joined in with swords and knives and muskets, until in the end between 200 and 300 bodies lay dead or dying on a ledge at the foot of a precipice on Salamji where they had been pushed and thrown. Almost all those killed were Galla, who, as infidels and traditional enemies of the Christian Amhara, were generally the first to suffer from the emperor's anger. It seems that on this occasion few, if any, of his own people were molested.

At six o'clock the following morning Waldmeier was summoned to join Theodorus on the heights of Fala, where he was watching the approach of the British forces. It was Good Friday, 10 April. The emperor was still in what Waldmeier described as a dark and dangerous mood, and he made the loyal and long-suffering Swiss missionary say a dramatic farewell to his wife, and then walk barefoot as if he were

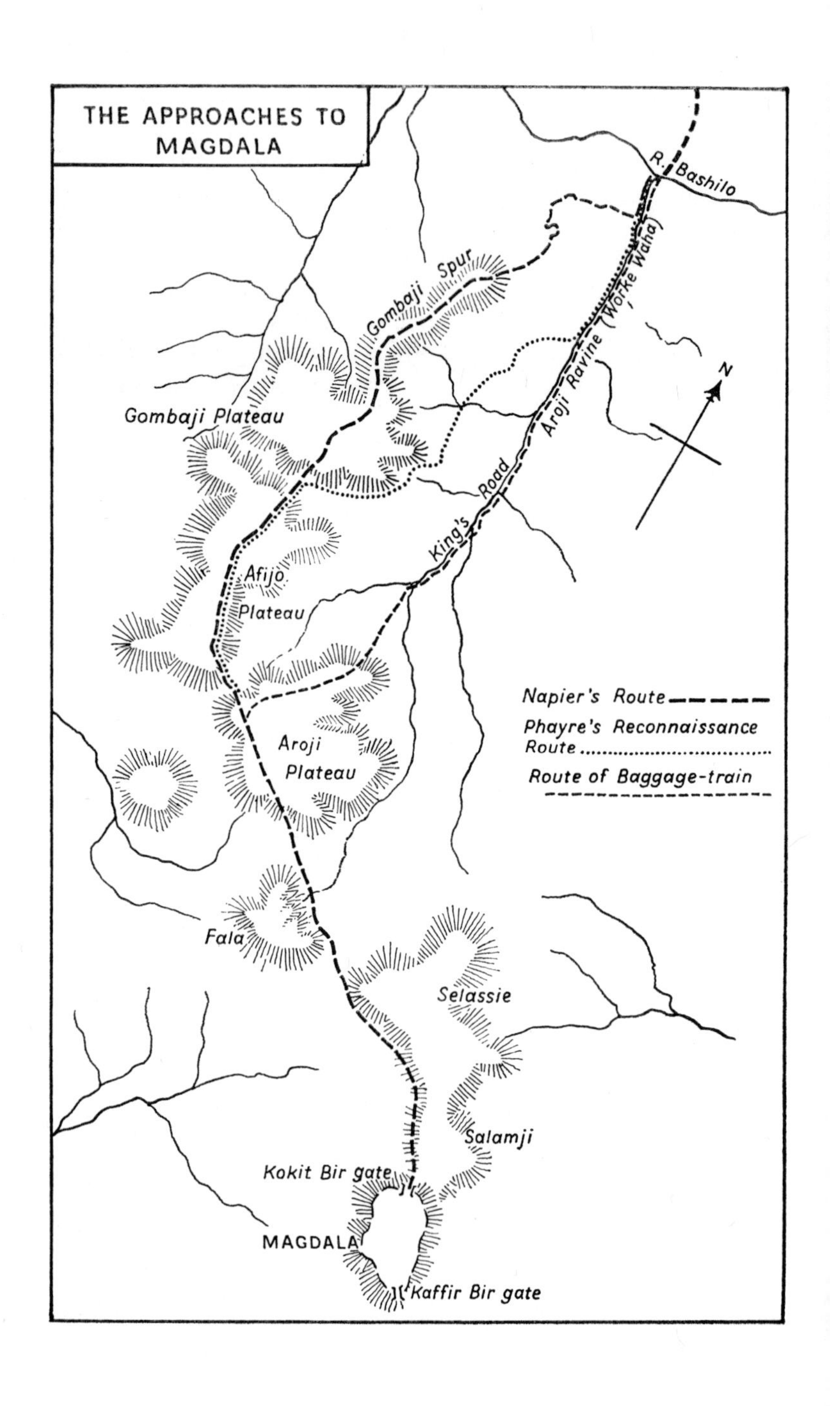
THE APPROACHES TO MAGDALA
R. Bashilo
Gombaji Spur
Worke Waha
Aroji Ravine
N
Gombaji Plateau
King's Road
Afijo
Plateau
Napier's Route
Phayre's Reconnaissance Route
Route of Baggage-train
Aroji
Plateau
Fala
Selassie
Salamji
Kokit Bir gate
MAGDALA
Kaffir Bir gate

Adi Woka, from a sketch by R. R. Holmes

The Taccaze Valley

The Storming of Magdala, as seen from Salamji

The head of Theodorus, sketched by R. R. Holmes immediately after the emperor's death.

A twentieth-century Ethiopian oil-painting of events at the capture of Magdala. Profile conventionally denoted evil.

going to his execution. Soon afterwards the emperor's mood changed. He reappeared in a flowing robe adorned with gold and silver thread, and started to move some of his guns from Salamji to Fala. It was at this point that Napier's letter of 3 April was at last delivered. But the die was cast, and he would not read it. 'Let the letter be kept in the messenger's pocket, and it can go back to its master because I shall not receive it; it would not change my mind.'

By this time Theodorus had concentrated most of his troops on Fala and Selassie, leaving only a few on Salamji to fire and guard the guns, and no more than 50 inside the fortress itself. Early in the afternoon, as the British troops began to move up towards the fortress, he addressed his forces. 'My children,' he said, 'be not afraid of these English soldiers because they are like the Philistines who made war against David; but remember David smote them, and in the name of God I shall conquer.' Then, taking on the role of the dead Abuna Salama, he absolved all those who should fall in battle. From his vantage-point on Fala the emperor later saw what appeared to be a column of 600 or 700 British and Indian soldiers coming up the valley on the road which he and Waldmeier had made to bring the guns up to Magdala from the Bashilo. The column contained a large number of mules, and Theodorus took it to be a baggage-train which for some unaccountable reason had been sent on ahead. According to Waldmeier, Theodorus wanted to wait and see what was coming on behind, but his troops were impatient to attack what seemed such a rich and easy target, and in the end he ordered his guns to open fire, and soon afterwards let his forces go. Moments later thousands of his excited soldiers and horsemen were moving silently and with menacing speed down the precipitous slope of Fala towards the seemingly unsuspecting and unprepared enemy in the valley below.

When Napier began his advance on the morning of 10 April the last thing he had in mind was a battle. He knew from careful reconnaissance that the descent to the bed of the Bashilo would be hard going. It meant a drop of 3900 feet in four and a half miles by a series of steep and awkward terraces. The river itself was at that time only waist-deep, but with rain about, and heavy clouds in the morning sky, it could quickly become a dangerous torrent. The climb up the other side of the river was equally steep, and appeared to involve a march of several miles before a possible camp-site could be reached. Moreover the country on the south side of the Bashilo looked particularly difficult. The *Times* correspondent said that it looked as if it had been cut up by a knife—'one huge, tangled, inextricable mass of hills, scarps and ravines lying like the labyrinth which protected Fair Rosamund'.[1] In view of this, Napier naturally did not want his troops to have to fight on the same day as they crossed the Bashilo. All he wanted at this stage was to send forward a sufficient force to carry out a detailed survey of the approaches to the fortress of Magdala without getting so close as to provoke an attack. This difficult task he entrusted once again to Colonel Phayre, supported by a balanced force of about 1800 men under the command of General Staveley.

The easiest and shortest route to the Aroji plateau, which Napier set as the limit and the probable camping-place of the first day's advance, was by the King's Road. But this route had two serious disadvantages. It followed the line of a dry river-bed known as Worke Waha, or the Aroji ravine, whose steep, rocky slopes and narrow bed made it particularly easy for an enemy to ambush. The other disadvantage was that it was the one Napier would be expected to choose. He therefore issued orders to Staveley and to Phayre that the King's Road and the Aroji ravine were not to be used. He told them that instead they must find a way up on the right by the steep ridge marked on the map as the Gombaji spur.[2] The commander of the 1st Brigade, Brigadier-General Schneider, was instructed to occupy this ridge and camp for the night at some suitable place in that vicinity, while the orders to the Royal Engineers and the Indian sappers and miners were to improve the way up to the Gombaji plateau and make it passable for the mules and the elephants which were following on behind with the guns and the rations. Phayre's precise orders were to reconnoitre forward from the spur 'towards Arrogie and Fahla'.

The first to move that morning were the forward units of the 1st Brigade, who left their camp on the plateau above the gorge of the Bashilo at dawn. With them went Colonel Phayre with his reconnaiss-

[1] Fair Rosamund was one of Henry II's mistresses, who, to quote the antiquary John Stow, 'dyed at Woodstocke where King Henry made for her a house of wonderful working so that no man or woman might come to her but that he had been instructed by the King. This house after some was called Labyrinthus, or Dedalus worke, wrought like unto a knot in a garden called a maze; but it was commonly said that lastly the queene Elianor came to her by a clue of thriddle or slike, and so dealt with her that she lived not long after. . . .'

[2] Also spelt Gombage, Gumbaji, Gombagee, and Gunborji.

ance party. The 2nd Brigade followed at 10 o'clock, and with them went Napier himself and his staff. The descent was even harder going than had been expected, and the marching troops noted with irreverent satisfaction that the staff were undergoing the rare experience of having to use their feet while they dragged their reluctant horses behind them. It was hot and humid and airless in the 4000-foot gorge, and with the river glinting in the sun below, many of the soldiers disobeyed orders and drank all the water in their bottles on the march down; when they reached the river and found that the water was too dirty to drink they naturally blamed everyone but themselves. The going was so bad that a rest was ordered on the banks of the river. The men also had orders to take off their boots and socks for the crossing, with the result that the 2nd Brigade began to arrive before the last of the 1st Brigade had crossed, put on its boots again, and was ready to start the climb up the other side. There was thus considerable congestion and confusion in the wide and partially dry river bed, and it was fortunate for the expeditionary force that there were no enemy forces there to take advantage of the situation.

Soon after midday, the British and Indian infantry units of the 1st Brigade started the long, hard climb up the Gombaji spur to the flat tableland above, a description which prompted the comment that, if this was a tableland, then the bloody table had been put the wrong way up and they were climbing up and down the bloody legs. General Staveley went with them, but he had been suffering from rheumatism, and the hard going made him short-tempered with his staff. But Colonel Phayre and his party of sappers and miners went another way. They followed the King's Road up the Aroji ravine for about half a mile before they branched off and made their way up the steep right-hand side of the ravine to a small plateau called Afijo, which was between the Gombaji spur and the Aroji plateau. Why exactly Phayre took this route, despite Napier's written orders, is not clear, but the most likely explanation seems to be that a closer inspection of the terrain of the Gombaji spur made him realize that this steep, cross-country route might be all right for infantry but that it simply could not be made passable in the time available for the mules and elephants bringing up the guns and the essential supplies of the advance force, and that the direct way up the King's Road would therefore have to be risked. Whatever his reasons, Phayre must have been very relieved to find no signs of the enemy in the Aroji ravine, and to be able to see with his own eyes when he got to the top of the hill on the right, that it really was undefended and free of ambushers. He thereupon sent a message back to General Staveley, who was still making his slow and painful way up the Gombaji spur, to tell him that the route up the Aroji ravine by the King's Road was safe, and to this he added an assurance that the head of the Aroji ravine had already been secured. Staveley sent this message straight back to Napier, who by this time had reached the bank of the river, where he had planned to camp for the night with the 2nd Brigade. When Napier got this news he changed his plans. He ordered the guns and the baggage of the 1st Brigade to go up the King's Road at once and to meet the infantry in the vicinity of the Aroji plateau, and he and his staff then set off at speed on their horses up the Gombaji spur in the track of the infantry. Napier was still under the impression that Phayre and his sappers had gone this way too, according to their orders, and he was surprised to see no signs that the sappers had been at work improving the track. He was even more surprised when he reached a vantage-point on the Afijo plateau to look down to the head of the Aroji ravine, where the road came out of the valley, and to see no evidence that it had been secured by his troops as Phayre's message had said.

It was a critical situation, not only for Napier but also, one imagines, for General Staveley and Colonel Phayre, who had joined him there. There was, however, no time for explanation or recrimination. The head of the column of guns and supplies which Napier had sent up the King's Road, could already be seen emerging from the ravine, and it was clear that as soon as they reached the open ground of the Aroji plateau they would be exposed both to the emperor's guns on Fala and Salamji, and to surprise attack. With all the urgency and command that he could muster Napier ordered the Sikhs of the 23rd Pioneers to go down at speed from Afijo and occupy the head of the valley, and at the same time he sent his A.D.C. off at the gallop to rush up the British troops of the King's Own Royal regiment, who were coming slowly on behind. He must have had his doubts about their effectiveness at that particular juncture as, not long before, he had himself passed them on his horse, looking and sounding exhausted, discouraged, and thoroughly bloody-minded at the steepness and roughness of the climb, at the heaviness of their greatcoats and blankets, and at their lack of water. When Napier's urgent message reached them many were lying flat out on their backs. But when they got their orders they were for the most part quickly on their feet, and moving forward. Officious staff officers in a hurry on horseback were a common enough phenomenon, but the prospect of some action, and perhaps some looting on the side, evoked an immediate response.

It was now about 4 o'clock in the afternoon. From his commanding position on the Afijo plateau Napier had been looking anxiously at the guns which Theodorus had positioned on Fala; but the general opinion was that at 3000 yards they were probably too far away to be a danger. There were other guns on Salamji and Selassie, but they were even further away. Suddenly there was a puff of smoke. A moment later a ball of heavy roundshot thudded into the ground behind where Napier sat on his horse, a deliberately conspicuous figure in a white tunic for the benefit of his troops. Although the silhouettes of the guns and the gun-crews on the crest of Fala were visible to the British troops, there was no sign of any other soldiers. But as the other guns on Fala began to open fire, the outline of the hill started to change, and, as suddenly as the first gun had opened fire, the summit of the hill was seen to be lined from end to end with an unbroken line of horses and men.

Fast as they moved down the steep slope, it took the Abyssinian forces some time to cover the distance of 3000 yards and the fall of 1400 feet between their starting-point on Fala and the flat ground at the head of the Aroji ravine. While their troops streamed down the hillside the Abyssinian cannonade continued. Most of the shot were round balls of stone, but some consisted of two halves of a ball joined by links of chain like the old-fashioned chain-shot which was used at the Battle of Trafalgar to rake the decks and cut the rigging. They made a sinister and disturbing noise as they whistled through the air, and some members of Napier's staff had difficulty in emulating their chief's aplomb.

The emperor's fire was mainly directed against the troops at the head of the ravine, where the Punjabi Pioneers were now in position protecting the artillery and baggage coming up the King's Road. It was well-directed fire, but it was largely ineffective, partly because excessive charges of powder were used, which caused the shot to overcarry, but mainly because the guns were situated so high up that the shot fell out of the sky, so to speak, and only did damage where they landed instead of raking the ground and harming what was in the way.

As the Abyssinian forces were coming down the slope of Fala, the tired soldiers of the King's Own regiment were negotiating the fall of 700 feet and the distance of about 1200 yards which separated the crest of Afijo from the plain of Aroji. Many of them dropped their heavy packs as they ran forward, with the tough but poorly armed mountain tribesmen of the 27th Baluchi regiment, and detachments of Royal Engineers and Indian sappers and miners in close support. They moved with such speed that they were all in position across the width of the Aroji plateau by the time the first of the Abyssinian troops reached the bottom of the slope, and had paused briefly to reform before they started to come forward in a solid mass of horsemen and foot soldiers nearly 1500 yards wide and six or seven men deep.

They were an awesome sight. The forces which the emperor unleashed against Napier's soldiers that afternoon came down from Fala with the proud, confident bearing of soldiers used to winning, and unafraid of death.[1] They were soon complemented by others coming down the slopes from Selassie on the left. There were no distinct bodies of cavalry to be seen, but about five hundred of the leaders and the vanguard were mounted on fast, sure-footed mountain ponies or tough-looking mules. Some of the leading men wore shirts and cloaks of crimson or scarlet silk, and as they advanced at a steady, purposeful trot they looked in the swirling mountain mist more colourful than the men of the King's Own in their stained and dusty khaki.

The first on the British side to open fire were the Naval Rocket Brigade with their new and comparatively untried light metal tubes which projected long-distance 6 lb rockets with fiery tails of smoke that looked and sounded more alarming than they were.[2] They were firing over the heads of their own troops from their position near Napier on Afijo, and they were, according to the man from *The Times*, more dangerous at first to friend than to foe. The enemy's main thrust at this point was on the flat ground of the Aroji plateau, where they were faced by the British soldiers of the King's Own. There were in fact less than three hundred men of the regiment on the plateau as two companies had been detached to guard the baggage train and were at that moment strung along the length of the King's Road in the Aroji ravine. The British troops may have been few in number, and they were

[1] Estimates by eye-witnesses varied from 3500 to 7000.

[2] The Naval Rocket Brigade was by many accounts the élite of the British force. Its sailors, who were armed with cutlasses as well as the latest quick-firing Snider rifles, were particularly well-turned out, cheerful, hard-working, and well-disciplined. They were notably careful in loading their mules, and generally treated them with a kindness which was repaid with amiability and stoicism on the part of the mules. The sailors struck up a great friendship with the Sikhs of the Punjabi Pioneers, and they made a point of camping next to one another for mutual jollity. The fact that few had a word in common did not seem to matter.

tired and thirsty after their long climb up the spur but they had one overwhelming advantage. They were armed with the latest breech-loading Snider rifles which, as explained earlier, could fire six or seven rounds a minute.[1] These Snider rifles were effective at 500 yards, but Colonel Cameron, who was commanding the King's Own, held his soldiers' fire until the advancing Abyssinians were 250 yards from the British troops.

The first burst of fire caused many casualties; among them, picked out by several marksmen under the impression from his dress that he was the emperor, was Theodorus' oldest and most trusted general, Fitaurari Gabri, who had led the advancing troops down the slope and across the plain in a tunic of crimson laced with gold. The Abyssinian soldiers were accustomed to losing men in the first burst of fire, and the first British volley did not halt their steady advance. Brandishing their guns and spears, they shouted their defiance and their menace as they closed in for the kill, as was their custom, during the interval while their opponents were reloading. But this time there was no interval. They were met instead by an almost continuous blaze of fire. It was the first time they had encountered breech-loading rifles which could fire at such a rapid rate. Hundreds fell and hundreds died before the line of soldiers wavered and broke, and scattered. But they did not run far. They were astonished and dismayed, but not demoralized or defeated, and they took what cover they could behind rocks and bushes, and returned their enemy's fire with their cumbersome and slow-firing muzzle-loading muskets. One group of sixty or seventy men did not waver, and managed to get within 100 yards of the British line before they too turned aside and went for cover. Another group even tried unsuccessfully to get round the flank of the British line. When they believed that the Abyssinian assault had been finally contained and repulsed, the British troops began to follow them across the plain. By now the swirling mountain mist had turned first to drizzle and then to steady rain. The clouds were low and threatening, and it was getting dark. Napier had watched the battle from his vantage-point on Afijo, and when he thought his troops had gone far enough he gave the order to halt and break off the engagement.

As the main body was advancing towards the British troops on the Aroji plateau, part of the Abyssinian forces which had come down from

[1] One of these rifles is on display in the exhibit of the Abyssinian War of 1868 in the National Army Museum in London.

Fala and Selassie veered round to their right and made for what looked like the vulnerable and tempting line of baggage mules coming up the King's Road. A train of heavily laden baggage mules indeed it was, but the mistake the Abyssinians made was that the mules in front were not carrying rations or tents but the guns of a light mountain battery. The guns were quickly unloaded and set up, but accounts differ of how effective their fire was in arresting the Abyssinian advance. The guns had been set up in a semi-circle in order to concentrate their fire, and they did not start firing until the enemy was four or five hundred yards away. Even so they failed to halt the Abyssinian assault, and in the end it was the Sikhs of the Punjabi Pioneers who stopped it. Although they fired a volley or two at the advancing thousands, the old, smooth-bored muzzle-loaders with which the Sikhs were armed were too slow and inaccurate to hold such a fearless and determined enemy. The Sikhs' muzzle-loaders may have been ineffective as firearms but they did have bayonets. In hand-to-hand fighting few could match the bearded, strongly built, and ruthless Sikhs. In half an hour the bands of lithe, light-boned Amhara warriors were destroyed.

Some of the Abyssinians on the far right of the attack managed to avoid the Punjabi Pioneers and made straight for the mules of the transport train, only to be met by the detachment of the King's Own which was escorting them. Here again the power of the Snider rifles was decisive. Faced with their rapid and accurate fire, the Abyssinians turned, and tried to escape up the line of the King's Road. But the triumphant Sikhs were waiting for them on the slopes of the ravine, and those who escaped the bayonets there were cut down on the plain by the guns of the mountain battery firing over open sights. In the pouring rain and the rumbling thunder the remnants of Theodorus' defeated army scrambled up the slopes of Fala, or crouched behind bushes and rocks for the darkness to cover their retreat.

Napier's soldiers spent the night on the battlefield, each man standing by his arms in case of another surprise attack. Many had had nothing to eat all day, and no water to drink since the morning. They were not allowed to light fires and to put up tents, and they had to lie on the ground huddled in their greatcoats, cold, wet, and hungry. Napier's troops did not really expect another attack after the afternoon's massacre, but nevertheless they kept a careful watch; it was some time before they realized that the lights moving on the slopes of Fala and Selassie were the torches and flares of comrades and womenfolk looking for the dead, the dying, and the wounded Abyssinian soldiers. It was a long, miserable night for everyone, and it was made piteous and hideous by the cries of the wounded calling for help, and the chattering and snuffling of the hyaenas and jackals. As soon as it got light, parties of British and Indian soldiers went out to bury the Abyssinian dead. Their orders may have been largely based on reasons of hygiene, but it seems to have been just ordinary compassion which moved some of the British soldiers to bring nearly a hundred of the wounded into their field hospitals, and to offer their water-bottles to those who could or would not be moved. These British soldiers noted with admiration that none of the Abyssinian soldiers had thrown away their arms to facilitate their escape, as they knew most European troops would have done; each man seemed to have died or fallen with his weapons still in his hands or close by his side.

The number of Abyssinian soldiers buried by Napier's troops that morning was 560, but it was estimated that altogether about 700 of the emperor's soldiers were killed in the battle of Aroji, and about 1500 wounded. The British expedition's casualties were 20, of whom two later died.

CHAPTER XV

The assault

The emperor was on Fala with his guns during the battle, and he remained there afterwards until well into the night. Waldmeier, who stayed with him, described him as being between anger and despair. His anger was sharpened by the realization that part of the fault was his own. When he ordered the guns to open fire, and allowed his impatient troops to attack, he believed that all that lay before them then was a baggage train of mules guarded by six or seven hundred soldiers. He did not know that the leading mules were carrying the steel guns of a light mountain battery, nor did he know that the main part of the advance force was moving up from the Gombaji spur, screened from his view by the scarp of Afijo. His outward show of anger was mainly directed against his gunners. Although Waldmeier and Saalmüller had aligned the guns and calculated the charges of gunpowder, the actual loading and firing was under the direction of an Egyptian Copt, and a man described afterwards by Dr Blanc as 'the half-Abyssinian son of a converted Bengali Jew'. The ineffectiveness of the artillery which he had so laboriously dragged all the way from Debra Tabor and of which he was so proud, particularly vexed the emperor, and he became dangerously angry, 'trembling with rage and gnashing his teeth in his fury', when one of his largest and most prized guns called Theodorus burst its barrel the first time it was fired. The despair was caused by the rout of his army by what he now realized was merely the vanguard of the British force. His defeat was made all the harder to bear by the cries of his wounded and dying soldiers, and by the lamentations of the women.

It was late at night when he left Fala and returned to his tent on Salamji. Near midnight he sent for Waldmeier and Flad, and told them to take a message to Rassam, who, with the other captives, was still confined in the fortress. It was a verbal message. 'I, the King of Ethiopia, was under the impression that I was the only strong man in my country but God has shown me stronger men. I ask thy advice about a reconciliation'. Rassam composed the kind of petition that he thought the emperor had in mind, and suggested that Prideaux and Martin Flad should be sent to General Napier's camp to deliver it, accompanied by an Abyssinian emissary of the emperor's choice and an interpreter. Theodorus at first seemed disposed to agree, but, as was apt to happen, his mood suddenly changed: 'There is no hurry about sending to the English. Let God do what he pleases. Now go to sleep.' At four o'clock in the morning he changed his mind again, and at dawn the following morning his emissary and an interpreter set off with Prideaux and Flad for Napier's camp under a flag of truce. The emperor watched their progress through his telescope. He saw too that during the night Napier's forces on the Aroji plateau had doubled in size with the arrival of the 2nd Brigade, and that the light mountain guns and naval rockets had been supplemented by the much more powerful Armstrong guns and the heavy mortars which had been brought up in the night by the elephants.[1]

Napier made a special point of showing both the elephants and the heavy artillery to the emperor's emissary when he arrived, and, while he treated him with a courtesy and respect which did not go unnoticed, he made it clear verbally that unless the emperor gave up both himself and all his Europeans, he and his army would be destroyed wherever they might go and however long it might take. Napier's written reply was more conciliatory in its tone, but its meaning was equally clear:

> Your Majesty has fought like a brave man, and has been overcome by the superior power of the British Army. It is my desire that no more blood may be shed. If, therefore, your Majesty will submit to the Queen of England, and bring all the Europeans now in your Majesty's hands, and deliver them safely, this day, in the British camp, I guarantee honourable treatment for yourself, and all the members of your family.

Lieutenant Prideaux recorded afterwards how the emperor had received these messages when they were taken back to him. 'His lips, always thin as a sword's, quivered nervously and the horseshoe on his forehead grew deeper. "What do they mean", he asked, "by honourable treatment? Do they mean to treat me honourably as their prisoner, or do they intend to assist me in recovering my country from the rebels?"'

[1] The Armstrong guns, which weighed nearly 1000 lbs each, originally had teams of eight horses to draw them, but after a number of accidents on the steep slopes, and other occasions when the guns had to be dragged by men with ropes, Napier had two elephants attached to each battery for their carriage.

Prideaux and Flad, who had returned somewhat reluctantly to the emperor's camp, wisely avoided trying to answer questions to which it was unlikely that anyone, including Napier, knew the ultimate answer. In the end Theodorus told Prideaux and Flad to wait outside his tent while he considered, and then dictated his reply to Napier's letter. He began as he meant to continue: 'Thus Kassa, whose trust is in God, speaks . . .'. He went on: 'Believing myself to be a great lord I gave you battle; but by reason of the worthlessness of my artillery all my pains were as nought. I had intended, if God so decreed, to conquer the whole world, and it was my desire to die if my purpose could not be fulfilled. Since the day of my birth till now no man has dared to lay hands on me. . . .' He ended his letter on the same note: 'A warrior who has dandled strong men in his arms like infants will never suffer himself to be dandled in the arms of others.'

Prideaux and Flad were told to take this letter to General Napier, 'that servant of a woman', as Theodorus scornfully called him in front of his own supporters. To make his refusal to surrender more pointed and provocative, he sent back Napier's own letter as well. Waldmeier again recounted how, after they had gone, the emperor sat on a rock looking once more 'gloomy and dark as night'. Then he stood up, drank some water, and started to pray. After making the sign of the cross, he drew a pistol, put it in his mouth, and pulled the trigger. It failed to fire the first time, and his attendants managed to wrest the pistol from the emperor's hand before it eventually went off and the bullet grazed his head. They then did their best to persuade Theodorus to make some gesture of conciliation to Napier before it was too late. In the end he agreed. Soon after 4 o'clock in the afternoon of 11 April he told Rassam to go with his fellow captives and make their way to the British camp. Rassam, treading warily as a cat and hardly daring to believe that the moment of release had really come, decided to put on his official uniform, and pay his last respects to the emperor. He went alone. He was not the only one to fear that if Theodorus set eyes on the others, or if one of them said or did something out of turn, he might still change his mind. The captives' last sight of the emperor was of him standing defiantly on a ledge in the gathering dusk, surrounded by some twenty of his followers and holding a double-barrelled rifle as if he and his small company were still ready to take on the whole British force on their own.

It was well after dark by the time the Magdala captives reached the

British lines, and were shown into the tent where Napier sat austerely in the light of a single lamp. There were ten of them in all—Rassam and Blanc, together with Prideaux, whom they had met on the way returning to Magdala after delivering the emperor's letter, Cameron with his Irish secretary, Kerans, and Pietro, his Italian manservant, Stern and Rosenthal, the two Jews' Society missionaries, and Mrs. Rosenthal and her child. Mrs. Flad had stayed in the fortress with her husband.

It should have been an occasion of great elation and relief both for the captives, and for Napier and his forces. This was the moment the captives had waited for, month after month, and in some cases year after year. For Napier these were the persons on whose behalf the whole expedition had been mounted, and whose release was his principal objective. When the time came, however, something was lacking on both sides. There was a certain holding back of applause and sympathy on the part of Napier and his men at the discovery that those whose piteous lamentations had generated so much heat and hurt national pride, and had launched such a complex and costly expedition, should in the end turn out to look so sleek, well-nourished, and well-dressed.[1] The captives, for their part, experienced a sense of disappointment and anticlimax when they found that, in contrast to their well organized and well-servanted style of living at Magdala, they had to sleep on the ground in a crowded tent like the officers and men who had come to rescue them, and that, instead of the elegant dinner at a well-laid table followed by brandy and cigars which they had looked forward to, all they got, even in the commander-in-chief's own mess, was a soldier's ration of tough beef and chapattis washed down with sugarless and milkless tea.

The next day was Easter Sunday, 12 April. Early in the morning another messenger arrived in Napier's camp with a letter from the emperor. It was a very different letter from the one he had sent the day before, and unlike the earlier letter it was properly sealed. Translated, it ran:

> In the name of the Father, the Son, and the Holy Ghost, one God;
> The King of Kings, Theodorus: May it reach the servant of the great Queen of England.

[1] The photograph with the shabby clothes and the chains facing p. 210 was taken later for the benefit of the Press and the captives' relations and friends. In fact Rassam, Blanc, and Prideaux wore their uniforms and highly polished boots, and, like Cameron, they all sported monocles which was something that particularly incensed the egalitarian Stanley. Stern was equally well turned out.

I am writing to you without being able to address you by name as our intercourse has arisen so unexpectedly. I am grieved at having sent you my writing of yesterday, and at having quarrelled with you, my friend. When I saw your manner of fighting, and the discipline of your army, and when my people failed to execute my orders, then I was consumed with sorrow to think that, although I killed and punished my soldiers, yet they would not return to the battle. While the fire of jealousy burned within me Satan came to me in the night, and tempted me to kill myself with my own pistol. But reflecting that God would be angry with me if I were to go in this manner, and leave my army without a protector, I sent to you in a hurry lest I might die, and all things be in confusion before my message should reach you. After my messenger had gone I cocked my pistol, and putting it in my mouth, pulled the trigger. Though I pulled and pulled, yet it would not go off. But when my people rushed upon me, and laid hold of the pistol, it was discharged just as they had drawn it from my mouth. God having thus signified that I should not die but live, I sent to you Mr. Rassam that same evening, that your heart might be made easy.

Today is Easter; be pleased to allow me to send a few cows to you.

The reason for my returning to you your letter yesterday was that I believed at that time that we should meet one another in heaven but never on earth.

I let the night pass without sending for the body of Fitaurari Gabri, because I thought that after my death we should both be buried together; but since I have lived, be pleased to allow him to be buried.

You require from me all the Europeans, even my best friend Waldmeier. Well, be it so; they shall go. But, now that we are friends, you must not leave me without artisans, as I am a lover of the mechanical arts. . . .

There seems little doubt that when Theodorus wrote this letter he believed, and had been led by Rassam and the Swiss artisans to believe that, if he released all the Magdala captives, and the other Europeans in his service, then Napier would probably regard the main objects of the expedition as having been achieved, and thus leave the emperor and his fortress alone, and return to his own country. Whether or not Rassam and Cameron, and the missionaries, really thought themselves this was true, they certainly did their best to persuade the emperor and his advisers that it was, as the best means of securing their own safety and eventual release. The emperor's offer of cows was a traditional Abyssinian gesture of peace, and their acceptance would similarly be taken as a sign that Napier regarded hostilities as being at an end. The Abyssinian court official and intermediary who carried this letter, was therefore instructed by Theodorus to find out from Rassam privately when he arrived at the British camp whether or not General Napier was willing to accept the cows. Neither the question nor the answers were put in writing. This, added to the fact that both the Amharic and the English versions of most of the letters and verbal messages had as a rule to be translated through the medium of Arabic, meant that there were often serious doubts about what was actually said or meant. What probably happened in this case is that when he was asked, Napier, thinking that, as stated in the letter, no more than a few cows were involved, and being assured that in this case no special significance need be attached to them, told Rassam that he would accept them, and that this reply was duly conveyed to the emperor. With this message about the cows, Napier also sent back the body of Fitaurari Gabri, an act which was not surprisingly taken by Theodorus as an additional assurance of peace and goodwill.

In view of this gesture and the assurance, Theodorus despatched the cows to Napier, and at the same time told all the missionary artisans to get ready to leave. When Napier learnt from Colonel Thesiger later that the 'few cows' which were on their way were in fact a traditional Abyssinian peace-offering of 1000 cows and 500 sheep, he at once realized the significance of the emperor's gestures, and the consequences of his acceptance. He immediately gave orders, therefore, that the livestock should not be allowed into the British camp. His terms for peace were still that the emperor must surrender not only all his Europeans but himself as well.

Theodorus watched the progress of his gift of livestock through his telescope. When he saw that the cows and the sheep were not being allowed through the British lines he played his last card. He told the artisans and the others to go to the British camp with their families and belongings. When they had gone, he turned to his followers and said, 'Surely it is peace, now that they have taken my power from me—surely it is peace.'

The party of Swiss artisans and other Europeans together with their various households was a large one. The Europeans themselves and their families amounted to over fifty people, and they took with them 187 Abyssinian servants and 323 domestic animals. They also had quantities of tents and baggage belonging both to them, and to the Magdala captives who had been released the previous day. It took this large concourse some time to make the journey down the hill and through the outposts and outer perimeters of the British camp on the Aroji plateau, and it was late in the afternoon before the Emperor Theodorus, watching the proceedings again through his telescope, realized that his last card had been played in vain. His gift of cows and sheep was still finally excluded from the British lines. Now he knew that the only courses left to him and his followers were to surrender, to flee, or to fight.

When Napier had sent his ultimatum to the emperor on Saturday 11 April, he had given him 24 hours to reply. By the morning of Easter Monday Theodorus had surrendered the captives and the rest of the Europeans but he had not surrendered himself. Napier therefore gave orders for his troops to be drawn up for an assault on the fortress.

There must have been moments as Napier waited that morning for news of the emperor's movements, when he wondered whether he should press on with the assault or not. His original instructions from London were imprecise in several respects, but it was clear that the release of the British captives, and to a lesser extent that of the other Europeans, was the real objective of the expedition, and that no punitive action against the person or territory of the emperor was envisaged unless he harmed the prisoners. The demand that Theodorus should give himself up was Napier's own condition, and he knew therefore that he could hardly be criticized or arraigned by either the civil or the military authorities to which he was responsible if he now decided not to enforce this part of his ultimatum. Apart from this, Napier had now seen for himself at close quarters that the natural defences of Fala and the natural and man-made defences of Magdala itself, were very strong indeed, and that if they were well defended he could not expect to capture them without incurring heavy losses. In one of his despatches he described the fortress of Magdala as one of the strongest he had ever seen. He did not doubt that his troops would fight if they had to, but he had sensed that since the battle of Aroji a certain diminution of bellicose enthusiasm had spread, like some mild infectious disease, through the ranks of his officers and men. This feeling had two quite separate causes. One was that a close view after the battle of the terrible wounds inflicted by the Snider rifles and the British artillery, and the memory of the courage and determination of the Abyssinian soldiers, made many of the English soldiers in particular feel that it was an unequal contest and a one-sided slaughter which they had no wish to repeat. The other was the condition of the host captives released from the emperor's camp the previous afternoon. Rassam and the other Magdala captives had come in unaccompanied and unobtrusively the night before, but even they bore few visible signs of the privations and cruelties about which they and their supporters in England had so loudly complained. But it was the size, and the composition and the complexion, of the party which came on that Sunday afternoon which caused the initial sympathetic cheers of the troops to die away, and be replaced first by silence and finally by open laughter. Only two were British, and they were both Irishmen who had avoided the rigours of imprisonment at Magdala by offering their services to Theodorus; the others were Germans, Swiss, Hungarians, Austrians, or Frenchmen. One or two of them had wholly European wives of particularly prim and glum appearance; the rest had lively looking local consorts, and they had over the years acquired between them numbers of children who chattered among themselves excitedly in a strange mixture of German and Amharic.[1] But even the derisive laughter of the British soldiers developed a hollow ring when they discovered that the 61 Europeans they had suffered such discomforts to rescue possessed more tents between them than the total allowed to the whole military division of 5000 men.

In weighing up the pros and cons of pressing on with the assault on the emperor's fortress, General Napier had a number of other factors to consider too. The 5000 men in his advance division were already short of food. There was only one small spring on the Aroji plateau, and many of the pack mules normally used for bringing up the rations had had to be diverted to carrying barely drinkable water up from the muddy river Bashilo. An equally disturbing factor was the rain. There had been a heavy thunderstorm on the day of the battle of Aroji, and it had rained in the afternoon for several hours. Situated as he was, with 400 miles of difficult hilly country and several river gorges between him and his coastal base, he did not want to prolong his stay a day longer than he had to.

Napier had to balance these facts and arguments against an equally strong case for resuming and pushing on with his offensive. He had given his terms to his opponent. Rightly or wrongly, he had demanded that Theodorus should give himself up. All his training and experience in India disposed him against modifying his terms, whatever the

[1] In his autobiography Peter Ustinov claims descent from Magdalena, the daughter of 'a Swiss missionary and an Ethiopian lady', who was said to have been born in a tent during the assault on Magdala. The family folk-lore on which this claim is based does not name the Swiss missionary, but the evidence available suggests that it was Saalmüller: see p. 116. The usually unreliable Stanley speaks of a baby being born at this juncture, but her parents were a Pole, Moritz Hall, and his half-Abyssinian/half-Armenian wife (p. 117), and she was called Theodora.

difficulties, until all his conditions for peace had been met. As Napier himself put it in his official despatch

Moreover, we could not have reached Magdalla in this season unless we had been aided by the country. Kassa's supplies of flour had rendered us for the time independent of the failure of Zoulla to supply us. The grain of Enderta and Agame had enabled our transport animals to live and advance, but this aid was given in the full belief that we would rid the people of Theodore; and had we failed to do so, we should probably have had to fight our way out of the country. . . .

General Napier had been careful in his dealings with Kassai and with Gobazey's deputy not to commit himself in writing to removing the emperor from the scene, but there is no doubt that the help which they had already given to the expedition, and the help that would be expected of them on the way back, rested on the tacit understanding that he would be removed. As far as the Galla were concerned, Mir Akbar Ali had several times assured them that the emperor would be toppled, and Napier had eventually felt obliged to confirm this in writing to Imam Ahmed, the young son of Queen Mastiat. 'We have come this far with the army', he told him, 'to punish Theodorus for his ill-treatment of British and European servants.'

While Napier and his staff were debating these difficult decisions, news reached them that during the night the emperor had rallied some two thousand of his closest supporters with the intention of leaving the fortress by one if its southern exits, and making their way unencumbered by possessions or dependants to some remote province. The attempt was foiled by the encirclement of the bloodthirsty Galla tribesmen, who had been calling out in the night to the beleaguered Amhara with cries of 'O, come my beloved, come to my arms!', and whose vigilance that morning had been sharpened by Napier's offer of a reward of the equivalent of ten thousand pounds for the capture of the emperor, dead or alive. Another reason why the emperor's attempt to flee failed was that in the end many of his followers refused to go with him, preferring when it came to the point to face the British rather than the Galla. Seeing that escape was impossible, Theodorus returned to his camp on Salamji and told his soldiers that he himself would now remain and fight to the end. Some elected to stay with him. He gave permission for the rest to go—to escape or to make what terms with the British they could.[1]

[1] The actual reports which Napier received at the time were somewhat less precise and more conflicting; the details given here are based on a statement made later by the emperor's gun-bearer, Wolde Gabri.

This news was brought to Napier's camp that morning by some of the chiefs and commanders who had taken advantage of this permission to leave the emperor's camp. Among them were the commanders of the Abyssinian forces on Fala and Selassie. Napier had always looked on Fala as the key to Magdala's defences, and his original plan of attack was based on taking it from the flank where his attacking forces would be screened from the guns on both Fala itself and on Selassie and Salamji. He knew that Theodorus had removed some of the guns from Fala after the battle, and now that the commander of its garrison had offered to surrender it in exchange for the safety of himself and his soldiers, Napier simply sent the troops he had originally earmarked for this part of his attack to carry out an unopposed occupation. The same thing happened in the case of Selassie. The commander of its garrison offered to surrender it if Napier would protect him and his forces from the dismembering knives of the Galla, and Waldmeier, who knew every inch of the terrain, then showed the British forces the best ways up its difficult approaches. There must have been many poignant moments for the emperor as, one by one, his commanders gave up the strong outer defences of his fortress without a fight, as even Waldmeier, whom he had liked and trusted more than any other European since John Bell, volunteered to show his enemies the secret paths and crevices.

With these twin bastions secured, Napier was able to send his assault force straight up the King's Road to Salamji, the saddle of open ground between Fala and Selassie, and immediately below the gates of the fortress. The flat ground on the Aroji plateau allowed the troops to assemble in proper, parade-ground style, after which they marched up the valley with the Duke of Wellington's regiment now in the lead again and marching cockily to the tune of Yankee Doodle played by the regimental band. They met no opposition or gunfire on the way, and the only things which hampered their advance were a gradient of 1 in 3, and large numbers of surrendering Abyssinian soldiers who, together with their women and children, were trying to make their way down the valley at the same time as the solders were going up. It was estimated that between twenty-five and thirty thousand people came out of the fortress of Magdala and its outposts that day, of whom about a third were armed with weapons of some kind. It was an extraordinary concourse of men, women, and children, with their flimsy nomad tents and household pots and jars, and their flocks of sheep and goats, and it reminded many of those who witnessed it of biblical pictures of the flight of the Israelites from Egypt. The men laid down their arms, and touched their heads to the ground in submission as they passed the British troops; and the women trilled *li! li! li!*, in the traditional salute reserved for yesterday's enemies who had become today's victorious friends.

Two other events of dramatic quality occurred before the curtain went up on the last act. When the first British troops reached Salamji they noticed a pungent smell. Looking over the edge of the plateau on the far side, they saw its causes on some ledges below the steep scarp. There were piles of naked human bodies, some three hundred in all, lying where they had fallen or been flung by the emperor and his soldiers four days before.

For several years people both in Britain and in India had been learning from their daily papers and the numerous weekly and monthly periodicals of that time, from reports of proceedings in parliament, from public lectures and private chatter, and frequently from sermons in church as well, that 'Theodore, the wicked king of Abyssinia', not only imprisoned consuls and ill-treated missionaries, but was a tyrannical savage, a monster of depravity and drink, and above all extremely cruel. The initial zeal engendered by these impressions had, however, begun to diminish even before the battle of Aroji. The nearer everyone got to Magdala, and the more they saw and heard for themselves in Abyssinia itself, the suspicion started to grow that the emperor Theodorus was just as likely to be a brave, resourceful, and energetic ruler, whose good intentions and patriotic ambitions were being thwarted by the ignorance and short-sightedness of his own subjects; and that the captives and other Europeans in his power were partly, and perhaps more than partly, to blame for the situation in which they found themselves. This change of attitude had, as has been seen, been accelerated by the battle itself and by the events of the following two days. And it was one which was by no means confined to the rank and file of the British expedition. It was indeed probably strongest at the top, in Napier himself, for example, and among some of his staff. It was one which was also shared, in their hearts if not always in their prose, by most of the correspondents of the Press. The pile of naked bodies rotting in the sun on Easter Monday provided a jolt to these impressions, and suddenly seemed to give a purpose and a rightness to the expedition which up to then had sometimes been lacking. Some of the bodies had been savaged during the night by hyaenas and jackals, but it was clear that others had been slashed and dismembered in the slaughter, and General Napier was not the only one who felt that it was an act of cruelty on the part of the emperor which justified, indeed necessitated, his capture or his destruction.

On the small plateau of Salamji there now occurred another event which underlined the medieval quality of nineteenth-century Abyssinia, and the Byzantine nature of the emperor himself, in an entirely different way. When what was left of the emperor's followers had finally abandoned Salamji and retreated to the protection of the fortress of Magdala, they had taken most of their guns with them, but a few had been left behind. One was the giant mortar Sebastopol, which had never been fired and was too heavy to be moved in the face of an advancing enemy.[1] It was left perforce to lie where it had been positioned on Selassie like the skeleton of a monster whose size was the cause of its own extinction. But some of the guns were small brass cannon, and suddenly the astonished British troops on the plateau saw a body of men, led by less than a dozen horsemen, come down from the fortress gate and try to carry the cannon away. One of the horsemen was dressed with deliberately conspicuous splendour in a white tunic of gold embroidered silk and a lion's-skin mantle, and was armed with a rifle, a spear, and a sword. Captain Speedy recognized him at once as the emperor. In a show of stylized bravery and defiance, Theodorus and his fellow horsemen galloped towards the British troops, firing their rifles in the air and brandishing their spears, shouting loudly as custom decreed of their own prowess in battle, and of the cowardice of their opponents. Finally the emperor issued a challenge calling on anyone who dared, and on General Napier in particular, to settle the whole issue in single combat. Captain Speedy, with his six foot six inches of height and his fine reputation with the lance, asked to be allowed to accept the challenge. The British officer in command of the plateau felt obliged to refuse. There was a short, efficient burst of artillery fire as a sharp reminder that the year was 1868. The galloping and the shouting died away; the cannon were abandoned, and Theodorus and his small band of gallant, outmoded knights made their way back to their medieval castle and shut the wooden doors inside the gate.

At 3 o'clock in the afternoon of 13 April, with the distractions of

[1] Ethiopian tradition has it that the gunners refused to fire the giant mortar because 'the power of its voice will cause miscarriages to all the pregnant women in the country, and people who are gravely ill will die'.

prisoners of war, refugees, and romantic gestures out of the way, Napier began his assault on Magdala. The fortress consisted of a flat-topped plateau roughly three-quarters of a mile long and half a mile wide. The sides were sheer or almost sheer scarps of rock, except in two places. One was the entrance known as the Kaffir Bir on the far or southern side; it was from this gate that the emperor had planned to escape the previous night. The other place was the entrance called the Kokit Bir. Here there were two separate gates: an inner one linked to an outer gate by a short and very steep path between high boulders. The outer gate was about 300 feet above the level of the Salamji plateau where the British assault forces had been assembled; the only way to reach the gate was by an exposed, precipitous track with a very steep gradient.

Napier had spent some time that morning on the heights of Selassie trying to see with his telescope exactly what forces the emperor had with him inside the fortress, and how they were disposed. There were, in fact few soldiers to be seen, but like a prudent general he assumed that they were concealed behind the masonry of the gateway and the rough stone walls and thorn hedges of the ramparts on either side. He knew, from observation and from what Rassam and the others had told him, that the further parts of the fortress were largely taken up by non-combatant items—a Coptic church, the quarters where the emperor's family lived, the huts which housed his remaining Abyssinian hostages and prisoners, his treasury and stores, and the collection of religious books and paintings which Theodorus had amassed over the years for the church and monastery he one day hoped to build at Magdala.

In the end Napier positioned some of his artillery 1300 yards away on Selassie, and others twice as far away on Fala, in the expectation that most of its still somewhat unpredictable projectiles would fall roughly on the area of the gate and the ramparts, and leave the civilian areas more or less untouched. Although he still did not know how numerous the emperor's remaining forces inside the fortress were, he knew that he was up against a position of great natural and roughly fortified strength, and he decided to take no chances. Before he sent his infantry and sappers in to storm the fortress he used all the guns and mortars at his disposal to bombard the fortress in order, as he put it, 'to overpower the enemy's resistance and prevent the heavy casualties which I should otherwise have incurred'. It was a formidable assembly of the latest and most expensive ordnance—four 12-pounder Armstrong guns, twelve 7-pounder steel mountain guns, two 8-inch mortars, and 16 rocket tubes of the Naval Rocket Brigade. They continued their concentrated fire on the gate and ramparts of the fortress for more than an hour.

Precisely at 4 o'clock the British artillery, except for the more accurate light mountain guns, broke off the bombardment, and the assault troops started to go in. They looked a fine body of men, with a detachment of Royal Engineers and a force of Indian sappers from Madras leading the way in their scarlet uniforms, followed by ten companies of the Duke of Wellington's regiment in battle-dress khaki. They carried their regimental colours with them as they and other regiments had done since the eighteenth century. This was, as it happened, the last time they were ever to do so, but on this occasion they served a useful purpose. The young officer who carried them into action had been told to hold the colours up aloft where they could be seen by Napier and his staff as a signal that the fortress had been taken.

These sappers and the Duke of Wellington's regiment, the 33rd, were only the spearhead. There was considerably more in support, and in reserve—two further regiments of British infantry, the 45th Foot regiment and the 4th or the King's Own; another two companies of Indian sappers from Bombay together with the formidable Baluchis and the Punjabi Pioneers. The plan was for half the 33rd regiment to provide covering fire while the sappers went in to force or blow up the gate, and make a way for the rest of the regiment, and if needs be, the other assault troops, to take the fortress by storm.

As the sappers and the infantry began the steep ascent it started to rain. It was a heavy, blinding rain, and it hampered the advance rather more than the desultory enemy musket fire which was encountered on the way up. This musket fire, allied to the prospect of loot, liquor, and licence, seems to have excited the Irish soldiers, and despite the orders of their more prosaic English officers, they were soon 'firing and shout-like madmen'. It is unlikely that they hit any of the enemy at this stage, and it is more probable that the few superficial wounds suffered by the British and Indian sappers were mostly caused by this burst of Celtic enthusiasm. The situation of the leading sappers had indeed become very awkward at this point, with the heavily barricaded fortress gate barring their way in front, and the wild Irishmen of the 33rd regiment firing excitedly at their heels. In spite of the hour's bombardment by the British artillery the Kaffir Bir was still intact, and the sappers were unable to force its wooden doors open because, as was discovered afterwards, Theodorus had had a wall of stones 15 feet thick and 12 feet high piled up behind them. The call therefore went up for gunpowder to blast the gateway, for handsaws and axes to break down the ramparts, and for escalading ladders to climb them. No one answered the call. The truth was that, incredible though it now seems, the gunpowder, the saws, the axes, and the ladders had all been left behind. The official history of the campaign expressed the situation less directly. 'On arriving at the gateway the progress of the assailants was arrested, for it was closed, and the engineers had not at hand the powder-bags with which to blow it.' In his official despatch Napier, who was a loyal member of the Royal Engineers himself, disposed of the incident more obliquely: 'The Royal Engineers and Sappers, and leading sections of the 33rd Regiment were long before they could force an entrance, and during that time nine officers and men of the Royal Engineers and Sappers received wounds or contusions.'

Faced with the delay while powder and ladders were fetched, and the vulnerable position in which he and his men were placed, Major Cooper, the commander of the 33rd, decided that the only thing to do was to try and find a way into the fortress by breaching or scaling the ramparts on either side of the gateway. The cliffs of the fortress were in most places 'so precipitous that a cat could not climb them', as Austin put it, and in the vicinity of the gateway the natural hazards of the cliff had been reinforced with ramparts of stone surmounted by sharp stakes and hedges cut from thornbush with particularly nasty thorns. At one point, however, the scarp was no more than six or seven feet high, and an Irish soldier named Bergin, who was a very tall man, managed to get a toehold, and used his bayonet to clear a gap in the thornbush above. He then invited a small, lightweight drummer named Magner to get up on his shoulders from where he could just reach the top of the ramparts with his fingers. A vigorous push in the posterior with the butt of Bergin's rifle lifted him up and over the wall. Magner in turn reached down, and helped Bergin up. Bergin then gallantly protected the gap with rifle fire while others scrambled up in the same way until there were enough of them inside the fortress to attack the outer gate from the rear. The few visible defenders there retreated up the steep path to the upper gate, and an excited Ensign Wynter raised and waved the regimental colours of the 33rd as a sign that the main defences of the fortress had been successfully stormed.

The upper gate had not been closed behind the retreating Abyssinian soldiers, and when the leading British troops reached it they found that it was undefended, and that most of the enemy had laid down their arms. They did, however, see one man with a pistol in his hand. He quickly moved out of sight behind a stack of grass. Following him the soldiers heard the sound of a shot, and by the time they turned the corner the body was lying on the ground enveloped in a cloak. They turned the body over cautiously with their feet, with their bayonets at the ready, until they saw the gaping wound in the back of the head and knew that the man must be dead. The dead man's pistol was by his side. It was a handsome piece, with an inscribed silver plate let into the butt. The inscription read:

Presented
by
VICTORIA
Queen of Great Britain and Ireland
to
THEODORUS
Emperor of Abyssinia
As a slight token of her gratitude
For his kindness to her servant PLOWDEN
1864

From statements made later by Abyssinians who had stayed with the emperor to the end, it appeared that he had been defending the gate during the assault with no more than fifty to a hundred men, while another two hundred soldiers had retreated or been sent to other parts of the fortress. The emperor had taken cover during the bombardment, but despite this his chief minister and old friend Ras Engada was blown to pieces by a shell in front of his eyes. Theodorus showed no outward sign of emotion. All he said was, 'How can one fight with people who use such terrible missiles?' before he retreated to a safer position and changed into less conspicuous clothes. When the British infantry finally scaled the ramparts and turned the gate's defences, the emperor had told his followers to withdraw to the upper gate, and there he had released them from their allegiance and given them leave to go. Some tried to persuade him to lay down his own arms and surrender. But he refused, saying, 'Let us not fall into men's hands; they have no pity. Let us fall into God's'. Soon afterwards he had put his pistol into his mouth, and pulled the trigger.

From calculations made after the battle it appeared that the British artillery barrage had killed about twenty Abyssinian soldiers and civilians, and wounded a hundred and twenty others. The Snider rifles of the Royal Engineers and the Duke of Wellington's regiment accounted for a further 45 dead during the infantry assault. The British casualties were ten wounded, and five slightly hurt. One had a spear wound, and three were hit with splinters of rock. The rest were gunshot wounds from weapons not specified in the official reports.

Private Bergin and Drummer Magner were awarded the Victoria Cross, and there were numerous other rewards for bravery and devotion to duty. The Battle of Magdala, as it was called in the newspapers and periodicals of the day, was generally reported as a great victory for British arms, but, as a staff officer who was writing for *Blackwood's* at the time remarked, there was in truth 'little of stirring military incident or military prowess to record'. The *Times* correspondent, who tried hard to be fair and forgiving, added sadly: 'as a patriot, perhaps the less I say of this siege the better.'

CHAPTER XVI

The aftermath

Although it was not mentioned in Napier's despatches or in the official history of the expedition, the first thing the British and Indian soldiers did when they got into the fortress of Magdala was to plunder. It was still a common military practice, and no one, least of all in Abyssinia, would have expected anything else. But while it was a custom almost universally practised and accepted in the field, it had by 1868 become one of the comfortable illusions of those who remained at home in Victorian Britain that it belonged to the past; something that could, therefore, should it inconveniently ever come to light, be smugly condemned in the Press, in parliament, and the pulpit. By the standards of the time the British troops at Magdala seem to have been considerate and undemanding plunderers. What they, and particularly the Irish soldiers, wanted most was liquor. Next came saleable loot, then food. Women do not seem to have been high on their list of needs; they certainly evoked no mention as plunder even in the most critical and sensation-seeking of Press reports or in the most candid private diaries and letters.

In fact the pickings for the soldiers were poor, apart from copious supplies of *tej*, a kind of honey beer or mead which is apt to vary considerably in quality and taste. Food was harder to find. It was discovered that the provident and ruthless Emperor Theodorus had collected enough grain at Magdala to supply the garrison's needs for a six months' siege, but what both the officers and the men of British expeditionary force were looking for were tastier things to vary the monotony of their own basic rations; yet the most that young Ensign Wynter, for example, could find were 'some hen's eggs, being awfully hungry we ate them raw'. The stores looked more promising; among a chaotic disarray, Captain James saw

> arms from every country under the sun. Beautiful English breech-loading rifles in their cases, silver-mounted shields and spears. Harmoniums, Amharic and Arabic books, priestly vestments, crowns, censers, crosses, children's trains and toy soldiers, photographic apparatus and chests of beautiful

English tools. A hut full of salt bricks, another of sulphur, another hides and yokes. State umbrellas, silver drums, records of State blowing about, multitudes of English and Persian carpet silk. . . .

When it came to plunder, no one in Napier's army was apparently a match for any of what Stanley described as 'these gentlemen in black', the late emperor's missionary artisans who had the advantage of knowing where exactly to look and what to look for. One of their richest finds at Magdala was the coffin of Abuna Salama, who had been buried in his full canonical robes with his regalia. No one knows who took what, but when the coffin came to be officially examined, a diamond cross said to have been worth thousands of pounds was found to be missing.

With an experienced sense of judgement and timing Napier allowed the looting to take its course for a while in the knowledge that the only exits from the fortress were by gateways where everyone could be questioned and, if need be, searched. Everything taken inside the fortress was then collected and later put up for auction, and the prize money thus gained was divided equally among the troops. As the value of the booty was thought to be no more than £3000, the officers relinquished their share; in spite of this gesture, and the fact that the bidding was o brisk that the auction realized over £5000,[1] all each soldier got in the end was 15 rupees and 11 annas, or about twenty-five shillings. The only things which were not auctioned were weapons 'taken at the point of the bayonet', which were exempted under a very old rule of military lore, and a number of items which found their way illicitly or by special arrangement into private hands or regimental museums and messes.[2]

[1] The best bidder was Dr. Holmes of the British Museum. He used most of his allowance of £1000 to outbid everyone else and secure some 350 of the books from Theodorus' splendid collection of Ethiopian religious books and illuminated manuscripts. In making his choice he had the advice of the versatile and scholarly Munzinger, who obligingly wrote the title of each volume in English inside the front cover. Three hundred and forty-eight of these truly magnificent volumes, roughly but firmly bound in leather by Ethiopian craftsmen, are now in the Department of Printed Oriental Books in the British Museum. One of the books, a copy of the especially treasured Kebra Nagast which Theodorus is said to have kept under his pillow, was returned to Abyssinia in 1872.

[2] Among them was a crown which one of the Prussian officers attached to the expedition bought for £4 from a British soldier, and smuggled home under cover of what amounted to diplomatic immunity. He presented it to Prince Bismarck, who refused when asked to give it back to the British government. Other items, such as those taken by the Naval Rocket Brigade, are now in the Victoria and Albert Museum in South Kensington.

The emperor's crown and the royal seal were kept by Napier himself, and later presented to Queen Victoria.[1]

During their search for plunder the leading troops discovered the emperor's wife, Terunesh. They did not know who she was, and she was at first subjected to some coarse military humour, but when her identity as the emperor's abandoned wife became known one of the British soldiers slapped her cheerfully on the back and assured her that 'Todros was *mafish*'. To save her from further molestation Napier took her under his protection, so that the *Times* correspondent was able to observe that her features were 'delicate and well cut, the hands and feet small and exquisitely shaped'. Captain James was more direct, and called her 'a really pretty, fair girl about 25 with large eyes and long hair'. She was a sad, quiet girl by all accounts, and some of her delicate bloom was the transient beauty of the consumptive. She shared her quarters at Magdala with the emperor's current favourite, a plump, earthy, good-natured Galla girl whom everybody liked. With them too lived Alamayu, the only child of Theodorus' church marriage with Terunesh, who was described by James as 'a nice looking boy of about 8 years old', and by Dr. Austin as 'an intelligent, fine looking boy who is said to be like his father'. Theodorus had been very attached to his son and brought him up to play the part of a prince from an early age. Before he died at Magdala he made his peace with his wife, from whom he had been estranged for many years, and asked her in the event of his death to hand Alamayu over to the care and upbringing of the English.

Napier sent Theodorus' body to his family[2] for burial. Before doing so the careful Napier had a post-mortem examination carried out for

[1] This crown was happily returned to Ethiopia in 1925 as a gesture of Anglo-Ethiopian friendship. It was handed by George V personally to Ras Tafari, as the late Haile Selassie was known before he became Emperor of Ethiopia.

[2] When Napier offered Theodorus honourable treatment for himself and his family, the emperor facetiously replied that this would be expensive for the British government because his family was more numerous than the hairs on his head. In fact his family at Magdala consisted of his church-marriage wife, Terunesh, and her son, Alamayu; Mashesha, the recognized son of an earlier civil marriage, a man of about 30, who held several important posts under his father and later had his father's remains taken from Magdala and buried in Kwara; Hailu Kasa, another recognized son of a civil marriage to a Galla woman; a daughter of about 20, who had as a younger girl been given to Menelik as a temporary wife while he was held as a hostage at Magdala and who, after Menelik escaped, was given in more permanent marriage to a chief called Bareay; and two other daughters aged 5 and 3, whose mother came from Begemder.

confirmation that the emperor had died by his own hand. The emperor's body was then cleaned and clothed, and laid out on an Abyssinian bedstead in a circular hut. Many came to view it. Some of the Europeans who came had their expectations confirmed, and described his face as cruel and sensuous. Others had different impressions. Captain Hayward of the Sherwood Foresters thought that he must have been a 'fine looking man, tall and spare with rather a fine head'. The *Times* correspondent, whose first impression had been poor, revised his opinion when he had had a closer look. He found the emperor's face 'very striking, the features finely cut but more expressive of power and strength than delicacy or refinement—the brow massive and thoughtful, the lips thin and closely drawn, indicative of rare determination'. One of the last to see Theodorus' body was Lieutenant Prideaux. He thought he saw the trace of a smile on the dead man's lips, and was moved to record that, were it not for his cruelties, 'we might be tempted to forget our sufferings, and be glad that, having fought his fight well as a soldier in his youth, he had died as a soldier in his age'.

The body of the Emperor Theodorus, the son of Solomon, the Slave of Christ, the King of all the Kings of Ethiopia, was buried without ceremony in a shallow grave in unconsecrated ground by the ramshackle church of Medhani Alam at Magdala. As the usually compassionate Dr. Austin put it, in prim language that he knew would be understood by the hierarchical, church-going readers of *The Times*, 'as a suicide Theodorus could not of course be given Christian burial or military honours'. The shallow grave was filled in with stones, and then covered in straw. A few days later the church, like the rest of the fortress, went up in flames.

The emperor's suicide may have offended the establishment susceptibilities of Church and State in mid-Victorian England, but it solved what might otherwise have been one of Napier's, and ultimately H.M.G.'s most awkward problems. To have allowed him to remain in Abyssinia as a free man would, as Napier had already reported, have been regarded as a breach of faith and an act of weakness by his enemies and rivals which might well have prejudiced the expedition's safe return; while to have handed him over to those rivals would have been to condemn him to a fate which would have been in breach of the undertaking Napier had given him. To have taken him out of Abyssinia and accorded him the honourable treatment which was promised him would have provoked potent growls of displeasure in many quarters in Britain and in India, while harsher treatment would have provoked almost equally potent noises of protest from the liberal, the compassionate, and the sentimental. Comfortable, but not too comfortable exile to some remote but tolerably healthy place like St. Helena or the Seychelles would probably have attracted roughly equal disapproval from both sides, and would therefore have been the solution most likely to appeal to Her Majesty's Government.

There were, however, other problems. General Napier wanted to leave Magdala as soon as he possibly could, and get back with his soldiers to his Red Sea base before the coming rains and other hazards interferered with their return. There were nevertheless some things which he felt that in either duty, conscience, or prudence he ought to do before he left. The core of these problems was the disposal of the fortress of Magdala itself. The thousands and thousands of soldiers and civilians who had fled from it before and after the assault were already huddled in insanitary closeness against the unenthusiastic flanks of the British and Indian troops on Aroji, but the empty huts, the rifled stores and treasuries, and the formidable natural defences were still there. So too were the late emperor's guns and mortars, and his stores of ammunition.

Magdala lay within territory which had long ago been taken from the Amhara by the Galla, and had been held by them until it was recaptured by Theodorus some ten years before. It was therefore, immediately claimed as of right by each of the two rival Galla queens, and both hurried to Napier's camp to be the first to press their case in person.[1] Before he saw them Napier told Munzinger to speak to Mashasha, in case his master, the Wagshum Gobazey of Lasta, felt inclined to have it. The reason which Napier gave officially for this preference was that as a Christian, Gobazey could use the fortress to halt the advance of the Muslim Galla. One suspects, however, that, with 30,000 Christian Amhara refugees on his hands, he also saw the advantages of being able to leave them with a reasonably clear conscience in the care of a ruler who shared their religion and their language, instead of having to shoulder the burden himself of escorting them out of the reach of the waiting Galla. Gobazey declined the offer. His natural boundary, he

[1] The last ruler, Abu Shir, had, like a good Muslim, left more than one widow; and two of them, Mastiat and Werkait, were engaged in a bitter struggle for the throne.

explained through Mashasha, was the river Bashilo, and he had neither the troops nor the arms to hold an outpost in Galla territory. He showed more interest in the late emperor's guns, and even hinted that he might be prepared to take over all the British army's responsibilities at Magdala if the guns were handed over too. As Napier rightly guessed that this would impair his own relations with Ras Kassai, through whose territory he still had to pass, he reluctantly braced himself to receive the Galla queens and to listen with suitably British aplomb to their eloquent inexactitudes and insincerities.

The first queen to arrive was Werkait. Napier was impressed neither with her claim nor with her person. Werkait, whose son had been earlier taken hostage and killed by Theodorus, had the twin disadvantages of being middle-aged and having no male heir. Napier confined himself to urging her to make peace with her rival, to which Werkait replied, 'When two persons are striving for a crown how can peace be made between them? If Mastiat were to make peace with me today in your presence, she would betray me tomorrow.'

Napier's meeting with Queen Mastiat was more productive and more entertaining. Mastiat, whom Stanley described as 'fair, fat and forty', not only had a more attractive personality but she also had a male heir, a boy of six or seven, a splendidly attired and handsome youth who captivated everyone who met him. Nor was Mastiat herself without charm. She arrived for her meeting with the British general muffled up to the eyebrows, for mystery rather than for modesty, and armed with a sword, a spear, and a shield, and looking, as the *Times* correspondent noted, 'quite capable of leading her army anywhere'. Under the influence of Napier's hospitality and the arrival of a photographer she revealed more of her person and her personality, and impressed Napier and his staff, and the Press correspondents too, with her earthy humour and her capacity for food and liquor. Many of the dishes set before her by Napier's well-trained Indian cooks were new to her, and as Stanley put it, she ate her way through the menu in her own way, 'pudding before beef, blancmange with potatoes, drinking coffee before finishing her *fricandeau*, emitting labial smacks like pistol cracks when a more savory dish than common pleased her palate'. When Napier suggested that she too might make her peace with her rival she replied that if that Werkait were to swear friendship on the Koran itself today, she would violate her oath tomorrow.

In the end Napier decided that the best thing to do with Magdala was

Captain Speedy

European prisoners after their release, posed to show off their shackles. Left to right – on ground: Pietro, Lt. Prideaux, Kerans; seated: Rassam, Mrs. Rosenthal and child, Consul Cameron, Dr. Blanc; standing: Rosenthal, Stern.

Alamayu, portrait by William Simpson shortly after the storming of Magdala

Alamayu in England

to destroy all that the emperor Theodorus had put there—the guns, the fortifications, and all the makeshift buildings—and then leave it to the rival parties to fight it out. When he conveyed this decision to Mastiat, who stayed in his camp as his guest for several days, she agreed demurely that nothing but fire could purify such a wicked place. Napier and Mastiat seem to have understood one another, and it was perhaps no coincidence that when the promised destruction took place a day or two later, Queen Mastiat and her forces were in the right place at the right time to be the first to see if anything had escaped the flames, and to take possession of what remained of Theodorus' great fortress.

The destruction of Magdala took place on the afternoon of 17 April. The first to be destroyed were the guns and mortars, 37 in all, which Theodorus had acquired or had made in the home-made foundries of his missionary artisans. The guns had been examined by Napier's gunners and found to be in good condition, with adequate supplies of ammunition in the shape of cannon-balls made of stone, and metal casings filled with bullets or iron filings held in place by cow-dung. One of the largest pieces had, as mentioned, accidentally burst its barrel on Fala. The rest were now deliberately burst with excessive charges of powder. One was too large to be destroyed in this way. This was the huge mortar named Sebastopol. It was tipped from its carriage, and left to lie on the ground, where it still lies to this day.

When the guns had been destroyed or immobilized, the gates and the ramparts were blown up, and the huts set on fire. There were few stone buildings on Magdala; they were almost all made of rough timber and thatch, or of mud and wattle, and they did not take long to burn. It had been intended that the ragged church would be spared, but in the end it too caught fire and was completely destroyed. The ashes were still hot when the Galla started to move in through the drifting pall of smoke which could be seen, as it was meant to be seen, for a score of miles in all directions.

By 18 April all the British troops had been withdrawn from the area, and had crossed the Bashilo. The following day they started on their long 400-mile march back to the coast. Their progress was hampered for the first few days by the close presence of the thousands of refugees from the fortress—the soldiers who had been relieved of their muskets but not of their spears and swords, the wounded, the women and children who walked with their herds of cattle or sheep during the day and camped at night as close to the troops as they could for protection against the marauding Galla. There were times when the British troops had to open fire to repel the marauders, and the *Times* correspondent was moved to observe that 'the British had far more difficulty in protecting Theodore's army than they ever had in conquering them'. Once they had crossed the river Jidda and were in undisputed Amhara territory, the refugees began to disperse to their homes, and by the time the Taccaze was reached they had all left.

The only remaining Abyssinians left on Napier's hands were a number of the emperor's hostages and prisoners whom the British troops had found and released at Magdala, some of whom were being escorted towards their homes. There was also the emperor's widow and her son Alamayu. Terunesh had been ill and confused when she started on her journey. She had promised Theodorus before he died that she would hand Alamayu over to the care of the British, and she realized that in any case his chances of survival if he remained in Abyssinia were now slight. She herself had at first asked to go back to her own people in Semien, but, when the time came, she said she wanted to stay with her son whether he went to Bombay, as was at first proposed, or to England. In the end she did not have to make any choice. Her illness got progressively worse, and she eventually died on the march near Antalo. She was buried with honour in the church of the Trinity at Chelicut. The band of the King's Own regiment escorted the body to the slow ceremonial beat of the 'Dead March' in *Saul*.

The return of the expeditionary force to Zula was planned and executed with precision and forethought, but it was not as easy and happy as had been hoped. In the personal letters which he wrote to the Duke of Cambridge on the march home, Napier conceded that 'we have had a most distressing march for the troops. Storms almost daily. . . . The constant rain and exposure coming upon men who had had insufficient food threw a number of them into the hospitals during our return.' Cuts and bruises took a long time to heal, the gums of the teeth became swollen and sore. The troops put their ill health down to the lack of rum and sugar, but the medical authorities put the blame on 'great alterations of temperature, bad water and insufficiently cooked food'. Privately, however, they, like everyone else, could not fail to notice that as soon as the transport position improved and the daily issues of rum and sugar and tobacco were resumed, the health as well as the spirits of the soldiers improved. Bottles of beer, port, and brandy did the same for the officers and the Press correspondents. By the time the troops reached the last highland base at Senafay many of the men's uniforms were in unmilitary tatters, with their boots bound in rags to keep them together. Their faces were toughened and roughened by the wind and the rain and the sun, and by a marked diminution of daily washing and shaving, but their spirits revived when at last they marched off to face the final hazards of the Suru defile, and the heat, dust, glare, flies, and sandstorms of the coastal plain. The ones to suffer most in the last stages were the animals. The mules died or were abandoned in hundreds, and five of the more carefully cherished and much-more expensive elephants had to be shot.

Although the health and the spirits of the soldiers caused Napier and his commanders much concern, they were not their only worries. It was said that Napier had always regarded the rainy season in Abyssinia as more dangerous than the emperor, and as the rainstorms grew heavier and more frequent, the rivers rose, the steep slopes became slippery, and the marshy places became bogs. General Napier pushed his tired and hungry troops as hard as he could, and in the end the return journey became as much a race against time as the outward march had been. And no one forgot that near the finish the Suru defile could be transformed by a sudden fall of rain into a lethal torrent in a matter of minutes. Napier had had an alternative route surveyed and prepared in case it was needed, but, with the good fortune which so often attended him during the campaign, on the day he made the descent himself there was no rain at all.

Another cause for concern was the attitude of the people of the provinces through which they had to pass. They were for the most part noticeably less friendly and more predatory than they had been on the expedition's outward journey to Magdala. They had learnt from experience that they had little to fear from an army that paid for its needs, and did not cut off the hands and the feet of assailants and thieves. They had also learnt to look for the expedition's weak points—the stragglers, the lame mules, and those who for one reason or another wandered off the line of march without an escort. There was also another reason for their change of attitude. Theodorus, alive, had been widely feared and often hated, and at first the British were looked upon as heaven-sent means whereby rebellions might prosper, private quarrels could be pursued, and ancient wrongs avenged. But Theodorus, dead, quickly became a hero and a martyr, a man whose brave victories, clever deceptions, and effective cruelties were soon recounted with national and racial pride, while those who had destroyed him became outsiders in every sense, foreigners to be harried and cheated at every turn. The astute Wagshum Gobazey, for example, carefully avoided meeting Napier to the end. He had sensed from the beginning that in order to command the wide religious and political support he needed to succeed Theodorus as emperor, the less direct contact he had with the foreign invaders the better. The position of Ras Kassai was different. Then, as now, the rulers and people of Tigrai and what is now called Eritrea wanted to assert their independence and their separate identity, and Kassai therefore continued to help and supply the British expeditionary force on its way home, and to meet General Napier again publicly with ceremony and warmth. He guessed too that he would be well rewarded for his co-operation, and his guess was well founded. He got a number of mortars and field guns, 850 muskets, and nearly half a million rounds of ammunition. The itinerant Shoho, who lived outside Kassai's control in the passes and plains, had no such expectations, and they harried the stragglers and rearguards to the end.

By 10 June 1868 Napier had marched his fighting troops the four hundred miles to the coast, and had completed the embarkation of the whole of his force in the fleet of transport ships which meticulous staff work had assembled and assigned to them, unit by unit. A small rear party remained for a few days to deal with what could not be taken away or sold on the spot. It was not long before the drifting sand, the consuming sun, and the abrasive wind had combined with the acquisitive Shoho tribesmen to erase almost all trace of the expedition except for the railway embankments and the stone jetties which, over the course of six months, had brought in a total of 63,756 men, and taken most of them out again.[1]

Thanks to the telegraph between Suez and London, and the much criticized lack of one between Zula and Suez, the news of the release of the captives and the fall of Magdala reached London on 25 and 26 April. The news was received with an acclamation sharpened by anxious relief, and warmed by several degrees of moral satisfaction. In the

[1] Figures vary from report to report and from book to book. The total given here comes from the Report of the Select Committee on the Abyssinian War, i.e., 14,700 combatant troops and 49,056 non-combatants and camp-followers.

House of Commons, Disraeli, now Prime Minister, took his customary surfeit of verbal advantage from the situation. 'As a feat of arms it would be difficult, probably impossible to find its parallel for completeness and precision. . . .' It resembled, he said, more than any other event in history, the advance of Cortez into Mexico but with the difference that 'we did not enter Abyssinia to despoil the innocent but in a spirit of justice, humanity, religion and civilization, and that we are about now to vacate the country in a manner which will prove to the world the purity of our purpose'. *The Times* produced a more succinct and realistic judgement: 'Never surely in the history of war has there been an expedition undertaken with such reluctance, planned with such prevision and perfected with such despatch.'[1]

The Times, like the Prime Minister, was keen to extract as much virtue as possible from the decision to withdraw from Abyssinia. Certainly few people in Europe believed that Britain would do so once it had the fair and fertile, and possibly minerally profitable, land of Abyssinia at its mercy. The French view in particular was that the expedition was a typically perfidious excuse for occupying the Red Sea coast, and thus controlling the southern exits and entrances of France's nearly completed Suez canal. The British decision to withdraw was based, like most foreign policy decisions, on a pragmatic Foreign Office assessment of where on balance Britain's best interests lay, but this did not of course stop *The Times* from protesting, like a middle-aged lady whose virtue has been called in question by the neighbours, that Napier's announcement that the army would return immediately 'will be a complete answer to the insinuations of foreign nations'.

All parliament and the Press had to go on at this point were Napier's brief but dramatic telegrams, and it was some time before the details of the Battle of Aroji, the release of the captives, the assault on Magdala, and the emperor's suicide reached London. In the meantime people began to press the government both in and out of parliament for fuller statements and explanations, and for gestures and acts of public satisfaction with which to match the nation's euphoric mood. In the face of these pressures the government became increasingly embarrassed by the length of time which Napier's last official despatches were taking to

[1] Lord Stanley's own journal entry for 26 April was less assertive: '. . . thus ends more fortunately than we could have expected, a war on which we embarked with extreme reluctance and only from a sense of the impossibility of doing otherwise. . . .'

arrive; the last one in fact did not reach London until 29 June, by which time, as one honourable member of the House of Commons pointed out, there were already gentlemen in town who had been present in Abyssinia at the events it described. But, with his triumph safely tucked into his belt, Napier was not a man to be hurried by the impatience of civilians in Whitehall and Westminster. 'I regret', he wrote, 'that I have not been able to complete my despatch earlier but owing to the marching in difficult country, which has occupied the greater part of the days, and the many demands on my time, it has been quite out of my power.'

It was a popular victory nevertheless, and the journals and periodicals of the day lavished paragraphs of praise on Napier and his army. If more attention was paid in their prose and illustrations to the part played by red-blooded and blue-blooded Englishmen than the facts truly warranted, the Fenian troubles and the memories of the recent Indian mutiny were, perhaps, partly to blame. Votes of thanks to all who took part in the campaign were, however, carried by acclamation in both houses of Parliament. In the House of Commons it was proposed by Disraeli as Prime Minister, and seconded by Gladstone as leader of the opposition; and in the House of Lords the royal Duke of Cambridge himself went out of his way to reiterate the congratulations which the Queen and he had privately bestowed on Napier, and on both the Indian and the British troops under his command. Parliament also conferred a pension of £2000 a year on General Napier and 'the male heir of his body', and when he arrived in London in July he was made a peer,[1] and given the Freedom of the City of London. 'The Abyssinian Gallop,' with words and music especially composed 'for the piano forte', had a brief but spirited vogue, and 'The Death of Theodore' was exhibited in dioramic pictures 'daily at quarter to 2 and quarter past 7' at the Royal Polytechnic.

The euphoria lasted through a summer of dinners and speeches, but there were already whispers and rumblings of criticism and discontent. The persistent Sidney Buxton complained in the Commons that mule-

[1] *The Times* commented that it was 'a mistake to make a hereditary peer of a man whose profession makes it impossible for him to leave his family in a position to support it', and argued with good sense that a life peerage would be more appropriate in such cases. This realistic view was later endorsed by some of Napier's descendants, whose inheritance was not improved by the fact that in two marriages Napier had fifteen children.

drivers had been 'flogged daily by fifties', and as early as 22 May a question was put, asking

> whether H.M.G. would defend this gallant officer in the event of certain members of this House conspiring with certain persons out of the House to persecute Sir Robert Napier for causing the death of King Theodore and others by bombardment after the release of the captives.

The most serious and persistent criticism was, as befitted a nation of shopkeepers, over the cost of the war and the way the money had been spent. It was concentrated to start with on rumours of a big difference between the first estimates of what the war would cost which had been made by Disraeli when he was Chancellor of the Exchequer, and what it had actually cost. There was a demand for the appointment of a Select Committee to enquire why there had been such 'a monstrous miscalculation', and why it had cost us more to subdue primitive Abyssinia in 1868 than it had cost Prussia to conquer one of the greatest European powers in 1866. In the end the Conservative Government widened the terms of reference of the committee to cover the causes as well as the cost of the war in order to ensure that if there was to be any criticism, the Liberals, who had been in power in the period before the war, should get as much of the blame as the Tories who had made the estimates and spent the money. When another 2d had to be added to the standard rate of income tax to meet the final bill, one could almost hear the political surgeons of both parties sharpening their scalpels for the post-mortem.

The Select Committee sat for well over a year, and recorded over 700 pages of evidence. It found that when all the bills had been paid, the total cost of the war was nearly £9,000,000. This was more than four times Disraeli's first tentative estimate of £2,000,000, and more than double the figures he gave when he had had time to go into the matter more fully. In a small masterpiece of political verbiage the all-party committee concluded that the vast difference between the estimated and the real cost 'is attributable to the inadequacy of the estimate on the one hand and to the profuse and enormous cost on the other'. The Select Committee's report went on nevertheless to uncover a series of horrific miscalculations, inefficiencies, and laxities. They resulted in many cases in large losses to the taxpayer, and to corresponding gains in some cases to private concerns and individual public officials, like the consuls, for instance, who had been allowed to take a five per cent commission on the cost of the mules they had so gracelessly gathered from the waterfronts and back streets of the Mediterranean and the Middle East.

Not surprisingly it was these hurried and often careless arrangements made for the collection and delivery of transport animals which came in for most criticism. But having ascertained that out of a total of 36,000 animals landed, the number 'destroyed or abandoned' in Abyssinia was 28,673, the Committee concluded that 'the money waste in the purchase of mules is as nothing compared with the money cost (about a million pounds) resulting from their loss'. It also had some uncomfortable things to say about supplies. Over 35,000 tons of forage, for example, had been shipped to Abyssinia, but only 7000 tons was actually put ashore; the rest remained on board and was never used. In several cases the same stores were ordered both from India and from England, and had arrived embarrassingly close together, and 'it was a matter of no little surprise to your Committee to learn that the Home Government had sent 38 tons of rice and sugar to India'. The greatest criticism, however, was about the rates paid for the hire of transport ships, which cost the taxpayer £3,500,000, and for the supply of coals, which accounted for close on another £1,000,000. In this respect the Committee noted that the main recipients of the excessive charges were the well-known and highly respectable British India Steam Navigation Company and the Peninsular and Oriental Steamship Company, and that in a number of cases lower tenders were rejected by the government because it 'did not wish to excite competition in the home market against the P. and O. Company'.

The Committee seems to have carried out its investigations in a diligent, thorough, and conscientious way, but when it came to answer the questions which it properly posed to itself: 'why such profusion, and who is to blame?', it reached the happy conclusion that they would 'best discharge their duty by clearly and sharply defining the facts, leaving conclusions and inferences . . . to the judgement of parliament'. And there the matter rested, and eventually went to sleep. The trouble was that the home government, in its anxiety for someone else to do the work, had virtually given a free hand to General Napier and the Governor of Bombay to make the arrangements and to carry out the task, while still agreeing to pay the bill. In the circumstances there was probably little else they could have done, but there were inevitably elements of risk in giving even the best-intentioned such a limitless blank cheque. Napier himself confided to the Select Committee that expense was 'quite out of his province'; that his business was to take Magdala, and 'he never thought of the cost'. The important thing was that he had taken Magdala and achieved the objects of the expedition with little loss of British life. In these circumstances there was not much parliament could do except to note the Committee's view that 'the traditions of the professions of arms have tended to inspire military men with a feeling very much akin to contempt for everything in the nature of business', and hopefully to accept its recommendation 'that a more perfect business organisation and business training than exists at present should be worked into our military system'.

Napier's expeditionary force was not the only subject of criticism. Both Rassam and Cameron were asked to submit detailed accounts and explanations of their conduct, When these had been studied in the Foreign Office and the Treasury, Cameron's appointment was terminated, and he was somewhat frostily given no more than his ordinary consular pension of £350 a year. Rassam and his companions, Blanc and Prideaux, were, however, congratulated on their actions and demeanour, and more generously treated. Rassam got a special award of £5000, and the others £2000 each. Cameron died soon afterwards, a sick and disappointed man, continually complaining and petitioning about his poverty and ill-treatment, but Hormuzd Rassam, born of Kurdish parents in Mosul in 1826, lived to marry an English wife, and to die in his bed in Brighton in 1890, when he was 74. General Napier continued, as Lord Napier of Magdala, to serve the crown with distinction in India and as Governor of Gibraltar, and died, a respected national figure, in 1910, when he was 80. He was buried in St. Paul's, and an equestrian monument was erected in a peaceful setting of plane trees and pigeons at the top of Queen's Gate in Kensington.

When Napier and his army left Abyssinia in the summer of 1868 they left a vacuum. H.M.G. made it clear, with an ostentatious impartiality easily mistaken for indifference, that it had no wish to fill it, or to influence the way it was filled. When Napier and the India Office suggested that Munzinger should be made British consul at Massawa to preserve some British presence and influence in that area, James Murray at the Foreign Office took the opportunity to sum up, in a precise and elegant minute, what he thought British policy towards Abyssinia and the Red Sea coast should be. The minute proposed to the Foreign Secretary that when Lord Napier came to discuss his suggestion, Murray should say 'that no advantage but the contrary had resulted from the establishment of a consulship in that place; that we could not see that any trading interest as regards England would have to be protected; and that politically I thought that we might not unreasonably say that the appointment had involved us in complications which it was most desirable for the future to avoid'. Lord Stanley gave his approval to this statement of policy, and the post of British consul at Massawa was left unfilled.

There was, however, no lack of others to fill the vacuum left by the British withdrawal. The Egyptians had purposefully purchased Massawa from their nominal Turkish overlords in 1866, and, when the British left after Magdala,they moved in to consolidate their position along the whole African shore of the Red Sea and the Gulf of Aden as far south as Berbera; by 1874 they had even pushed inland from Berbera and occupied Harar. When the British government had declined to appoint Munzinger as consul in Massawa, it was the more imperialistic Egyptians again who employed his local knowledge and skills as their own agent on the Red Sea coast. Inside Abyssinia itself, the vacuum left by the death of the emperor and the British departure was more keenly contested. Wagshum Gobazey of Lasta, Kassai of Tigrai, and young Menelik of Shoa jockeyed for position like feudal barons, and each in turn, and sometimes simultaneously, sought arms and other forms of support from the reluctant British and the less reluctant and more far-seeing French, and eventually from the Italians too. Gobazey was the first to make a decisive move and proclaim himself emperor under the title of Tekla Giyorgis II, but when he tried to bring Kassai and Tigrai under his sway he was heavily defeated at Adowa in 1872. With the agreement of Menelik, Kassai now assumed the title of emperor as Yohannes IV, leaving Menelik to consolidate and extend his rule in the southern half of Ethiopia, and eventually to succeed him as emperor when he died.

While Theodorus' ancient enemies quarrelled and intrigued and fought over his inheritance, the true heir, Theodorus' son Alamayu was being brought up by the British Government to be an officer and a gentleman in the English mould. General Napier had brought Alamayu back with him to London, and the seven-year-old boy was for a time entrusted to the care of the unconventional Captain Speedy, for whom he had developed a strong affection, and in whose house he lived happily for a time on the Isle of Wight, and in India. Queen Victoria asked to see Alamayu at Osborne and took a great liking to him, and thereafter maintained a special interest in his problems and welfare. Eventually, however, the parsimony and orthodoxy of the Treasury, which was paying the bills, proved a more powerful force, and against his own wishes and the Queen's desire, Alamayu was given into the charge of the headmaster of Cheltenham College. As the headmaster was in holy orders, the Treasury could conveniently argue that this arrangement would also be better for the boy's religious education. From Cheltenham, Alamayu's new mentor moved to Rugby, and Alamayu went with him to finish his schooling there. Although the Queen and several other well-meaning people, including Napier, continued to take a close interest in the young Abyssinian boy, he seems to have missed the boisterous company and warm affection of the Speedy household, and Speedy's exciting and authentic stories of hunting, fighting, and intrigue in Abyssinia. As he wrestled without enthusiasm or success with the curriculum and the cricket and the often insensitive rough-and-tumble of an English public school Alamayu grew more and more lonely, unhappy, and depressed.

When he was 18, he was sent to the Royal Military Academy at Sandhurst, the idea being that he might be commissioned into a good Indian regiment. When she heard about Alamayu going to Sandhurst, the Queen asked Sir Stafford Northcote, who was still Secretary of State for India, to tell the authorities there 'what an interest she takes in Alamayu in his sad and homeless condition, and that she hopes kindness will be shown by *all*, and that he will not be *teazed* or chaffed'. On 31 July 1879 Northcote told the Queen that he did not think that Alamayu should return to Sandhurst; 'He is doing no good there, and he is unhappy.' In October he became seriously ill with what was diagnosed by his English doctors as pleurisy but which he himself was convinced, as if by some innate Abyssinian instinct, was deliberate poisoning. He refused all food and medicine, and on 14 November he died. He was 19 years old.

That evening Queen Victoria wrote up her journal:

Was very grieved and shocked to hear by telegram that good Alamayu had passed away this morning. It is too sad. All alone in a strange country, without seeing a person or relative belonging to him, so young and so good, but for *him* one cannot repine. His was no happy life, full of difficulties of every kind, and he was so sensitive, thinking that people stared at him because of his colour, that I fear he would never have been happy. Everyone is very sorry.

By the Queen's wish a biblical text was added to the wording on the memorial which she had put up for him in the Chapel Royal at Windsor, 'He was a stranger,' it went, 'and ye took him in.'

Appendixes

APPENDIX A

List of corps and units in the Abyssinian Expeditionary Force

Cavalry	3rd Dragoon Guards 10th Regiment Bengal Lancers 12th Regiment Bengal Lancers 3rd Regiment Bombay Light Cavalry 3rd Regiment Sind Horse
Artillery	G Battery 14th Brigade Royal Artillery (Armstrong guns) A Battery 21st Brigade Royal Artillery, with mountain train B Battery 21st Brigade Royal Artillery, with mountain train 5th Battery 25th Brigade Royal Artillery, with mountain train 1st Company Bombay Native Artillery Naval Rocket Brigade: two batteries
Engineers	10th Company Royal Engineers Bombay Sappers and Miners: four companies Madras Sappers and Miners: three companies
Infantry	4th Foot (King's Own Royal Regiment) 26th Foot (Cameronians) 33rd Foot (Duke of Wellington's) 45th Foot (Sherwood Foresters) 21st Bengal Native Infantry 23rd Bengal Native Infantry (Punjabi Pioneers) 2nd Bombay Native Infantry (Grenadiers) 3rd Bombay Native Infantry 5th Bombay Native Infantry 8th Bombay Native Infantry 10th Bombay Native Infantry 18th Bombay Native Infantry 21st Bombay Native Infantry 25th Bombay Native Infantry 27th Bombay Native Infantry (Baluchis)

APPENDIX B

Composition of advance division as shown in appendix to General Napier's Despatch of 29 March 1868

Abyssinian Field Force
Strength of Advanced Force encamped at Santara, 30 March 1868

	British		Native	
	Officers	Non-commissioned, Rank and File	Officers	Non-commissioned, Rank and File
General Staff	22	—	1	26
First, or Sir C. Staveley's Division				
1st Brigade				
Brigadier-General Schneider, and Brigade Staffs	8	—	—	—
3rd Regiment Sind Horse	9	—	13	231
A/21 Steel Battery	8	115	—	—
10th Company, Royal Engineers	3	29	—	—
Head Quarters, 4th King's Own Regiment	26	483	—	—
Ditto, ditto, 1st Baluchi Battalion	5	—	8	318
2 Companies, Punjabi Pioneers	2	—	4	178
2nd Brigade				
Brigadier-General Wilby and Brigade Staff	4	—	—	—
Head Quarters, 3rd Light Cavalry	8	—	12	163
B/21, Steel Battery	6	103	—	—
Naval Rocket Brigade	6	83	—	—
Head Quarters, 33rd D.o.W. Regiment	30	689	—	—
Ditto, ditto, 4 Companies, Punjabi Pioneers	6	—	8	331
Sind Horse (detachment)	—	—	2	100
3rd Brigade				
Brigadier-General Field, and Brigade Staff	4	—	—	—
Head Quarters, 12th Bengal Cavalry	4	—	4	140

3 Companies Sappers and Miners (1 Madras, 2 Bombay)	6	—	6	344
1 Company 4th Foot	1	55	—	—
2 Companies Punjabi Pioneers	2	—	4	178
Head Quarters, 4 Companies 10th Regiment	4	—	8	209
Total of Royal Artillery: 4 guns, 8/14, Royal Artillery; 2 8-inch mortars	6	120	—	—

3rd Brigade, two marches in rear, escorting, and clearing roads for elephants, with guns and mortars.

Total:—British Officers	170	Men	1,677
Native ,,	70	,,	2,218
Grand Total	240		3,895

Bibliography of principal works consulted

Bibliography of principal works consulted

OFFICIAL PAPERS, PUBLICATIONS, AND MANUSCRIPT SOURCES

Public Record Office

Foreign Office files on Abyssinia 1808–78 F.O. 1/1–29, confidential prints 1846-63 F.O. 401/1, 1864–68 F.O. 401/2, further papers 1852–67 F.O. 401/3–5.

India Office library

Abyssinia: Original correspondence vols I–III
Military despatches to Bombay L/Mil/3/2421
Aden Residency: General correspondence R.20/AIA
Secret compilation R.20/AIA
Napier papers R.20/AIA
Rassam donation R.20/AIA

Royal Archives Windsor Castle

misc. pp. dealing with Abyssinia RA 18/37
pp. of H.R.H. the Duke of Cambridge RA. ADD. MSS E/1 (nos. 5549 *et seq.*; nos. 5818–5958)

The Royal Geographical Society has a collection of MS. letters addressed to E. Hertslet of the Foreign Office by Captain Cameron and other captives from Magdala in 1866 and 1867.

National Army Museum

Carter, Brigadier B. W. 'A subaltern in Abyssinia.'
Field, Sir John 'Jottings from an Indian journal.'
James, Capt. Frank Extracts from journal during the Abyssinian campaign.
Roberts, Lt-Col. F. S. Notebooks: Abyssinia 1868.
Scott, Lieut. W. W. Letters from Abyssinia 1868.
Vine, P. A. L. 'By train to Abyssinia; the Zula to Kumayli railway of 1868.'
Hayward, Major H. B. Diary during the Abyssinian expedition of 1868.

ACCOUNTS AND PAPERS PRINTED BY ORDER OF THE HOUSE OF COMMONS AND PAPERS PRESENTED BY COMMAND

Papers relating to the imprisonment of British subjects in Abyssinia; 1865.
Further Correspondence respecting British captives in Abyssinia; 1865–67.
Correspondence respecting Abyssinians at Jerusalem, 1850–1867; 1867–68.
Correspondence respecting Abyssinia, 1846–1868; 1867–68.
Papers connected with the Abyssinian Expedition; 1867–68.
Further Papers; 1867–68.
Two despatches from Sir Robert Napier to the Secretary of State for India, dated respectively 14 April and 12 May 1868, giving particulars of the release of the captives, the attack on, and capture of, Magdala; the death of King Theodore, &c.
Return of the number of European officers with each native regiment in the expedition to Abyssinia, and the number of native commissioned and non-commissioned officers and men of each regiment; 1867–68.
Routes in Abyssinia; 1867–68.
Report from Mr. Rassam respecting his mission to Abyssinia; 1868–69.
Report from Consul Cameron respecting his imprisonment in Abyssinia; 1868–69.
Report from the Select Committee on the Abyssinian War; 1868–69.

ARTICLES IN JOURNALS AND PERIODICALS

The Times Dec. 1867–June 1868. Reports from special correspondent.
Blackwood's 1868. vols I and II. Letters from a staff officer with the Abyssinian expedition.
Pall Mall Gazette 1868. Articles by Lieut. Prideaux.
Chojnacki, S. 'William Simpson and his journey to Ethiopia 1868', *Journal of Ethiopian Studies*, 1968.
Crummey, D. 'Tewodros as Reformer', *Journal of African History*, 1969, x.
— 'The Violence of Tewodros', *Journal of Ethiopian Studies*, 1971, xi.
Hooker, J. R. 'The Foreign Office and the Abyssinian captives', *Journal of African History*, 1961, ii.
Millward, Col. 'Abyssinian Journal 1868', *Journal of Ethiopian Studies*, 1969, vii.
Morgan, M. 'Communities and tradition in Ethiopian history: the reign of Tewodros', *Ethiopian Observer*, 1969, xii.
Jeśman, C. 'Theodore II of Ethiopia', *History Today*, 1972.
— 'The tragedy of Magdala', *Ethiopian Observer*, 1966, x.
Pankhurst, Rita 'The library of Tewodros at Magdala', *Bulletin of S.O.A.S.* 1973.

PRINTED BOOKS

Acton, Roger *The Abyssinian Expedition and the Life and Reign of King Theodore*, with engravings from the *Illustrated London News*, London 1870.
Blanc, Dr. Henry *A Narrative of Captivity in Abyssinia*, London 1868.
Bruce, James *Travels to Discover the Source of the Nile*, Edinburgh 1790.
Cooper, C. I. *The King's Own*, Oxford 1939.
Crummey, Donald *Priests and Politicians: Protestant and Catholic Missions in Orthodox Ethiopia 1830–1868*, Oxford 1972.
Dufton, F. *Narrative of a journey through Abyssinia in 1862–3*, London 1867.
Henty, G. A. *The March to Magdala*, London 1869.
Holland, T. J. and Hozier, H. M. *Record of the Expedition to Abyssinia*, London 1870.
Isaacs, A. A. *Life of H. A. Stern*, London, 1886.
Krapf, J. L. *Travels, Researches and Missionary Labours*, London 1860.
Lee, A. *History of the 33rd Foot*, Norwich 1922.
Lejean, G. *Théodore II. Le nouvel empire d'Abyssinie et les intérêts français dans le sud de la Mer Rouge*, Paris 1865.
Leslau, W. *Falasha Anthology*, New Haven 1951.
— *Coutumes et croyances des Falachas*, Paris 1957.
Markham, Clement *A History of the Abyssinian Expedition*, London 1869.
Mathew, David *Ethiopia*, London 1947.
McMunn, Sir George *History of the Sikh Pioneers*, London 1936.
Myatt, F. *The March to Magdala*, London 1970.
Pankhurst, Richard *The Ethiopian Royal Chronicles*, Addis Ababa 1967.
Parkyns, Mansfield *Life in Abyssinia*, London 1853.
Plowden, W. C. *Travels in Abyssinia and the Galla country with an account of a mission to Ras Ali in 1848*, London 1868.
Rassam, Hormuzd *Narrative of the British Mission to Theodore, King of Abyssinia*, London 1869.
Rubenson, Sven *King of Kings, Tewodros of Ethiopia*, Addis Ababa 1965.
Stanley, Lord *Disraeli, Derby and The Conservative Party. The Political Journals of Lord Stanley, 1849–69*, Brighton 1977.
Stanley, H. M. *Coomassie and Magdala*, London 1874.
Stern, H. A. *Wanderings among the Falashas in Abyssinia*, London 1862.
—*The Captive Missionary*, London, n.d.
Ullendorff, Edward *The Ethiopians*, London 1960.
Veitch, W. D. *Notes from the journal of Martin Flad*, London 1860.
Waldmeier, T. *Autobiography*, London, n.d.

Index

Index